- ॐ -

श्रीमद्भगवद्गीता

śrīmadbhagavadgītā

- ॐ -

Bhagavad Gita

The Holy Book of Sanatana Dharma

Belongs to ______________________

I0389582

ॐ

A Classic of Indian Spirituality

ॐ

Sanskrit Text with English Translation/Transliteration & Dotted-Lined-Margin for Taking Notes

Published by: only **RAMA** only
(an Imprint of e1i1 Corporation)

Title: Bhagavad Gita for Notetaking
Sub-Title: Holy Book of Sanatana Dharma with Sanskrit Text, English Translation/Transliteration
& Dotted-Lined-Margin for Taking Notes

This is a derived work from the epic Mahabharata composed in Sanskrit millenniums ago by
Bhagwan Shri Veda Vyasa
of prehistoric India

Translator/Author: Sushma, Vidya Wati

Identifiers
ISBN: 978-1-945739-55-2 (Paperback)
ISBN: 978-1-945739-56-9 (Hardcover)

—o—

Versions of this Book are also available in these formats (& more):

My Bhagavad Gita Journal--A Daily Journey of Self Discovery ISBN: 978-1-945739-39-2
(Journal Book - size 8"x8" 365 pgs for taking notes/journaling your daily thoughts alongside the verses)

Bhagavad Gita, The Holy Book of Sanatana Dharma ISBN: 978-1-945739-43-9
(Convenient 4"x6" Pocket-Sized Edition)

Bhagavad Gita, Holy Book of Sanatana Dharma ISBN: 978-1-945739-36-1/978-1-945739-37-8
(Original Sanskrit Text with English Translation & Transliteration, size 6.1"x9.2")

—o—

श्रीमद्भगवद्गीता śrīmadbhagavadgītā

6 • ध्यानम् – Invocations

11 • प्रथमोऽध्यायः – अर्जुनविषादयोगः I – Despondency of Arjuna

22 • द्वितीयोऽध्यायः – साङ्ख्ययोगः II – The Path of Sāṅkhya

40 • तृतीयोऽध्यायः – कर्मयोगः III – The Path of Karma

51 • चतुर्थोऽध्यायः – ज्ञानकर्मसंन्यासयोगः IV – The Path of Knowledge

62 • पञ्चमोऽध्यायः – संन्यासयोगः V – Renunciation of Action

70 • षष्ठोऽध्यायः – ध्यानयोगः VI – The Path of Meditation

82 • सप्तमोऽध्यायः – ज्ञानविज्ञानयोगः VII – The Path of Knowledge and Realization

90 • अष्टमोऽध्यायः – अक्षरब्रह्मयोगः VIII – Path to the Supreme Spirit

98 • नवमोऽध्यायः – राजविद्याराजगुह्ययोगः IX – The Path of Royal-Knowledge Royal-Science

107 • दशमोऽध्यायः – विभूतियोगः X – Glories of the Divine

118 • एकादशोऽध्यायः – विश्वरूपदर्शनयोगः XI – Vision of the Universal Divine Form

133 • द्वादशोऽध्यायः – भक्तियोगः XII – The Path of Bhakti

138 • त्रयोदशोऽध्यायः – क्षेत्रक्षेत्रज्ञविभागयोगः XIII – Of the Body and the Embodied-Soul

147 • चतुर्दशोऽध्यायः – गुणत्रयविभागयोगः XIV – Discernment of the Three *Gunas*

154 • पञ्चदशोऽध्यायः – पुरुषोत्तमयोगः XV – Path to the Supreme God-Head

160 • षोडशोऽध्यायः – दैवासुरसम्पद्विभागयोगः XVI – Divine and Demoniacal Attributes

166 • सप्तदशोऽध्यायः – श्रद्धात्रयविभागयोगः XVII – Of the Three Kinds of Shraddhā

174 • अष्टादशोऽध्यायः – मोक्षसंन्यासयोगः XVIII – The Path of Renunciation

194 • गीतामाहात्म्यम् – gītāmāhātmyam

A Brief Note on the Context of The Bhagavad-Gītā

The Bhagavad-Gītā is a synthesis and compendium of spiritual ideas on Dharma, Bhakti, Karma, Moksha, Yoga etc. Alongside Rāmāyana, the Gītā is considered an important Scripture of Sanatana Dharma and is counted amongst the classics of Indian spirituality. It is a collection of 700 verses culled from the Bhīshma-Parva of the epic Mahābhārata. Unlike the Vedas and Upanishads, scriptures like Mahābhārata and Rāmāyana, are historical records known as Itihāsas, which literally means 'Thus-happened...'—or History.

Bhagavad-Gītā is a dialogue between Arjuna and his charioteer Lord Krishna that takes place in the middle of the battle-field of Kurūkshetra when Arjuna suddenly becomes overcome with quandary and despair to the violence and death about to be unleashed on the battle field—for what was at hand was an epic war-of-wars where many armies from the pan Indian sub-continent stood gathered to battle it out in what was essentially a dispute over the kingdom of Hastināpur, and that too between two warring factions related by blood: the Pāndavas and Kauravas.

Arjuna is the third of five brothers: Yudhishthira, Bhīma, Arjuna, Nakula and Sahadeva, collectively called the Pāndavas. Their father was King Pāndu and upon Pāndu's premature death—and because all his children were still underage—Pāndu's brother Dhritarāshtra was asked by the ministerial council to take over the reins of Hastināpur. Upon coming of age Yudhishthira, the eldest Pāndava and the prince regent, was to be crowned the King but by then Dhritarāshtra's own ambitions and avarice had come a long way, much spurred by his evil sons. Dhritarāshtra had many sons and they grew up to be a salacious immoral bunch given to unrighteous evil ways who openly indulged in unchaste activities. They were the very opposite of the five Pāndavas who were not only brave but bright, moral, and righteous. The eldest of Dhritarāshtra's sons was Duryodhana and he wanted the dominion for himself and his brothers. These brothers, since they belonged to the Kuru family, were called the Kauravas which word, over time, has come to represent unrighteousness. So the war of Kurūkshetra of the Gītā is a war between Pāndavas and Kauravas, between Dharma and Adharma, between good and evil, right and wrong.

Krishna, the incarnation of Lord Vishnu, was related to these families of Pāndavas and Kauravas—albeit distantly. The Pāndava brothers—by dint of their good moral life—had forged a close bond with Krishna whom they regarded to be their friend, philosopher and guide. Krishna did his best to avert the war and used every diplomatic means to mediate peace between Pāndavas and Kauravas. He even proposed that the Pāndavas be given just five villages for the sake of truce, but prince Duryodhana refused to yield even an inch of land. When the war became inevitable, Krishna asked both rivals to choose either Krishna himself, or his army, to fight on their side in the upcoming battle. Arjuna happily chose Krishna—even though it meant getting the assistance of only one person alone; while Duryodhana regaled as he chose Krishna's vast army to be his partner in the upcoming battle. Further because he had vowed that he would not lift any weapon to fight, so Krishna took only a passive physical role in the battle—that of being Arjuna's charioteer. Of course Lord Krishna remained Pāndavas leading counselor and guide, and it was only by Krishna's guidance and grace that the Pāndavas would later emerge victorious.

Other than Krishna and Arjuna, the other two people whose dialogues are found in the Gītā are Sanjay and Dhritarāshtra. We already know King Dhritarāshtra to be the ambitious father of the evil Kaurava brothers. He was blind by birth and the narration of the battlefield is being described to him by Sanjay, a councilor of his. By Vyāsa's grace Sanjay had become possessed of the boon of divine sight and so he is able to see and hear everything happening remotely in the battlefield of Kurūkshetra, as if he himself stood there in person—akin to present day telecast.

The Bhagavad-Gītā opens with Dhritarāshtra asking Sanjay to narrate the happenings on the battlefield. There Arjuna tells Krishna to draw his chariot between the two armies so that he could see all his adversaries. When Arjuna actually saw his teachers relatives, friends etc., up close and realized that many of them will inevitably be killed within hours and days and on both sides, his mind begins to reel and he almost faints. Most of these were men whom Arjuna had known since childhood and grew up with, and so his tender feelings naturally become kindled. He throws down his bow and arrows and declares to Krishna that he will not fight and would rather renounce everything and live on alms. In the discourse which follows, Lord Krishna helps Arjuna to overcome his weakness and see clearly and do the right thing.

INVOCATIONS

ध्यानम् — dhyānam.

ॐ श्री परमात्मने नमः

— om śrī paramātmane namaḥ —

[Om—I bow down to the Supreme-Energy, Supreme-Being]

त्वमेव माता च पिता त्वमेव । त्वमेव बंधुश्च सखा त्वमेव ।

tvameva mātā ca pitā tvameva ,
tvameva baṁdhuśca sakhā tvameva ,

त्वमेव विद्या द्रविणं त्वमेव । त्वमेव सर्वं मम देवदेव ॥

tvameva vidyā draviṇaṁ tvameva ,
tvameva sarvaṁ mama devadeva .

Thou art my mother and my father, Thou alone my kin, kith, friend; Thou alone my wisdom, knowledge, wealth; Thou alone—O God of gods—my all, and everything! (1)

— ॐ —

शान्ताकारं भुजगशयनं पद्मनाभं सुरेशं

śāntākāraṁ bhujagaśayanaṁ padmanābhaṁ sureśaṁ

विश्वाधारं गगनसदृशं मेघवर्णं शुभाङ्गम् ।

viśvādhāraṁ gaganasadṛśaṁ meghavarṇaṁ śubhāṅgam ,

लक्ष्मीकान्तं कमलनयनं योगिभिर्ध्यानगम्यं

lakṣmīkāntaṁ kamalanayanaṁ yogibhirdhyānagamyaṁ

वन्दे विष्णुं भवभयहरं सर्वलोकैकनाथम् ॥

vande viṣṇuṁ bhavabhayaharaṁ sarvalokaikanātham .

I venerate Shri Vishnu—of a serene appearance who slumbers upon the serpent *Shesha-Nāga*, from whose navel has sprung the lotus of creation, who presides over as the God of gods, who is the substratum of the universe, boundless and infinite like the sky. Of a dark hue like the clouds, of a form radiating everlasting auspiciousness, with eyes beautiful like lotus petals, who is the beloved of Devī Lakshmī, who is reachable only through devotional meditation by Yogīs, who removes all fears of worldly existence—upon Him, Vishnu, the One Great Lord of all the worlds, I meditate. (2)

— ॐ —

यं ब्रह्मा वरुणेन्द्ररुद्रमरुतः स्तुन्वन्ति दिव्यैः स्तवैः
yaṁ brahmā varuṇendrarudramarutaḥ stunvanti divyaiḥ stavaiḥ

वेदैः साङ्गपदक्रमोपनिषदैर्गायन्ति यं सामगाः ।
vedaiḥ sāṅgapadakramopaniṣadairgāyanti yaṁ sāmagāḥ ,

ध्यानावस्थिततद्गतेन मनसा पश्यन्ति यं योगिनो
dhyānāvasthitatadgatena manasā paśyanti yaṁ yogino

यस्यान्तं न विदुः सुरासुरगणा देवाय तस्मै नमः ॥
yasyāntaṁ na viduḥ surāsuragaṇā devāya tasmai namaḥ .

Unto That Supreme—whom Brahammā, Varuna, Indra, Rudra and the Mārutas praise with excellent holy hymns; who is versified throughout the Vedas and Upanishads by the chanters of Sāma; who—in perfect meditations deep—the yogis see within their own minds while absorbed in "That-One"; whose beginning and end, even gods and demi-gods never know of—unto That Supreme-Being, I offer my many venerations. (3)

ॐ ॐ ॐ ॐ ॐ ॐ ॐ ॐ ॐ ॐ ॐ ॐ ॐ ॐ ॐ ॐ ॐ

— ॐ — ॐ — ॐ — ॐ — ॐ —

VENERATIONS

— ॐ — स्तुतिः — ॐ — stutiḥ — ॐ —

— ॐ —

पार्थाय प्रतिबोधितां भगवता नारायणेन स्वयम्
pārthāya pratibodhitāṁ bhagavatā
nārāyaṇena svayam

व्यासेनग्रथितां पुराणमुनिना मध्ये महाभारते ।
vyāsenagrathitāṁ purāṇamuninā
madhye mahābhārate ,

अद्वैतामृतवर्षिणीं भगवतीमष्टादशाध्यायिनीम्
advaitāmṛtavarṣiṇīṁ bhagavatīmaṣṭādaśādhyāyinīm

अम्ब त्वामनुसन्दधामि भगवद्गीते भवेद्वेषिणीम् ॥
amba tvāmanusandadhāmi bhagavadgīte bhavedveṣiṇīm .

O Thou Bhagavad-Gītā—with whom Pārtha was enlightened by the Lord Nārāyana himself; who was integrated into the Mahābhārata by the ancient sage Vyāsa; O Thou blessed Mother—who with her eighteen Cantos shower humanity with the nectar of Advaita; O Thou destroyer of rebirths, upon Thee—O Bhagavad-Gītā, O loving Mother—I meditate. (1)

— ॐ —

नमोऽस्तु ते व्यास विशालबुद्धे फुल्लारविन्दायतपत्रनेत्र ।
namo'stu te vyāsa viśālabuddhe phullāravindāyatapatranetra ,
येन त्वया भारततैलपूर्णः प्रज्वालितो ज्ञानमयः प्रदीपः ॥
yena tvayā bhāratatailapūrṇaḥ prajvālito jñānamayaḥ pradīpaḥ .

Salutations to Thee O Vyāsa—of a mighty intellect and with eyes large like the petals of a full-blossomed lotus; by whom has been forever lit in this world the Lamp-of-Wisdom, filled with the oil in the form of the great epic: Mahābhārata. (2)

— ॐ —

प्रपन्नपारिजाताय तोत्रवेत्रैकपाणये ।
prapannapārijātāya totravetraikapāṇaye ,
ज्ञानमुद्राय कृष्णाय गीतामृतदुहे नमः ॥
jñānamudrāya kṛṣṇāya gītāmṛtaduhe namaḥ .

He—who is the wish-granting tree of the suppliant—in whose one hand is held the rope for cow and with the other hand who holds the Yogic posture of *Jnana*—who is the milcher of the nectar known as Gītā—unto Him, Krishna, my repeated venerations. (3)

— ॐ —

सर्वोपनिषदो गावो दोग्धा गोपालनन्दनः ।
sarvopaniṣado gāvo dogdhā gopālanandanaḥ,
पार्थो वत्सः सुधीर्भोक्ता दुग्धं गीतामृतं महत् ॥
pārtho vatsaḥ sudhīrbhoktā
dugdhaṁ gītāmṛtaṁ mahat .

All the Upanishads are the cows; the milcher is the joy of cowherds, Krishna; Pārtha is the calf; the man of purified understanding is the partaker; and the milk is verily the supreme nectar known as Gītā. (4)

— ॐ —

वसुदेवसुतं देवं कंसचाणूरमर्दनम् ।
vasudevasutaṁ devaṁ kaṁsacāṇūramardanam ,
देवकीपरमानन्दं कृष्णं वन्दे जगद्गुरुम् ॥
devakīparamānandaṁ kṛṣṇaṁ vande jagadgurum .

I worship the charioteer, the Lord-God, the destroyer of Kamsa and Chānura, the supreme joy of Devakī, the son of Vāsudeva—Shri Krishna, the Universal Guru. (5)

— ॐ —

भीष्मद्रोणतटा जयद्रथजला गान्धारनीलोत्पला
bhīṣmadroṇataṭā jayadrathajalā gāndhāranīlotpalā
शल्यग्राहवती कृपेण वहनी कर्णेन वेलाकुला ।
śalyagrāhavatī kṛpeṇa vahanī karṇena velākulā ,
अश्वत्थामविकर्णघोरमकरा दुर्योधनावर्तिनी
aśvatthāmavikarṇaghoramakarā duryodhanāvartinī
सोत्तीर्णा खलु पाण्डवैरणनदी कैवर्तकः केशवः ॥
sottīrṇā khalu pāṇḍavairaṇanadī kaivartakaḥ keśavaḥ .

That terrible battle-river—which had Bhīṣma and Droṇa as its two banks, and Jayadrathaja as its waters; which had the king of Gāndhāra as its blue lotus, and Śalya as its shark; whose currents and billows were Kṛipā and Karṇa; which had Aśvatthāmā and Vikarṇa as its terrible alligators; and of which Duryodhana was the deadly whirlpool—that ferocious river could be forded by the Pāṇḍavas only because they had Keśava as their helmsman. (6)

— ॐ —

पाराशर्यवचः सरोजममलं गीतार्थगन्धोत्कटं
pārāśaryavacaḥ sarojamamalaṁ gītārthagandhotkaṭaṁ
नानाख्यानककेसरं हरिकथासम्बोधनाबोधितम् ।
nānākhyānakakesaraṁ harikathāsambodhanābodhitam ।
लोके सज्जनषट्पदैरहरहः पेपीयमानं मुदा
loke sajjanaṣaṭpadairaharahaḥ pepīyamānaṁ mudā
भूयाद्भारतपङ्कजं कलिमलप्रध्वंसिनः श्रेयसे ॥
bhūyādbhāratapaṅkajaṁ kalimalapradhvaṁsinaḥ śreyase .

May this Lotus called Mahābhārata—which was born on the lake of the words of Vyāsa—which is perfumed with the fragrance of the Import-of-Gītā—which has its innumerous stories as the pollen—which became fully bloomed through the discourses of Hari—which is the destroyer of the sins of the Kali-Yuga—which is everyday partaken joyously by the bees in the shape of good people of the world—may it bestow all goodness upon us. (7)

— ॐ —

मूकं करोति वाचालं पङ्गुं लङ्घयते गिरिम् ।
mūkaṁ karoti vācālaṁ paṅguṁ laṅghayate girim ,
यत्कृपा तमहं वन्दे परमानन्दमाधवम् ॥
yatkṛpā tamahaṁ vande paramānandamādhavam .

I salute the Supreme-Being of the nature of supreme bliss, by whose very grace the dumb become eloquent and the cripples step across mountains. (8)

— ॐ —

ॐ पूर्णमदः पूर्णमिदँ पूर्णात् पूर्णमुदच्यते ।
om pūrṇamadaḥ pūrṇamidaṁ̐
pūrṇāt pūrṇamudacyate ,
पूर्णस्य पूर्णमादाय पूर्णमेवावशिष्यते ।
pūrṇasya pūrṇamādāya
pūrṇamevāvaśiṣyate ,
ॐ शान्तिः शान्तिः शान्तिः ॥
om śāntiḥ śāntiḥ śāntiḥ .

Om—That One (the unmanifest Brahma)—is infinite, complete, Entire; this (the manifest universe) is entire; And from That One fullness has emerged this entire universe here; And even when this entirety here is taken out of that One-Entire, It still abides complete in all Its entireness! Om, peace—let there be tranquility all around me! (9)

— ॐ — ॐ — ॐ — ॐ — ॐ — ॐ — ॐ — ॐ — ॐ — ॐ — ॐ —

प्रथमोऽध्यायः - अर्जुनविषादयोगः

prathamo'dhyāyaḥ - arjunaviṣādayogaḥ

:: Canto – I ::

- Despondency of Arjuna -

धृतराष्ट्र उवाच--
dhṛtarāṣṭra uvāca --

धर्मक्षेत्रे कुरुक्षेत्रे समवेता युयुत्सवः ।
dharmakṣetre kurukṣetre samavetā yuyutsavaḥ
मामकाः पाण्डवाश्चैव किमकुर्वत सञ्जय ॥ १-१ ॥
māmakāḥ pāṇḍavāścaiva kimakurvata sañjaya (1-1)

Dhritarāshtra said: On that holy *Dharmika* region of Kurūkshetra, gathered anxiously for the battle, what did my sons and the sons of Pāṇdu do, O Sanjay? (1.1)

सञ्जय उवाच --
sañjaya uvāca --

दृष्ट्वा तु पाण्डवानीकं व्यूढं दुर्योधनस्तदा ।
dṛṣṭvā tu pāṇḍavānīkaṁ vyūḍhaṁ duryodhanastadā
आचार्यमुपसङ्गम्य राजा वचनमब्रवीत् ॥ १-२ ॥
ācāryamupasaṅgamya rājā vacanamabravīt (1-2)

Sañjay said: Seeing the army of the Pāndavas drawn up for battle, King Duryodhana approached Guru Drona, and spoke these words: (1.2)

— ॐ —

पश्यैतां पाण्डुपुत्राणामाचार्य महतीं चमूम् ।
paśyaitāṁ pāṇḍuputrāṇāmācārya mahatīṁ camūm
व्यूढां द्रुपदपुत्रेण तव शिष्येण धीमता ॥ १-३ ॥
vyūḍhāṁ drupadaputreṇa tava śiṣyeṇa dhīmatā (1-3)

"O Guru, behold this vast army of the Pāndavas arrayed here against us by none other than Drupada's son—your own brilliant disciple. (1.3)

— ॐ —

अत्र शूरा महेष्वासा भीमार्जुनसमा युधि ।
atra śūrā maheṣvāsā bhīmārjunasamā yudhi
युयुधानो विराटश्च द्रुपदश्च महारथः ॥ १-४ ॥
yuyudhāno virāṭaśca drupadaśca mahārathaḥ (1-4)
धृष्टकेतुश्चेकितानः काशिराजश्च वीर्यवान् ।
dhṛṣṭaketuścekitānaḥ kāśirājaśca vīryavān
पुरुजित्कुन्तिभोजश्च शैब्यश्च नरपुङ्गवः ॥ १-५ ॥
purujitkuntibhojaśca śaibyaśca narapuṅgavaḥ (1-5)
युधामन्युश्च विक्रान्त उत्तमौजाश्च वीर्यवान् ।
yudhāmanyuśca vikrānta uttamaujāśca vīryavān
सौभद्रो द्रौपदेयाश्च सर्व एव महारथाः ॥ १-६ ॥
saubhadro draupadeyāśca sarva eva mahārathāḥ (1-6)

In this army are great heroes wielding mighty bows—the equals of Bhima and Arjuna in military prowess—fighters like Yuyudhana and Virāta and Drupada; there behold Dhrishtaketu and Chekitāna and the valiant king of Kāshi, and also Purujit and Kuntībhoja and the king of Shaiba—the best of champions; and there's the mighty Yuddhāmanyu, and the valiant Uttamauja, and also the son of Subhadrā and the sons of Draupadī—all of whom are mighty chariot-warriors. (1.4-1.6)

— ॐ —

अस्माकं तु विशिष्टा ये तान्निबोध द्विजोत्तम ।
asmākaṁ tu viśiṣṭā ye tānnibodha dvijottama
नायका मम सैन्यस्य संज्ञार्थं तान्ब्रवीमि ते ॥ १-७ ॥
nāyakā mama sainyasya saṁjñārthaṁ tānbravīmi te (1-7)

O best amongst the twice-born, be informed also of the distinguished warriors on our side—the leaders of my army; I shall name them for your consideration: (1.7)

— ॐ —

भवान्भीष्मश्च कर्णश्च कृपश्च समितिञ्जयः ।
bhavānbhīṣmaśca karṇaśca kṛpaśca samitiñjayaḥ
अश्वत्थामा विकर्णश्च सौमदत्तिस्तथैव च ॥ १-८ ॥
aśvatthāmā vikarṇaśca saumadattistathaiva ca (1-8)

There is yourself; and then Bhīshma, and Karna, and the ever victorious in battles—Kripā; and also Ashvatthāmā, and Vikarna, and as well the son of Saumadatta. (1.8)

— ॐ —

अन्ये च बहवः शूरा मदर्थे त्यक्तजीविताः ।
anye ca bahavaḥ śūrā madarthe tyaktajīvitāḥ
नानाशस्त्रप्रहरणाः सर्वे युद्धविशारदाः ॥ १-९ ॥
nānāśastrapraharaṇāḥ sarve yuddhaviśāradāḥ (1-9)

And there are so many other heroes as well—wielding versatile weapons, skilled in military warfare, and all determined to stake their life for my sake. (1.9)

— ॐ —

अपर्याप्तं तदस्माकं बलं भीष्माभिरक्षितम् ।
aparyāptaṁ tadasmākaṁ balaṁ bhīṣmābhirakṣitam
पर्याप्तं त्विदमेतेषां बलं भीमाभिरक्षितम् ॥ १-१० ॥
paryāptaṁ tvidameteṣāṁ balaṁ bhīmābhirakṣitam (1-10)

Immeasurable is this army of ours, perfectly protected by Bhīshma; and of sufficient extent is their army which stands guarded by Bhīma. (1.10)

— ॐ —

अयनेषु च सर्वेषु यथाभागमवस्थिताः ।
ayaneṣu ca sarveṣu yathābhāgamavasthitāḥ
भीष्ममेवाभिरक्षन्तु भवन्तः सर्व एव हि ॥ १-११ ॥
bhīṣmamevābhirakṣantu bhavantaḥ sarva eva hi (1-11)

Now all ye—keeping to your strategic positions at all fronts, diligently lend support to Bhīshma in every respect." (1.11)

— ॐ —

तस्य सञ्जनयन्हर्षं कुरुवृद्धः पितामहः ।
tasya sañjanayanharṣaṁ kuruvṛddhaḥ pitāmahaḥ
सिंहनादं विनद्योच्चैः शङ्खं दध्मौ प्रतापवान् ॥ १-१२ ॥
siṁhanādaṁ vinadyoccaiḥ śaṅkhaṁ dadhmau pratāpavān (1-12)

Then that powerful grand-patriarch Bhīshma—the eldest of Kurus—roared alike a lion and thundered forth on his conch-shell, gladdening the heart of Duryodhana. (1.12)

— ॐ —

ततः शङ्खाश्च भेर्यश्च पणवानकगोमुखाः ।
tataḥ śaṅkhāśca bheryaśca paṇavānakagomukhāḥ
सहसैवाभ्यहन्यन्त स शब्दस्तुमुलोऽभवत् ॥ १-१३ ॥
sahasaivābhyahanyanta sa śabdastumulo'bhavat (1-13)

And suddenly conches, kettledrums, horns, trumpets, bugles—blared forth all at once; and frightening and tumultuous was that sound. (1.13)

— ॐ —

ततः श्वेतैर्हयैर्युक्ते महति स्यन्दने स्थितौ ।
tataḥ śvetairhayairyukte mahati syandane sthitau
माधवः पाण्डवश्चैव दिव्यौ शङ्खौ प्रदध्मतुः ॥ १-१४ ॥
mādhavaḥ pāṇḍavaścaiva divyau śaṅkhau pradadhmatuḥ (1-14)

Thereafter seated on a glorious chariot yoked by white steeds, Lord Krishna, and also Arjuna, blew on their celestial conches. (1.14)

— ॐ —

पाञ्चजन्यं हृषीकेशो देवदत्तं धनञ्जयः ।
pāñcajanyaṁ hṛṣīkeśo devadattaṁ dhanañjayaḥ
पौण्ड्रं दध्मौ महाशङ्खं भीमकर्मा वृकोदरः ॥ १-१५ ॥
pauṇḍraṁ dadhmau mahāśaṅkhaṁ bhīmakarmā vṛkodaraḥ (1-15)

Shri Krishna sounded the divine conch Panchajanya, and Arjuna the Devadatta, and Bhīma—that voracious eater of ferocious deeds—blew on his strong conch Paundra. (1.15)

— ॐ —

अनन्तविजयं राजा कुन्तीपुत्रो युधिष्ठिरः ।
anantavijayaṁ rājā kuntīputro yudhiṣṭhiraḥ
नकुलः सहदेवश्च सुघोषमणिपुष्पकौ ॥ १-१६ ॥
nakulaḥ sahadevaśca sughoṣamaṇipuṣpakau (1-16)

And king Yudhishthira, the son of Kuntī, blew on the conch Ananta-Vijaya, and Nakula on Sughosha, and Sahadeva on the conch Mani-Pushpaka. (1.16)

— ॐ —

काश्यश्च परमेष्वासः शिखण्डी च महारथः ।
kāśyaśca parameṣvāsaḥ śikhaṇḍī ca mahārathaḥ

धृष्टद्युम्नो विराटश्च सात्यकिश्चापराजितः ॥ १-१७ ॥
dhṛṣṭadyumno virāṭaśca sātyakiścāparājitaḥ (1-17)

द्रुपदो द्रौपदेयाश्च सर्वशः पृथिवीपते ।
drupado draupadeyāśca sarvaśaḥ pṛthivīpate

सौभद्रश्च महाबाहुः शङ्खान्दध्मुः पृथक्पृथक् ॥ १-१८ ॥
saubhadraśca mahābāhuḥ śaṅkhāndadhmuḥ pṛthakpṛthak (1-18)

And that excellent archer the king of Kāshī, and the mighty Mahā-rathī Shikhandī, and Dhrishta-dyumna and Virāta and the invincible Sātyakī, and Drupada as well; as also the five sons of Draupadī, and the mighty-armed Abhimanyū—the son of Subhadrā—all of them, from both sides of the battlefield, blew on their respective conch-shells, O emperor. (1.17-1.18)

— ॐ —

स घोषो धार्तराष्ट्राणां हृदयानि व्यदारयत् ।
sa ghoṣo dhārtarāṣṭrāṇāṁ hṛdayāni vyadārayat

नभश्च पृथिवीं चैव तुमुलोऽभ्यनुनादयन् ॥ १-१९ ॥
nabhaśca pṛthivīṁ caiva tumulo'bhyanunādayan (1-19)

And that tumultuous sound, from every which direction, echoing through the heavens and earth, rent the hearts of the sons of Dhritarāshtra. (1.19)

— ॐ —

अथ व्यवस्थितान्दृष्ट्वा धार्तराष्ट्रान् कपिध्वजः ।
atha vyavasthitāndṛṣṭvā dhārtarāṣṭrān kapidhvajaḥ

प्रवृत्ते शस्त्रसम्पाते धनुरुद्यम्य पाण्डवः ॥ १-२० ॥
pravṛtte śastrasampāte dhanurudyamya pāṇḍavaḥ (1-20)

हृषीकेशं तदा वाक्यमिदमाह महीपते ।
hṛṣīkeśaṁ tadā vākyamidamāha mahīpate

अर्जुन उवाच --
arjuna uvāca --

सेनयोरुभयोर्मध्ये रथं स्थापय मेऽच्युत ॥ १-२१ ॥
senayorubhayormadhye rathaṁ sthāpaya me'cyuta (1-21)
यावदेतान्निरीक्षेऽहं योद्धुकामानवस्थितान् ।
yāvadetānnirīkṣe'haṁ yoddhukāmānavasthitān
कैर्मया सह योद्धव्यमस्मिन् रणसमुद्यमे ॥ १-२२ ॥
kairmayā saha yoddhavyamasmin raṇasamudyame (1-22)

Then seeing your sons arrayed against him in combat, and when weapons were just about ready to be discharged, Arjuna—who held the mark of Lord Hanumāna upon the flag of his chariot—took up his bow and spoke the following words to Hrishīkesha: "O Achyuta, place my chariot between the two armies so I can see those that are arrayed in this battlefield seeking war—so I can know with whom I have to contend in this great trial of arms. (1.20-1.22)

— ॐ —

योत्स्यमानानवेक्षेऽहं य एतेऽत्र समागताः ।
yotsyamānānavekṣe'haṁ ya ete'tra samāgatāḥ
धार्तराष्ट्रस्य दुर्बुद्धेर्युद्धे प्रियचिकीर्षवः ॥ १-२३ ॥
dhārtarāṣṭrasya durbuddheryuddhe priyacikīrṣavaḥ (1-23)

Let me look at the combatants gathered here: those who are eager to please this evil minded Duryodhana and have assembled by his side ready to fight." (1.23)

सञ्जय उवाच --
sañjaya uvāca --

एवमुक्तो हृषीकेशो गुडाकेशेन भारत ।
evamukto hṛṣīkeśo guḍākeśena bhārata
सेनयोरुभयोर्मध्ये स्थापयित्वा रथोत्तमम् ॥ १-२४ ॥
senayorubhayormadhye sthāpayitvā rathottamam (1-24)
भीष्मद्रोणप्रमुखतः सर्वेषां च महीक्षिताम् ।
bhīṣmadroṇapramukhataḥ sarveṣāṁ ca mahīkṣitām
उवाच पार्थ पश्यैतान्समवेतान्कुरूनिति ॥ १-२५ ॥
uvāca pārtha paśyaitānsamavetānkurūniti (1-25)

Sanjay said: Addressed thusly by Arjuna, Hrishīkesha drew up the magnificent chariot amidst the two armies—in front of Bhīshma, Drona and the other chieftains—and he said, "Here behold the Kauravas who are assembled hither, O Pārtha!" (1.24-1.25)

— ॐ —

तत्रापश्यत्स्थितान्पार्थः पितॄनथ पितामहान् ।
tatrāpaśyatsthitānpārthaḥ pitṝnatha pitāmahān
आचार्यान्मातुलान्भ्रातॄन्पुत्रान्पौत्रान्सखींस्तथा ॥ १-२६ ॥
ācāryānmātulānbhrātṝnputrānpautrānsakhīṁstathā (1-26)
श्वशुरान्सुहृदश्चैव सेनयोरुभयोरपि ।
śvaśurānsuhṛdaścaiva senayorubhayorapi
तान्समीक्ष्य स कौन्तेयः सर्वान्बन्धूनवस्थितान् ॥ १-२७ ॥
tānsamīkṣya sa kaunteyaḥ sarvānbandhūnavasthitān (1-27)
कृपया परयाविष्टो विषीदन्निदमब्रवीत् ।
kṛpayā parayāviṣṭo viṣīdannidamabravīt

And there on the battlefield, Arjuna saw his uncle-fathers, grandfathers, gurus, elders, dons, brothers, cousins, sons, grandsons, nephews, friends, fellows, in-laws, and other relatives—arrayed on both sides of the army. Seeing all the kinsmen gathered together and suddenly overcome with a great emotion, the son of Kuntī began to lament and he spoke with grief the following words: (1.26-1.27)

अर्जुन उवाच --
arjuna uvāca --

दृष्ट्वेमं स्वजनं कृष्ण युयुत्सुं समुपस्थितम् ॥ १-२८ ॥
dṛṣṭvemaṁ svajanaṁ kṛṣṇa yuyutsuṁ samupasthitam (1-28)
सीदन्ति मम गात्राणि मुखं च परिशुष्यति ।
sīdanti mama gātrāṇi mukhaṁ ca pariśuṣyati
वेपथुश्च शरीरे मे रोमहर्षश्च जायते ॥ १-२९ ॥
vepathuśca śarīre me romaharṣaśca jāyate (1-29)
गाण्डीवं स्रंसते हस्तात्त्वक्चैव परिदह्यते ।
gāṇḍīvaṁ sraṁsate hastāttvakcaiva paridahyate
न च शक्नोम्यवस्थातुं भ्रमतीव च मे मनः ॥ १-३० ॥
na ca śaknomyavasthātuṁ bhramatīva ca me manaḥ (1-30)

Arjuna said: "O Krishna, now that I see these kinsmen arrayed in battle before me, my limbs tremble, and my mouth is parched, and shivers run down my body, and my hair stands on end; I find my Gāndīva bow slipping away from my hand, and my skin burns all over, and my mind is reeling, and I can no longer hold myself steady. (1.28-1.30)

— ॐ —

निमित्तानि च पश्यामि विपरीतानि केशव ।
nimittāni ca paśyāmi viparītāni keśava
न च श्रेयोऽनुपश्यामि हत्वा स्वजनमाहवे ॥ १-३१ ॥
na ca śreyo'nupaśyāmi hatvā svajanamāhave (1-31)
न काङ्क्षे विजयं कृष्ण न च राज्यं सुखानि च ।
na kāṅkṣe vijayaṁ kṛṣṇa na ca rājyaṁ sukhāni ca
किं नो राज्येन गोविन्द किं भोगैर्जीवितेन वा ॥ १-३२ ॥
kiṁ no rājyena govinda kiṁ bhogairjīvitena vā (1-32)

O Keshava, all I can see are just adverse omens; I fail to see how any good can come from all the killings of our loved ones in the battle. I no longer desire any victory, or sovereignty, or pleasures, O Krishna. Of what use can kingdoms or luxuries or even life be to us, O Govinda? (1.31-1.32)

— ॐ —

येषामर्थे काङ्क्षितं नो राज्यं भोगाः सुखानि च ।
yeṣāmarthe kāṅkṣitaṁ no rājyaṁ bhogāḥ sukhāni ca
त इमेऽवस्थिता युद्धे प्राणांस्त्यक्त्वा धनानि च ॥ १-३३ ॥
ta ime'vasthitā yuddhe prāṇāṁstyaktvā dhanāni ca (1-33)
आचार्याः पितरः पुत्रास्तथैव च पितामहाः ।
ācāryāḥ pitaraḥ putrāstathaiva ca pitāmahāḥ
मातुलाः श्वशुराः पौत्राः श्यालाः सम्बन्धिनस्तथा ॥ १-३४ ॥
mātulāḥ śvaśurāḥ pautrāḥ śyālāḥ sambandhinastathā (1-34)

—Because those very people for whose sake we may want kingdoms, luxuries and joys—our gurus, fathers, sons, and our grandsires, uncles, brothers, in-laws, nephews, grandsons, and many, many kinsmen—they themselves are arrayed before us in battle, themselves prepared to lose their lives and wealth. (1.33-1.34)

— ॐ —

एतान्न हन्तुमिच्छामि घ्नतोऽपि मधुसूदन ।
etānna hantumicchāmi ghnato'pi madhusūdana
अपि त्रैलोक्यराज्यस्य हेतोः किं नु महीकृते ॥ १-३५ ॥
api trailokyarājyasya hetoḥ kiṁ nu mahīkṛte (1-35)

O Madhusūdana, though they may slay me, I no longer have any desire to kill them; nay, not even for the sake of sovereignty over the three worlds—much less for a mere kingdom here upon earth! (1.35)

— ॐ —

निहत्य धार्तराष्ट्रान्नः का प्रीतिः स्याज्जनार्दन ।
nihatya dhārtarāṣṭrānnaḥ kā prītiḥ syājjanārdana
पापमेवाश्रयेदस्मान्हत्वैतानाततायिनः ॥ १-३६ ॥
pāpamevāśrayedasmānhatvaitānātatāyinaḥ (1-36)
तस्मान्नार्हा वयं हन्तुं धार्तराष्ट्रान्स्वबान्धवान् ।
tasmānnārhā vayaṁ hantuṁ dhārtarāṣṭrānsvabāndhavān
स्वजनं हि कथं हत्वा सुखिनः स्याम माधव ॥ १-३७ ॥
svajanaṁ hi kathaṁ hatvā sukhinaḥ syāma mādhava (1-37)

O Janārdana, how can we hope to be happy slaying our brethren, these sons of Dhritarāshtra? Sin alone will accrue to us if we kill them—even these aggressors. It does not behoove us to kill the sons of Dhritarāshtra—who after all are our kinsmen. O Mādhava, how can we be happy killing our very own? (1.36-1.37)

— ॐ —

यद्यप्येते न पश्यन्ति लोभोपहतचेतसः ।
yadyapyete na paśyanti lobhopahatacetasaḥ
कुलक्षयकृतं दोषं मित्रद्रोहे च पातकम् ॥ १-३८ ॥
kulakṣayakṛtaṁ doṣaṁ mitradrohe ca pātakam (1-38)
कथं न ज्ञेयमस्माभिः पापादस्मान्निवर्तितुम् ।
kathaṁ na jñeyamasmābhiḥ pāpādasmānnivartitum
कुलक्षयकृतं दोषं प्रपश्यद्भिर्जनार्दन ॥ १-३९ ॥
kulakṣayakṛtaṁ doṣaṁ prapaśyadbhirjanārdana (1-39)

With their mind blinded by greed, even though these people perceive no evil in battling with friends and destroying the clan, but why shouldn't we—who can clearly see the evil accruing from such destruction of family—desist from this sin? (1.38-1.39)

— ॐ —

कुलक्षये प्रणश्यन्ति कुलधर्माः सनातनाः ।
kulakṣaye praṇaśyanti kuladharmāḥ sanātanāḥ
धर्मे नष्टे कुलं कृत्स्नमधर्मोऽभिभवत्युत ॥ १-४० ॥
dharme naṣṭe kulaṁ kṛtsnamadharmo'bhibhavatyuta (1-40)

With the destruction of family, time honored family traditions disappear; and when such virtues become lost, then vice takes hold of the entire race. (1.40)

— ॐ —

अधर्माभिभवात्कृष्ण प्रदुष्यन्ति कुलस्त्रियः ।
adharmābhibhavātkṛṣṇa praduṣyanti kulastriyaḥ
स्त्रीषु दुष्टासु वार्ष्णेय जायते वर्णसङ्करः ॥ १-४१ ॥
strīṣu duṣṭāsu vārṣṇeya jāyate varṇasaṅkaraḥ (1-41)

And with the preponderance of unrighteousness, the women of the family become defiled; and with the corruption of women, there arises Varnasankar in progeny, O descendant of Vrishni. (1.41)

— ॐ —

सङ्करो नरकायैव कुलघ्नानां कुलस्य च ।
saṅkaro narakāyaiva kulaghnānāṁ kulasya ca
पतन्ति पितरो ह्येषां लुप्तपिण्डोदकक्रियाः ॥ १-४२ ॥
patanti pitaro hyeṣāṁ luptapiṇḍodakakriyāḥ (1-42)

This Varnasankar (intermixture of Varnas), leads such destroyers of society and their families to hell; and then even departed ancestors fall—deprived as they are of the oblations of food and sap that is customarily offered by offsprings in the lineage. (1.42)

— ॐ —

दोषैरेतैः कुलघ्नानां वर्णसङ्करकारकैः ।
doṣairetaiḥ kulaghnānāṁ varṇasaṅkarakārakaiḥ
उत्साद्यन्ते जातिधर्माः कुलधर्माश्च शाश्वताः ॥ १-४३ ॥
utsādyante jātidharmāḥ kuladharmāśca śāśvatāḥ (1-43)

From these sins of the ruiners of family-order—that lead to the intermixture across Varnas—the established traditions of the clan and the long standing family customs become thoroughly decimated. (1.43)

— ॐ —

उत्सन्नकुलधर्माणां मनुष्याणां जनार्दन ।
utsannakuladharmāṇāṁ manuṣyāṇāṁ janārdana
नरके नियतं वासो भवतीत्यनुशुश्रुम ॥ १-४४ ॥
narake niyataṁ vāso bhavatītyanuśuśruma (1-44)

And such persons, whose family traditions are lost, are doomed to dwell perpetually in hell, O Janārdana, that's what we have heard. (1.44)

— ॐ —

अहो बत महत्पापं कर्तुं व्यवसिता वयम् ।

aho bata mahatpāpaṁ kartuṁ vyavasitā vayam

यद्राज्यसुखलोभेन हन्तुं स्वजनमुद्यताः ॥ १-४५ ॥

yadrājyasukhalobhena hantuṁ svajanamudyatāḥ (1-45)

Ah, what a heinous sin we are preparing to commit! Alas, merely for the sake of throne and enjoyments, we are intent upon killing our very own kinsmen! (1.45)

— ॐ —

यदि मामप्रतीकारमशस्त्रं शस्त्रपाणयः ।

yadi māmapratīkāramaśastraṁ śastrapāṇayaḥ

धार्तराष्ट्रा रणे हन्युस्तन्मे क्षेमतरं भवेत् ॥ १-४६ ॥

dhārtarāṣṭrā raṇe hanyustanme kṣemataraṁ bhavet (1-46)

It would be far better for me if the sons of Dhritarāshtra, weapons in hand, were to slay me in battle—even though I be unarmed and unresisting." (1.46)

सञ्जय उवाच --

sañjaya uvāca --

एवमुक्त्वार्जुनः सङ्ख्ये रथोपस्थ उपाविशत् ।

evamuktvārjunaḥ saṅkhye rathopastha upāviśat

विसृज्य सशरं चापं शोकसंविग्नमानसः ॥ १-४७ ॥

visṛjya saśaraṁ cāpaṁ śokasaṁvignamānasaḥ (1-47)

Sanjay said: And having spoken thusly, Arjuna cast aside his bow and arrows, and he sank down in his chariot upon the battlefield—completely overwhelmed with grief. (1.47)

ॐ तत्सदिति श्रीमद्भगवद्गीतासूपनिषत्सु

om tatsaditi śrīmadbhagavadgītāsūpaniṣatsu

ब्रह्मविद्यायां योगशास्त्रे श्रीकृष्णार्जुनसंवादे

brahmavidyāyāṁ yogaśāstre śrīkṛṣṇārjunasaṁvāde

अर्जुनविषादयोगो नाम प्रथमोऽध्यायः ॥

arjunaviṣādayogo.nāma prathamo'dhyāyaḥ

In this Yogic Scripture on the Science of Brahama—the Shrimada-Bhāgvada-Gītā Upanishad—
hereby ends the dialogue between Shrī Krishna and Arjuna entitled:
Arjuna-Vishāda Yoga, Canto I

द्वितीयोऽध्यायः - साङ्ख्ययोगः

dvitīyo'dhyāyaḥ - sāṅkhyayogaḥ

:: Canto – II ::

- The Path of Sāṅkhya -

सञ्जय उवाच --
sañjaya uvāca --

तं तथा कृपयाविष्टमश्रुपूर्णाकुलेक्षणम् ।
taṁ tathā kṛpayāviṣṭamaśrupūrṇākulekṣaṇam
विषीदन्तमिदं वाक्यमुवाच मधुसूदनः ॥ २-१ ॥
viṣīdantamidaṁ vākyamuvāca madhusūdanaḥ (2-1)

Sanjay said: To him thus overcome with pathos—distressed and grieving and with eyes full of tears—Madhusūdana spoke the following words: (2.1)

श्रीभगवानुवाच --
śrībhagavānuvāca --

कुतस्त्वा कश्मलमिदं विषमे समुपस्थितम् ।
kutastvā kaśmalamidaṁ viṣame samupasthitam
अनार्यजुष्टमस्वर्ग्यमकीर्तिकरमर्जुन ॥ २-२ ॥
anāryajuṣṭamasvargyamakīrtikaramarjuna (2-2)

Shri Bhagwāna said: "O Arjuna, wherefrom has this weakness—not entertained by noble souls, nor conducive to heaven, and which leads to great shame and dishonor—overtaken you at this hour of crisis? (2.2)

— ॐ —

क्लैब्यं मा स्म गमः पार्थ नैतत्त्वय्युपपद्यते ।
klaibyaṁ mā sma gamaḥ pārtha naitattvayyupapadyate
क्षुद्रं हृदयदौर्बल्यं त्यक्त्वोत्तिष्ठ परन्तप ॥ २-३ ॥
kṣudraṁ hṛdayadaurbalyaṁ tyaktvottiṣṭha parantapa (2-3)

Yield not to unmanliness, O Pārtha, this is totally unbecoming of you; shake off this petty timidity of heart, O scorcher of foes, and arise." (2.3)

अर्जुन उवाच --
arjuna uvāca --

कथं भीष्ममहं सङ्ख्ये द्रोणं च मधुसूदन ।
katham bhīṣmamaham saṅkhye droṇaṁ ca madhusūdana
इषुभिः प्रतियोत्स्यामि पूजार्हावरिसूदन ॥२-४॥
iṣubhiḥ pratiyotsyāmi pūjārhāvarisūdana (2-4)

Arjuna said: “In this battle, O Madhusūdana, how can I inflict arrows upon Bhīshma and Drona—who are worthy of the deepest respect? (2.4)

— ॐ —

गुरूनहत्वा हि महानुभावान् श्रेयो भोक्तुं भैक्ष्यमपीह लोके ।
gurūnahatvā hi mahānubhāvān śreyo bhoktuṁ bhaikṣyamapīha loke
हत्वार्थकामांस्तु गुरूनिहैव भुञ्जीय भोगान् रुधिरप्रदिग्धान् ॥२-५॥
hatvārthakāmāṁstu gurūnihaiva
bhuñjīya bhogān rudhirapradigdhān (2-5)

Rather than kill these reverend masters—honorable and esteemed, better it is to live on alms in the world; after all, whatever pleasures in the form of wealth and sense-enjoyments that I shall enjoy, will only be found drenched in the blood of these venerable souls. (2.5)

— ॐ —

न चैतद्विद्मः कतरन्नो गरीयो यद्वा जयेम यदि वा नो जयेयुः ।
na caitadvidmaḥ kataranno garīyo yadvā jayema yadi vā no jayeyuḥ
यानेव हत्वा न जिजीविषामस्तेऽवस्थिताः प्रमुखे धार्तराष्ट्राः ॥२-६॥
yāneva hatvā na jijīviṣāmaste'vasthitāḥ pramukhe dhārtarāṣṭrāḥ (2-6)

And we do not even know what is the preferred course—to fight or not to fight, and which outcome would be preferable—we conquering them, or they us. Killing whom we may not desire to live, those very kinsmen—these sons of Dhritarāshtra—stand gathered before us. (2.6)

— ॐ —

कार्पण्यदोषोपहतस्वभावः पृच्छामि त्वां धर्मसम्मूढचेताः ।
kārpaṇyadoṣopahatasvabhāvaḥ
pṛcchāmi tvāṁ dharmasammūḍhacetāḥ
यच्छ्रेयः स्यान्निश्चितं ब्रूहि तन्मे
yacchreyaḥ syānniścitaṁ brūhi tanme
शिष्यस्तेऽहं शाधि मां त्वां प्रपन्नम् ॥२-७॥
śiṣyaste'haṁ śādhi māṁ tvāṁ prapannam (2-7)

A niggardly weakness overwhelms my natural traits and I am bewildered in regards to duty. So I beseech to Thee: please tell me that which is decidedly good for me. I am Thy disciple, pray guide me—who have taken refuge in Thee. (2.7)

— ॐ —

न हि प्रपश्यामि ममापनुद्याद् यच्छोकमुच्छोषणमिन्द्रियाणाम् ।

na hi prapaśyāmi mamāpanudyād
yacchokamucchoṣaṇamindriyāṇām

अवाप्य भूमावसपत्नमृद्धं राज्यं सुराणामपि चाधिपत्यम् ॥२-८॥

avāpya bhūmāvasapatnamṛddhaṁ
rājyaṁ surāṇāmapi cādhipatyam (2-8)

Even if I were to obtain in this world unrivaled sovereignty over vast prosperous kingdoms, or gain lordship even over gods—still I see no means to drive away this grief of mine which is utterly drying up my senses." (2.8)

सञ्जय उवाच --

sañjaya uvāca --

एवमुक्त्वा हृषीकेशं गुडाकेशः परन्तप ।

evamuktvā hṛṣīkeśaṁ guḍākeśaḥ parantapa

न योत्स्य इति गोविन्दमुक्त्वा तूष्णीं बभूव ह ॥२-९॥

na yotsya iti govindamuktvā tūṣṇīṁ babhūva ha (2-9)

Sanjay said: O King, having spoken thusly unto Hrishīkesha, Gudākesha—the tormentor of foes—conclusively told Govinda, 'I shall not fight', and fell silent. (2.9)

— ॐ —

तमुवाच हृषीकेशः प्रहसन्निव भारत ।

tamuvāca hṛṣīkeśaḥ prahasanniva bhārata

सेनयोरुभयोर्मध्ये विषीदन्तमिदं वचः ॥२-१०॥

senayorubhayormadhye viṣīdantamidaṁ vacaḥ (2-10)

Then O king, unto him who was sorrowing in the midst of the two armies, Hrishīkesha spoke the following words—as if smiling: (2.10)

श्रीभगवानुवाच --

śrībhagavānuvāca --

अशोच्यानन्वशोचस्त्वं प्रज्ञावादांश्च भाषसे ।

aśocyānanvaśocastvaṁ prajñāvādāṁśca bhāṣase

गतासूनगतासूंश्च नानुशोचन्ति पण्डिताः ॥२-११॥

gatāsūnagatāsūṁśca nānuśocanti paṇḍitāḥ (2-11)

Shri Bhagwāna said: "You sit here lamenting for those who are not worthy of grieving, and you also speak many learned words like someone wise—but in truth the wise grieve neither for the dead nor for the living. (2.11)

— ॐ —

न त्वेवाहं जातु नासं न त्वं नेमे जनाधिपाः ।
na tvevāhaṁ jātu nāsaṁ na tvaṁ neme janādhipāḥ
न चैव न भविष्यामः सर्वे वयमतः परम् ॥२-१२॥
na caiva na bhaviṣyāmaḥ sarve vayamataḥ param (2-12)

Indeed there never was a time when I—or you or any of these kings—did not exist; nor it is that hereafter any of us shall cease to be. (2.12)

— ॐ —

देहिनोऽस्मिन्यथा देहे कौमारं यौवनं जरा ।
dehino'sminyathā dehe kaumāraṁ yauvanaṁ jarā
तथा देहान्तरप्राप्तिर्धीरस्तत्र न मुह्यति ॥२-१३॥
tathā dehāntaraprāptirdhīrastatra na muhyati (2-13)

Even as the embodied soul attains in this body the states of childhood, youth and old age—even so it obtains another body upon death; the wise do not get deluded witnessing these changes. (2.13)

— ॐ —

मात्रास्पर्शास्तु कौन्तेय शीतोष्णसुखदुःखदाः ।
mātrāsparśāstu kaunteya śītoṣṇasukhaduḥkhadāḥ
आगमापायिनोऽनित्यास्तांस्तितिक्षस्व भारत ॥२-१४॥
āgamāpāyino'nityāstāṁstitikṣasva bhārata (2-14)

From the contact of the sense-organs with sense-objects, there arise heat and cold, and even so pleasures and pains; but these are all transitory and fleeting and are subject to coming and going—so therefore just endure them, O Bhārata. (2.14)

— ॐ —

यं हि न व्यथयन्त्येते पुरुषं पुरुषर्षभ ।
yaṁ hi na vyathayantyete puruṣaṁ puruṣarṣabha
समदुःखसुखं धीरं सोऽमृतत्वाय कल्पते ॥२-१५॥
samaduḥkhasukhaṁ dhīraṁ so'mṛtatvāya kalpate (2-15)

One who is not afflicted by these changes—for whom pains and pleasures are all alike—that wise person of equipoise is fit for immortality. (2.15)

— ॐ —

नासतो विद्यते भावो नाभावो विद्यते सतः ।
nāsato vidyate bhāvo nābhāvo vidyate sataḥ
उभयोरपि दृष्टोऽन्तस्त्वनयोस्तत्त्वदर्शिभिः ॥२-१६॥
ubhayorapi dṛṣṭo'ntastvanayostattvadarśibhiḥ (2-16)

The unreal has no existence, and the real never ceases to be—the conclusion of both is clearly perceived at its stark reality by the knowers of Truth. (2.16)

— ॐ —

अविनाशि तु तद्विद्धि येन सर्वमिदं ततम् ।
avināśi tu tadviddhi yena sarvamidaṁ tatam
विनाशमव्ययस्यास्य न कश्चित्कर्तुमर्हति ॥२-१७॥
vināśamavyayasyāsya na kaścitkartumarhati (2-17)

That-One—by whom this entire universe stands pervaded—know That alone to be imperishable; verily no one can bring about the destruction of that Immutable Principle—(2.17)

— ॐ —

अन्तवन्त इमे देहा नित्यस्योक्ताः शरीरिणः ।
antavanta ime dehā nityasyoktāḥ śarīriṇaḥ
अनाशिनोऽप्रमेयस्य तस्माद्युध्यस्व भारत ॥२-१८॥
anāśino'prameyasya tasmādyudhyasva bhārata (2-18)

—whereas all the external material body sheaths of that eternal, imperishable, immeasurable embodied Self, will perish and must come to an end. Therefore fight on, O Bhārata. (2.18)

— ॐ —

य एनं वेत्ति हन्तारं यश्चैनं मन्यते हतम् ।
ya enaṁ vetti hantāraṁ yaścainaṁ manyate hatam
उभौ तौ न विजानीतो नायं हन्ति न हन्यते ॥२-१९॥
ubhau tau na vijānīto nāyaṁ hanti na hanyate (2-19)

He who thinks of It to be a slayer, and who thinks of It as slain, both of them are ignorant—for verily the Self neither kills, nor gets killed. (2.19)

— ॐ —

न जायते म्रियते वा कदाचिन् नायं भूत्वा भविता वा न भूयः ।
na jāyate mriyate vā kadācin nāyaṁ bhūtvā bhavitā vā na bhūyaḥ
अजो नित्यः शाश्वतोऽयं पुराणो न हन्यते हन्यमाने शरीरे ॥२-२०॥
ajo nityaḥ śāśvato'yaṁ purāṇo na hanyate hanyamāne śarīre (2-20)

The Self is never born, nor does It ever die; nor does It come into existence by the body coming into being. Verily the Soul is unborn, immutable, constant, eternal and ancient-most. Even though the body is slain, the indwelling Self always persists unslain. (2.20)

— ॐ —

वेदाविनाशिनं नित्यं य एनमजमव्ययम् ।
vedāvināśinaṁ nityaṁ ya enamajamavyayam
कथं स पुरुषः पार्थ कं घातयति हन्ति कम् ॥२-२१॥
kathaṁ sa puruṣaḥ pārtha kaṁ ghātayati hanti kam (2-21)

The realized one—who knows the Self to be imperishable, constant and eternal, free of birth, death, decay—how can that realized person kill anyone? Or cause any death? And by what means? (2.21)

— ॐ —

वासांसि जीर्णानि यथा विहाय नवानि गृह्णाति नरोऽपराणि ।
vāsāṁsi jīrṇāni yathā vihāya navāni gṛhṇāti naro'parāṇi
तथा शरीराणि विहाय जीर्णान्यन्यानि संयाति नवानि देही ॥२-२२॥
tathā śarīrāṇi vihāya jīrṇānyanyāni saṁyāti navāni dehī (2-22)

Discarding worn-out garments, just as a person puts on new garbs, in like fashion does the embodied Self—casting off decrepit, outworn bodies—enters into other newer ones. (2.22)

— ॐ —

नैनं छिन्दन्ति शस्त्राणि नैनं दहति पावकः ।
nainaṁ chindanti śastrāṇi nainaṁ dahati pāvakaḥ
न चैनं क्लेदयन्त्यापो न शोषयति मारुतः ॥२-२३॥
na cainaṁ kledayantyāpo na śoṣayati mārutaḥ (2-23)

Weapons do not cut the Self; and fires burn It not; and water cannot drench It; nor can It the winds dry. (2.23)

— ॐ —

अच्छेद्योऽयमदाह्योऽयमक्लेद्योऽशोष्य एव च ।
acchedyo'yamadāhyo'yamakledyo'śoṣya eva ca
नित्यः सर्वगतः स्थाणुरचलोऽयं सनातनः ॥२-२४॥
nityaḥ sarvagataḥ sthāṇuracalo'yaṁ sanātanaḥ (2-24)

Verily the Self is not capable of being cut, or burnt; nor can It perish in water, or become dried—because the Self is eternal, all-pervading, unchanging, immovable, primordial. (2.24)

— ॐ —

अव्यक्तोऽयमचिन्त्योऽयमविकार्योऽयमुच्यते ।
avyakto'yamacintyo'yamavikāryo'yamucyate
तस्मादेवं विदित्वैनं नानुशोचितुमर्हसि ॥२-२५॥
tasmādevaṁ viditvainaṁ nānuśocitumarhasi (2-25)

This Self is spoken of as unmanifest, uncomprehensible and unchangeable; so knowing it to be such, you ought never to grieve. (2.25)

— ॐ —

अथ चैनं नित्यजातं नित्यं वा मन्यसे मृतम् ।
atha cainaṁ nityajātaṁ nityaṁ vā manyase mṛtam
तथापि त्वं महाबाहो नैवं शोचितुमर्हसि ॥२-२६॥
tathāpi tvaṁ mahābāho naivaṁ śocitumarhasi (2-26)

However, even if you suppose that the Soul is perpetually born and perpetually dies, even then there's no reason to grieve, O mighty-armed. (2.26)

— ॐ —

जातस्य हि ध्रुवो मृत्युर्ध्रुवं जन्म मृतस्य च ।
jātasya hi dhruvo mṛtyurdhruvaṁ janma mṛtasya ca
तस्मादपरिहार्येऽर्थे न त्वं शोचितुमर्हसि ॥२-२७॥
tasmādaparihārye'rthe na tvaṁ śocitumarhasi (2-27)

Because in that case, death is inevitable for one who is born; and after death rebirth is equally certain. Therefore over that inevitability you ought not to grieve. (2.27)

— ॐ —

अव्यक्तादीनि भूतानि व्यक्तमध्यानि भारत ।
avyaktādīni bhūtāni vyaktamadhyāni bhārata
अव्यक्तनिधनान्येव तत्र का परिदेवना ॥२-२८॥
avyaktanidhanānyeva tatra kā paridevanā (2-28)

Beings have the Unmanifest as their beginning; and upon death they return to that Unmanifest again. Between birth and death—only during the interim—do the beings become manifest; so wherefore lament for any one, O Bhārata? (2.28)

— ॐ —

आश्चर्यवत्पश्यति कश्चिदेनमाश्चर्यवद्वदति तथैव चान्यः ।
āścaryavatpaśyati kaścidenamāścaryavadvadati tathaiva cānyaḥ
आश्चर्यवच्चैनमन्यः श्रृणोति श्रुत्वाप्येनं वेद न चैव कश्चित् ॥२-२९॥
āścaryavaccainamanyaḥ śṛṇoti śrutvāpyenaṁ veda na caiva kaścit (2-29)

Some realize and marvel at this wonderful Self; others discuss of this curious wonderment; while some just get to hear of this curiosity; but countless others, even after hearing etc., still cannot fathom the Self at all. (2.29)

— ॐ —

देही नित्यमवध्योऽयं देहे सर्वस्य भारत ।
dehī nityamavadhyo'yaṁ dehe sarvasya bhārata
तस्मात्सर्वाणि भूतानि न त्वं शोचितुमर्हसि ॥२-३०॥
tasmātsarvāṇi bhūtāni na tvaṁ śocitumarhasi (2-30)

The indwelling Self, within the bodies of all, is eternally indestructible, O Bhārata, therefore, you ought not to grieve for any being. (2.30)

— ॐ —

स्वधर्ममपि चावेक्ष्य न विकम्पितुमर्हसि ।
svadharmamapi cāvekṣya na vikampitumarhasi
धर्म्याद्धि युद्धाच्छ्रेयोऽन्यत्क्षत्रियस्य न विद्यते ॥२-३१॥
dharmyāddhi yuddhācchreyo'nyatkṣatriyasya na vidyate (2-31)

And considering your own duty as well, you should not waver—for there is no greater good-fortune for a Kshatriya than a righteous battle that stands before. (2.31)

— ॐ —

यदृच्छया चोपपन्नं स्वर्गद्वारमपावृतम् ।
yadṛcchayā copapannaṁ svargadvāramapāvṛtam
सुखिनः क्षत्रियाः पार्थ लभन्ते युद्धमीदृशम् ॥ २-३२ ॥
sukhinaḥ kṣatriyāḥ pārtha labhante yuddhamīdṛśam (2-32)

Fortunate is the Kshatriya who gets to fight in a battle that has thus come unsought; verily it's an open portal to heaven, O Pārtha. (2.32)

— ॐ —

अथ चेत्त्वमिमं धर्म्यं सङ्ग्रामं न करिष्यसि ।
atha cettvamimaṁ dharmyaṁ saṅgrāmaṁ na kariṣyasi
ततः स्वधर्मं कीर्तिं च हित्वा पापमवाप्स्यसि ॥ २-३३ ॥
tataḥ svadharmaṁ kīrtiṁ ca hitvā pāpamavāpsyasi (2-33)

If you do not fight this righteous war, then shirking your duty and losing your reputation, you will incur sin as well. (2.33)

— ॐ —

अकीर्तिं चापि भूतानि कथयिष्यन्ति तेऽव्ययाम् ।
akīrtiṁ cāpi bhūtāni kathayiṣyanti te'vyayām
सम्भावितस्य चाकीर्तिर्मरणादतिरिच्यते ॥ २-३४ ॥
sambhāvitasya cākīrtirmaraṇādatiricyate (2-34)

And people will forever speak of your unending dishonor and shame, and for one held in high esteem, infamy is worse than death. (2.34)

— ॐ —

भयाद्रणादुपरतं मंस्यन्ते त्वां महारथाः ।
bhayādraṇāduparataṁ maṁsyante tvāṁ mahārathāḥ
येषां च त्वं बहुमतो भूत्वा यास्यसि लाघवम् ॥ २-३५ ॥
yeṣāṁ ca tvaṁ bahumato bhūtvā yāsyasi lāghavam (2-35)

These mighty warriors will think that you have withdrawn from the battle out of fear; and having hitherto been held in high esteem, you will fall into utter disgrace. (2.35)

— ॐ —

अवाच्यवादांश्च बहून्वदिष्यन्ति तवाहिताः ।
avācyavādāṁśca bahūnvadiṣyanti tavāhitāḥ
निन्दन्तस्तव सामर्थ्यं ततो दुःखतरं नु किम् ॥ २-३६ ॥
nindantastava sāmarthyaṁ tato duḥkhataraṁ nu kim (2-36)

Disparaging you, your enemies will utter many unmentionable things decrying your prowess. Now what could be more painful than such humiliation? (2.36)

— ॐ —

हतो वा प्राप्स्यसि स्वर्गं जित्वा वा भोक्ष्यसे महीम् ।
hato vā prāpsyasi svargaṁ jitvā vā bhokṣyase mahīm
तस्मादुत्तिष्ठ कौन्तेय युद्धाय कृतनिश्चयः ॥२-३७॥
tasmāduttiṣṭha kaunteya yuddhāya kṛtaniścayaḥ (2-37)

Either killed in battle you shall attain to heavens, or emerging victorious you shall enjoy sovereignty upon earth. So arise O son of Kuntī, stand up determined to fight. (2.37)

— ॐ —

सुखदुःखे समे कृत्वा लाभालाभौ जयाजयौ ।
sukhaduḥkhe same kṛtvā lābhālābhau jayājayau
ततो युद्धाय युज्यस्व नैवं पापमवाप्स्यसि ॥२-३८॥
tato yuddhāya yujyasva naivaṁ pāpamavāpsyasi (2-38)

Treating everything alike—regarding happiness and sorrow, gain and loss, victory and defeat, all to be equal—make yourself ready for the duty to battle; fighting this way, you will not incur sin. (2.38)

— ॐ —

एषा तेऽभिहिता साङ्ख्ये बुद्धिर्योगे त्विमां शृणु ।
eṣā te'bhihitā sāṅkhye buddhiryoge tvimāṁ śṛṇu
बुद्ध्या युक्तो यया पार्थ कर्मबन्धं प्रहास्यसि ॥२-३९॥
buddhyā yukto yayā pārtha karmabandhaṁ prahāsyasi (2-39)

What has just been told to you is from the view of requisite mental attitude to be adopted concerning the Self; now hear of it from the viewpoint of Karma—being endowed with which perspective you shall rent asunder all bondages born of Karma. (2.39)

— ॐ —

नेहाभिक्रमनाशोऽस्ति प्रत्यवायो न विद्यते ।
nehābhikramanāśo'sti pratyavāyo na vidyate
स्वल्पमप्यस्य धर्मस्य त्रायते महतो भयात् ॥२-४०॥
svalpamapyasya dharmasya trāyate mahato bhayāt (2-40)

In this path there is no loss of endeavor, nor is there any fear of incurring sin; even the least bit of this Dharma saves one from great danger and fear. (2.40)

— ॐ —

व्यवसायात्मिका बुद्धिरेकेह कुरुनन्दन ।
vyavasāyātmikā buddhirekeha kurunandana
बहुशाखा ह्यनन्ताश्च बुद्धयोऽव्यवसायिनाम् ॥ २-४१ ॥
bahuśākhā hyanantāśca buddhayo'vyavasāyinām (2-41)

In this path, O Kurū-Nandana, there is a single one-pointed determination—as opposed to the undecided wanderings of the irresolute, in infinite directions. (2.41)

— ॐ —

यामिमां पुष्पितां वाचं प्रवदन्त्यविपश्चितः ।
yāmimāṁ puṣpitāṁ vācaṁ pravadantyavipaścitaḥ
वेदवादरताः पार्थ नान्यदस्तीति वादिनः ॥ २-४२ ॥
vedavādaratāḥ pārtha nānyadastīti vādinaḥ (2-42)
कामात्मानः स्वर्गपरा जन्मकर्मफलप्रदाम् ।
kāmātmānaḥ svargaparā janmakarmaphalapradām
क्रियाविशेषबहुलां भोगैश्वर्यगतिं प्रति ॥ २-४३ ॥
kriyāviśeṣabahulāṁ bhogaiśvaryagatiṁ prati (2-43)
भोगैश्वर्यप्रसक्तानां तयापहृतचेतसाम् ।
bhogaiśvaryaprasaktānāṁ tayāpahṛtacetasām
व्यवसायात्मिका बुद्धिः समाधौ न विधीयते ॥ २-४४ ॥
vyavasāyātmikā buddhiḥ samādhau na vidhīyate (2-44)

The dull-witted—who are full of worldly desires, who are devoted merely to the eulogistic verses of the scriptures, who look upon heaven as the supreme goal arguing that there is nothing else beyond—utter familiar ornate words to advocate various ritualistic rites producing birth, actions, and fruits, as the means towards enjoyments and power. Those who are attached to pleasures and worldly powers and whose minds get carried away by such flowery language, do not attain to the determinate intellect which leads to *Samādhi*—the absorption in the Absolute. (2.42-2.44)

— ॐ —

त्रैगुण्यविषया वेदा निस्त्रैगुण्यो भवार्जुन ।
traiguṇyaviṣayā vedā nistraiguṇyo bhavārjuna
निर्द्वन्द्वो नित्यसत्त्वस्थो निर्योगक्षेम आत्मवान् ॥ २-४५ ॥
nirdvandvo nityasattvastho niryogakṣema ātmavān (2-45)

The ritualistic scriptures deal with subjects that come under the dominion of the three *Gunas*, O Arjuna—but remaining indifferent to this three-fold domain, do thou dwell self-possessed. Rising above the pairs of opposites like pleasures and aversions, and going above revelry, and remaining unconcerned with acquisition and preservation, always dwell established within the Self. (2.45)

— ॐ —

यावानर्थ उदपाने सर्वतः सम्प्लुतोदके ।
yāvānartha udapāne sarvataḥ samplutodake
तावान्सर्वेषु वेदेषु ब्राह्मणस्य विजानतः ॥२-४६॥
tāvānsarveṣu vedeṣu brāhmaṇasya vijānataḥ (2-46)

All the purposes which a small reservoir serves, is served entirely by a vast lake full of water. Likewise the purpose which all the scriptures serve, is already attained by one who is in complete knowledge of Brahama. (2.46)

— ॐ —

कर्मण्येवाधिकारस्ते मा फलेषु कदाचन ।
karmaṇyevādhikāraste mā phaleṣu kadācana
मा कर्मफलहेतुर्भूर्मा ते सङ्गोऽस्त्वकर्मणि ॥२-४७॥
mā karmaphalaheturbhūrmā te saṅgo'stvakarmaṇi (2-47)

To work alone you have the right—but as to the fruits, do not lay any claims. Let not the outcome of actions be your motive—and be not attached to inaction either. (2.47)

— ॐ —

योगस्थः कुरु कर्माणि सङ्गं त्यक्त्वा धनञ्जय ।
yogasthaḥ kuru karmāṇi saṅgaṁ tyaktvā dhanañjaya
सिद्ध्यसिद्ध्योः समो भूत्वा समत्वं योग उच्यते ॥२-४८॥
siddhyasiddhyoḥ samo bhūtvā samatvaṁ yoga ucyate (2-48)

Established in Yoga, perform Karma renouncing all attachments, O Dhananjaya, remaining unconcerned as to the outcome—be it failure or success; this equanimity of mind is what is called Karma-Yoga. (2.48)

— ॐ —

दूरेण ह्यवरं कर्म बुद्धियोगाद्धनञ्जय ।
dūreṇa hyavaraṁ karma buddhiyogāddhanañjaya
बुद्धौ शरणमन्विच्छ कृपणाः फलहेतवः ॥२-४९॥
buddhau śaraṇamanviccha kṛpaṇāḥ phalahetavaḥ (2-49)

Compared to work done through such wisdom of equanimity, all other work is far inferior. Seek refuge in this equipoise of mind, O Dhananjaya—for those that yearn for fruit are wretched and miserable indeed. (2.49)

— ॐ —

बुद्धियुक्तो जहातीह उभे सुकृतदुष्कृते ।
buddhiyukto jahātīha ubhe sukṛtaduṣkṛte
तस्माद्योगाय युज्यस्व योगः कर्मसु कौशलम् ॥ २-५० ॥
tasmādyogāya yujyasva yogaḥ karmasu kauśalam (2-50)

Endowed with equanimity, one gets rid of both good and evil in life; therefore take to the path of Karma-Yoga—which leads to dexterity in performance of work. (2.50)

— ॐ —

कर्मजं बुद्धियुक्ता हि फलं त्यक्त्वा मनीषिणः ।
karmajaṁ buddhiyuktā hi phalaṁ tyaktvā manīṣiṇaḥ
जन्मबन्धविनिर्मुक्ताः पदं गच्छन्त्यनामयम् ॥ २-५१ ॥
janmabandhavinirmuktāḥ padaṁ gacchantyanāmayam (2-51)

Endowed with the wisdom of equanimity, and abandoning attachments to the fruits born of action, the Karma-Yogī is thereby freed of the shackles of births and deaths and attains to self-realization—ascending to that supreme Abode which is void of all sorrows. (2.51)

— ॐ —

यदा ते मोहकलिलं बुद्धिर्व्यतितरिष्यति ।
yadā te mohakalilaṁ buddhirvyatitariṣyati
तदा गन्तासि निर्वेदं श्रोतव्यस्य श्रुतस्य च ॥ २-५२ ॥
tadā gantāsi nirvedaṁ śrotavyasya śrutasya ca (2-52)

When your understanding has fully crossed the dense forest of delusions, then your mind shall go beyond words—beyond those already heard, or that which you think you yet need to learn. (2.52)

— ॐ —

श्रुतिविप्रतिपन्ना ते यदा स्थास्यति निश्चला ।
śrutivipratipannā te yadā sthāsyati niścalā
समाधावचला बुद्धिस्तदा योगमवाप्स्यसि ॥ २-५३ ॥
samādhāvacalā buddhistadā yogamavāpsyasi (2-53)

When your understanding, now perplexed by variegated hearing, has gone past that—to rest in Samadhi, unwavering and steady—then you shall have attained to steadfastness in Yoga." (2.53)

अर्जुन उवाच --
arjuna uvāca --

स्थितप्रज्ञस्य का भाषा समाधिस्थस्य केशव ।
sthitaprajñasya kā bhāṣā samādhisthasya keśava
स्थितधीः किं प्रभाषेत किमासीत व्रजेत किम् ॥२-५४॥
sthitadhīḥ kiṁ prabhāṣeta kimāsīta vrajeta kim (2-54)

Arjuna said: "O Keshava, what are the characteristics of a man of steady wisdom who has become established in Samādhi? How does such a one abide, how he walks, how he talks?" (2.54)

श्रीभगवानुवाच --
śrībhagavānuvāca --

प्रजहाति यदा कामान्सर्वान्पार्थ मनोगतान् ।
prajahāti yadā kāmānsarvānpārtha manogatān
आत्मन्येवात्मना तुष्टः स्थितप्रज्ञस्तदोच्यते ॥२-५५॥
ātmanyevātmanā tuṣṭaḥ sthitaprajñastadocyate (2-55)

Shri Bhagwāna said: "O Pārtha, when one has cast off all the cravings of the mind, and when one takes delight in the joy of the Self alone—then such a one is said to be of steady wisdom. (2.55)

— ॐ —

दुःखेष्वनुद्विग्नमनाः सुखेषु विगतस्पृहः ।
duḥkheṣvanudvignamanāḥ sukheṣu vigataspṛhaḥ
वीतरागभयक्रोधः स्थितधीर्मुनिरुच्यते ॥२-५६॥
vītarāgabhayakrodhaḥ sthitadhīrmunirucyate (2-56)

He who is unperturbed amidst sorrows, desireless amid pleasures; he who is innocent of attachments, fear, anger—he is said to be a man of steady wisdom. (2.56)

— ॐ —

यः सर्वत्रानभिस्नेहस्तत्तत्प्राप्य शुभाशुभम् ।
yaḥ sarvatrānabhisnehastattatprāpya śubhāśubham
नाभिनन्दति न द्वेष्टि तस्य प्रज्ञा प्रतिष्ठिता ॥२-५७॥
nābhinandati na dveṣṭi tasya prajñā pratiṣṭhitā (2-57)

He who is free of fondness, affection, attachment in every respect, who getting good or evil neither rejoices nor recoils—he is said to be established in perfect wisdom. (2.57)

— ॐ —

यदा संहरते चायं कूर्मोऽङ्गानीव सर्वशः ।
yadā saṁharate cāyaṁ kūrmo'ṅgānīva sarvaśaḥ
इन्द्रियाणीन्द्रियार्थेभ्यस्तस्य प्रज्ञा प्रतिष्ठिता ॥ २-५८ ॥
indriyāṇīndriyārthebhyastasya prajñā pratiṣṭhitā (2-58)

When one can altogether withdraw the senses from the sense-objects—even as a tortoise its limbs—then his wisdom is said to be steady. (2.58)

— ॐ —

विषया विनिवर्तन्ते निराहारस्य देहिनः ।
viṣayā vinivartante nirāhārasya dehinaḥ
रसवर्जं रसोऽप्यस्य परं दृष्ट्वा निवर्तते ॥ २-५९ ॥
rasavarjaṁ raso'pyasya paraṁ dṛṣṭvā nivartate (2-59)

Sense enjoyments can be restricted through physical restraint by an abstemious being, no doubt—but a relish for them may still persist; even this relish falls off when the highest bliss—the Bliss of the Supreme is realized. (2.59)

— ॐ —

यततो ह्यपि कौन्तेय पुरुषस्य विपश्चितः ।
yatato hyapi kaunteya puruṣasya vipaścitaḥ
इन्द्रियाणि प्रमाथीनि हरन्ति प्रसभं मनः ॥ २-६० ॥
indriyāṇi pramāthīni haranti prasabhaṁ manaḥ (2-60)

The senses are potent and turbulent, O Kuntī-son; they forcibly carry away the mind engaged in self-control—even those of the struggling wise. (2.60)

— ॐ —

तानि सर्वाणि संयम्य युक्त आसीत मत्परः ।
tāni sarvāṇi saṁyamya yukta āsīta matparaḥ
वशे हि यस्येन्द्रियाणि तस्य प्रज्ञा प्रतिष्ठिता ॥ २-६१ ॥
vaśe hi yasyendriyāṇi tasya prajñā pratiṣṭhitā (2-61)

So restraining all sense-organs, the self-controlled one should sit meditating directing them upon Me. One whose senses are thus under control—is said to be established in perfect wisdom. (2.61)

— ॐ —

ध्यायतो विषयान्पुंसः सङ्गस्तेषूपजायते ।
dhyāyato viṣayānpuṁsaḥ saṅgasteṣūpajāyate
सङ्गात्सञ्जायते कामः कामात्क्रोधोऽभिजायते ॥२-६२॥
saṅgātsañjāyate kāmaḥ kāmātkrodho'bhijāyate (2-62)

When one dwells upon the sense-objects, an attachment for them ensues as a matter of course; and from attachment springs desire; and of desires that become frustrated, anger is the instinctive outcome. (2.62)

— ॐ —

क्रोधाद्भवति सम्मोहः सम्मोहात्स्मृतिविभ्रमः ।
krodhādbhavati sammohaḥ sammohātsmṛtivibhramaḥ
स्मृतिभ्रंशाद् बुद्धिनाशो बुद्धिनाशात्प्रणश्यति ॥२-६३॥
smṛtibhraṁśād buddhināśo buddhināśātpraṇaśyati (2-63)

From anger arises delusion; from delusion comes bewilderment of cognition and memory; and this bafflement leads to loss of intelligence; and through loss of reason—one comes by complete ruin. (2.63)

— ॐ —

रागद्वेषविमुक्तैस्तु विषयानिन्द्रियैश्चरन् ।
rāgadveṣavimuktaistu viṣayānindriyaiścaran
आत्मवश्यैर्विधेयात्मा प्रसादमधिगच्छति ॥२-६४॥
ātmavaśyairvidheyātmā prasādamadhigacchati (2-64)

Avoiding all that, the self-controlled Sādhaka—with his senses governed by the Self, who is free from attachments and aversions—attains to peace and tranquility even though moving amidst sense-objects. (2.64)

— ॐ —

प्रसादे सर्वदुःखानां हानिरस्योपजायते ।
prasāde sarvaduḥkhānāṁ hānirasyopajāyate
प्रसन्नचेतसो ह्याशु बुद्धिः पर्यवतिष्ठते ॥२-६५॥
prasannacetaso hyāśu buddhiḥ paryavatiṣṭhate (2-65)

When this tranquility is attained, there ensues destruction of all sorrows, every misery; and forthwith, that serene-minded one becomes established in steady wisdom. (2.65)

— ॐ —

नास्ति बुद्धिरयुक्तस्य न चायुक्तस्य भावना ।
nāsti buddhirayuktasya na cāyuktasya bhāvanā
न चाभावयतः शान्तिरशान्तस्य कुतः सुखम् ॥ २-६६ ॥
na cābhāvayataḥ śāntiraśāntasya kutaḥ sukham (2-66)

For one bereft of control, there's no determinate intellect—and no meditation either; without meditation, there's no peace; and, for one bereft of peace—how can there be happiness? (2.66)

— ॐ —

इन्द्रियाणां हि चरतां यन्मनोऽनुविधीयते ।
indriyāṇāṁ hi caratāṁ yanmano'nuvidhīyate
तदस्य हरति प्रज्ञां वायुर्नावमिवाम्भसि ॥ २-६७ ॥
tadasya harati prajñāṁ vāyurnāvamivāmbhasi (2-67)

To whichsoever of the wandering senses the mind becomes engaged, that very one forcibly carries the mind away. A mind that yields to the wandering senses gets borne away perforce—just like the wind carries away ships sailing on the waterways. (2.67)

— ॐ —

तस्माद्यस्य महाबाहो निगृहीतानि सर्वशः ।
tasmādyasya mahābāho nigṛhītāni sarvaśaḥ
इन्द्रियाणीन्द्रियार्थेभ्यस्तस्य प्रज्ञा प्रतिष्ठिता ॥ २-६८ ॥
indriyāṇīndriyārthebhyastasya prajñā pratiṣṭhitā (2-68)

Therefore O mighty-armed, he whose senses are governed and controlled away from the sense-objects—he becomes established in perfect wisdom. (2.68)

— ॐ —

या निशा सर्वभूतानां तस्यां जागर्ति संयमी ।
yā niśā sarvabhūtānāṁ tasyāṁ jāgarti saṁyamī
यस्यां जाग्रति भूतानि सा निशा पश्यतो मुनेः ॥ २-६९ ॥
yasyāṁ jāgrati bhūtāni sā niśā paśyato muneḥ (2-69)

That which is night to all beings—that is where the self-restrained one abides completely awake; and that in which all beings are actively awake—that is a dark night unto the introspective sage. (2.69)

— ॐ —

आपूर्यमाणमचलप्रतिष्ठं समुद्रमापः प्रविशन्ति यद्वत् ।
āpūryamāṇamacalapratiṣṭhaṁ samudramāpaḥ praviśanti yadvat
तद्वत्कामा यं प्रविशन्ति सर्वे स शान्तिमाप्नोति न कामकामी ॥ २-७० ॥
tadvatkāmā yaṁ praviśanti sarve sa śāntimāpnoti na kāmakāmī (2-70)

One in whom all sense-objects enter like unto an ocean—which though being continually filled by entering rivers, always remains unagitated, unaffected—that one alone attains to tranquility, and not he who hankers after sense enjoyments. (2.70)

— ॐ —

विहाय कामान्यः सर्वान्पुमांश्चरति निःस्पृहः ।
vihāya kāmānyaḥ sarvānpumāṁścarati niḥspṛhaḥ
निर्ममो निरहङ्कारः स शान्तिमधिगच्छति ॥ २-७१ ॥
nirmamo nirahaṅkāraḥ sa śāntimadhigacchati (2-71)

He who, giving up all sense-objects, moves about unattached—free of egoism and devoid of the idea of ownership—he reaches that state of tranquility. (2.71)

— ॐ —

एषा ब्राह्मी स्थितिः पार्थ नैनां प्राप्य विमुह्यति ।
eṣā brāhmī sthitiḥ pārtha naināṁ prāpya vimuhyati
स्थित्वास्यामन्तकालेऽपि ब्रह्मनिर्वाणमृच्छति ॥ २-७२ ॥
sthitvāsyāmantakāle'pi brahmanirvāṇamṛcchati (2-72)

That is the Brāhmmī state, O Pārtha, attaining which one persists deluded no more. One who gets established in that state—even in the final moments of life—attains to the final Nirvāna in Brahama." (2.72)

ॐ तत्सदिति श्रीमद्भगवद्गीतासूपनिषत्सु
om tatsaditi śrīmadbhagavadgītāsūpaniṣatsu
ब्रह्मविद्यायां योगशास्त्रे श्रीकृष्णार्जुनसंवादे
brahmavidyāyāṁ yogaśāstre śrīkṛṣṇārjunasaṁvāde
साङ्ख्ययोगो नाम द्वितीयोऽध्यायः ॥
sāṅkhyayogo nāma dvitīyo'dhyāyaḥ .

In this Yogic Scripture on the Science of Brahama—the Shrimada-Bhāgvada-Gītā Upanishad—
hereby ends the dialogue between Shrī Krishna and Arjuna entitled:
Sānkhya Yoga, Canto II

तृतीयोऽध्यायः - कर्मयोगः

tṛtīyo'dhyāyaḥ - karmayogaḥ

:: Canto – III ::

- The Path of Karma -

अर्जुन उवाच --
arjuna uvāca --

ज्यायसी चेत्कर्मणस्ते मता बुद्धिर्जनार्दन ।
jyāyasī cetkarmaṇaste matā buddhirjanārdana
तत्किं कर्मणि घोरे मां नियोजयसि केशव ॥ ३-१ ॥
tatkiṁ karmaṇi ghore māṁ niyojayasi keśava (3-1)

Arjuna said: "O Janārdana, if you consider knowledge to be superior to action (karma), then why, O Keshava, do you urge me to engage in such direful karma? (3.1)

— ॐ —

व्यामिश्रेणेव वाक्येन बुद्धिं मोहयसीव मे ।
vyāmiśreṇeva vākyena buddhiṁ mohayasīva me
तदेकं वद निश्चित्य येन श्रेयोऽहमाप्नुयाम् ॥ ३-२ ॥
tadekaṁ vada niścitya yena śreyo'hamāpnuyām (3-2)

By these apparently conflicting words you are, as it were, befuddling my understanding; do please tell me the one definite thing which shall obtain my highest good." (3.2)

श्रीभगवानुवाच --
śrībhagavānuvāca --

लोकेऽस्मिन् द्विविधा निष्ठा पुरा प्रोक्ता मयानघ ।
loke'smin dvividhā niṣṭhā purā proktā mayānagha
ज्ञानयोगेन साङ्ख्यानां कर्मयोगेन योगिनाम् ॥ ३-३ ॥
jñānayogena sāṅkhyānāṁ karmayogena yoginām (3-3)

Shri Bhagwāna said: "Listen O sinless-one, at an earlier time a two-fold faith had been declared by Me unto mankind: the way of Knowledge (for the Sānkhyas), and the way of Karma (for the Yogīs). (3.3)

— ॐ —

न कर्मणामनारम्भान्नैष्कर्म्यं पुरुषोऽश्नुते ।

na karmaṇāmanārambhānnaiṣkarmyaṁ puruṣo'śnute

न च संन्यसनादेव सिद्धिं समधिगच्छति ॥ ३-४ ॥

na ca saṁnyasanādeva siddhiṁ samadhigacchati (3-4)

Do know that by not performing work, a person does not necessarily reach inactivity which leads one to flawlessness; nor does he inevitably attain perfection by merely relinquishing possessions. (3.4)

— ॐ —

न हि कश्चित्क्षणमपि जातु तिष्ठत्यकर्मकृत् ।

na hi kaścitkṣaṇamapi jātu tiṣṭhatyakarmakṛt

कार्यते ह्यवशः कर्म सर्वः प्रकृतिजैर्गुणैः ॥ ३-५ ॥

kāryate hyavaśaḥ karma sarvaḥ prakṛtijairguṇaiḥ (3-5)

Moreover know for certain that no one can remain inactive even for a moment—for all beings are helplessly driven to work by the qualities born of Prakriti. (3.5)

— ॐ —

कर्मेन्द्रियाणि संयम्य य आस्ते मनसा स्मरन् ।

karmendriyāṇi saṁyamya ya āste manasā smaran

इन्द्रियार्थान्विमूढात्मा मिथ्याचारः स उच्यते ॥ ३-६ ॥

indriyārthānvimūḍhātmā mithyācāraḥ sa ucyate (3-6)

The fool who—though outwardly restraining the organs of action—sits dwelling upon the senses-objects within the mind, that man of deluded intellect is called a hypocrite. (3.6)

— ॐ —

यस्त्विन्द्रियाणि मनसा नियम्यारभतेऽर्जुन ।

yastvindriyāṇi manasā niyamyārabhate'rjuna

कर्मेन्द्रियैः कर्मयोगमसक्तः स विशिष्यते ॥ ३-७ ॥

karmendriyaiḥ karmayogamasaktaḥ sa viśiṣyate (3-7)

But one who knows rightly—and consequently excels—is one who performs Karma-Yoga with the organs of actions outwardly while simultaneously remaining unattached within, with his sense-organs remaining within the control of his mind all the time. (3.7)

— ॐ —

नियतं कुरु कर्म त्वं कर्म ज्यायो ह्यकर्मणः ।

niyataṁ kuru karma tvaṁ karma jyāyo hyakarmaṇaḥ

शरीरयात्रापि च ते न प्रसिद्ध्येदकर्मणः ॥ ३-८ ॥

śarīrayātrāpi ca te na prasiddhyedakarmaṇaḥ (3-8)

Therefore do always perform your prescribed duties—because action is superior to inaction. Moreover, even the maintenance of the body is impossible if you resort to inactivity. (3.8)

— ॐ —

यज्ञार्थात्कर्मणोऽन्यत्र लोकोऽयं कर्मबन्धनः ।

yajñārthātkarmaṇo'nyatra loko'yaṁ karmabandhanaḥ

तदर्थं कर्म कौन्तेय मुक्तसङ्गः समाचर ॥ ३-९ ॥

tadarthaṁ karma kaunteya muktasaṅgaḥ samācara (3-9)

This world is subject to the bounds of Karma—other than such Karmas which are performed for the sake of Yajna. Therefore O Kuntī-son, do you efficiently perform your prescribed duties just for duty's sake—remaining free of attachments at the same time. (3.9)

— ॐ —

सहयज्ञाः प्रजाः सृष्ट्वा पुरोवाच प्रजापतिः ।

sahayajñāḥ prajāḥ sṛṣṭvā purovāca prajāpatiḥ

अनेन प्रसविष्यध्वमेष वोऽस्त्विष्टकामधुक् ॥ ३-१० ॥

anena prasaviṣyadhvameṣa vo'stviṣṭakāmadhuk (3-10)

At the time of Creation, Brahammā created yore beings so that they would subsist by dint of Yajna, and he ordained: 'Ye beings: by this Yajna, may thou prosper; and may it yield the covetable objects of thy wants. (3.10)

— ॐ —

देवान्भावयतानेन ते देवा भावयन्तु वः ।

devānbhāvayatānena te devā bhāvayantu vaḥ

परस्परं भावयन्तः श्रेयः परमवाप्स्यथ ॥ ३-११ ॥

parasparaṁ bhāvayantaḥ śreyaḥ paramavāpsyatha (3-11)

Through Yajna, foster the gods, and let the gods foster you in return; thus, mutually sustaining each other, you shall both attain to supreme good. (3.11)

— ॐ —

इष्टान्भोगान्हि वो देवा दास्यन्ते यज्ञभाविताः ।
iṣṭānbhogānhi vo devā dāsyante yajñabhāvitāḥ
तैर्दत्तानप्रदायैभ्यो यो भुङ्क्ते स्तेन एव सः ॥ ३-१२ ॥
tairdattānapradāyaibhyo yo bhuṅkte stena eva saḥ (3-12)

Delighted though Yajna, the gods will assuredly bestow on you the desired fruits. He who enjoys what has been conferred by gods—but without making an offering in return—is undoubtedly a thief. (3.12)

— ॐ —

यज्ञशिष्टाशिनः सन्तो मुच्यन्ते सर्वकिल्बिषैः ।
yajñaśiṣṭāśinaḥ santo mucyante sarvakilbiṣaiḥ
भुञ्जते ते त्वघं पापा ये पचन्त्यात्मकारणात् ॥ ३-१३ ॥
bhuñjate te tvaghaṁ pāpā ye pacantyātmakāraṇāt (3-13)

The virtuous—who partake of the remnants of Yajna—are absolved of all sins; and the sinful—who cook just for their own sake—partake of sin.' (3.13)

— ॐ —

अन्नाद्भवन्ति भूतानि पर्जन्यादन्नसम्भवः ।
annādbhavanti bhūtāni parjanyādannasambhavaḥ
यज्ञाद्भवति पर्जन्यो यज्ञः कर्मसमुद्भवः ॥ ३-१४ ॥
yajñādbhavati parjanyo yajñaḥ karmasamudbhavaḥ (3-14)

Beings are born of food; food is produced from rain; rain ensues from Yajna; and Yajna has its origin in Karma. (3.14)

— ॐ —

कर्म ब्रह्मोद्भवं विद्धि ब्रह्माक्षरसमुद्भवम् ।
karma brahmodbhavaṁ viddhi brahmākṣarasamudbhavam
तस्मात्सर्वगतं ब्रह्म नित्यं यज्ञे प्रतिष्ठितम् ॥ ३-१५ ॥
tasmātsarvagataṁ brahma nityaṁ yajñe pratiṣṭhitam (3-15)

And Karma originates from Brahammā, and Brahammā originates in Brahama—the Imperishable. Therefore the all-pervading Brahama abides everlastingly within the Yajna. (3.15)

— ॐ —

एवं प्रवर्तितं चक्रं नानुवर्तयतीह यः ।
evaṁ pravartitaṁ cakraṁ nānuvartayatīha yaḥ
अघायुरिन्द्रियारामो मोघं पार्थ स जीवति ॥ ३-१६ ॥
aghāyurindriyārāmo moghaṁ pārtha sa jīvati (3-16)

He who does not here follow this cycle which has been thus set revolving—who leads a sinful life and delights merely in the senses—in vain he lives, O Pārtha. (3.16)

— ॐ —

यस्त्वात्मरतिरेव स्यादात्मतृप्तश्च मानवः ।
yastvātmaratireva syādātmatṛptaśca mānavaḥ
आत्मन्येव च सन्तुष्टस्तस्य कार्यं न विद्यते ॥ ३-१७ ॥
ātmanyeva ca santuṣṭastasya kāryaṁ na vidyate (3-17)

But he who takes delight within the Self, who is satisfied with the Self, who is contented just only in the Self—he really has no works he needs perform. (3.17)

— ॐ —

नैव तस्य कृतेनार्थो नाकृतेनेह कश्चन ।
naiva tasya kṛtenārtho nākṛteneha kaścana
न चास्य सर्वभूतेषु कश्चिदर्थव्यपाश्रयः ॥ ३-१८ ॥
na cāsya sarvabhūteṣu kaścidarthavyapāśrayaḥ (3-18)

And he has no purpose to fulfill in the discharge of his duties, and he has no reason not to perform his prescribed work, nor has he any necessity to depend upon another being. (3.18)

— ॐ —

तस्मादसक्तः सततं कार्यं कर्म समाचर ।
tasmādasaktaḥ satataṁ kāryaṁ karma samācara
असक्तो ह्याचरन्कर्म परमाप्नोति पूरुषः ॥ ३-१९ ॥
asakto hyācarankarma paramāpnoti pūruṣaḥ (3-19)

So then, remaining unattached, always perform your prescribed duties. Verily a man attains the Supreme by performing unattached those Karmas which are ordained to be performed. (3.19)

— ॐ —

कर्मणैव हि संसिद्धिमास्थिता जनकादयः ।
karmaṇaiva hi saṁsiddhimāsthitā janakādayaḥ
लोकसङ्ग्रहमेवापि सम्पश्यन्कर्तुमर्हसि ॥ ३-२० ॥
lokasaṅgrahamevāpi sampaśyankartumarhasi (3-20)

It was only thusly—by performing Karmas bereft of any attachments—that people such as Janaka reached perfection. And even for showing the way to the world, you ought to take to the Path of Karma. (3.20)

— ॐ —

यद्यदाचरति श्रेष्ठस्तत्तदेवेतरो जनः ।
yadyadācarati śreṣṭhastattadevetaro janaḥ
स यत्प्रमाणं कुरुते लोकस्तदनुवर्तते ॥ ३-२१ ॥
sa yatpramāṇaṁ kurute lokastadanuvartate (3-21)

Because whatever an esteemed person does, others follow suit; and that which he accepts as definitive, others adopt the same. (3.21)

— ॐ —

न मे पार्थास्ति कर्तव्यं त्रिषु लोकेषु किञ्चन ।
na me pārthāsti kartavyaṁ triṣu lokeṣu kiñcana
नानवाप्तमवाप्तव्यं वर्त एव च कर्मणि ॥ ३-२२ ॥
nānavāptamavāptavyaṁ varta eva ca karmaṇi (3-22)

In all the three worlds, there is no duty for me to perform, nor anything to gain which's not already mine, O Pārtha—still I am ever engaged in Karma. (3.22)

— ॐ —

यदि ह्यहं न वर्तेयं जातु कर्मण्यतन्द्रितः ।
yadi hyahaṁ na varteyaṁ jātu karmaṇyatandritaḥ
मम वर्त्मानुवर्तन्ते मनुष्याः पार्थ सर्वशः ॥ ३-२३ ॥
mama vartmānuvartante manuṣyāḥ pārtha sarvaśaḥ (3-23)

If I were to cease being vigilantly engaged in action, then others too will follow my footsteps in every way, O Pārtha. (3.23)

— ॐ —

उत्सीदेयुरिमे लोका न कुर्यां कर्म चेदहम् ।
utsīdeyurime lokā na kuryāṁ karma cedaham
सङ्करस्य च कर्ता स्यामुपहन्यामिमाः प्रजाः ॥ ३-२४ ॥
saṅkarasya ca kartā syāmupahanyāmimāḥ prajāḥ (3-24)

If I cease to work, these worlds would perish, and I would prove to be the cause of disarray and the destruction of beings. (3.24)

— ॐ —

सक्ताः कर्मण्यविद्वांसो यथा कुर्वन्ति भारत ।

saktāḥ karmaṇyavidvāṁso yathā kurvanti bhārata

कुर्याद्विद्वांस्तथासक्तश्चिकीर्षुर्लोकसङ्ग्रहम् ॥ ३-२५ ॥

kuryādvidvāṁstathāsaktaścikīrṣurlokasaṅgraham (3-25)

Even as an ignorant person performs Karma—being attached to it—even so should the wise perform Karma—albeit unattached—with a view towards maintaining world-order. (3.25)

— ॐ —

न बुद्धिभेदं जनयेदज्ञानां कर्मसङ्गिनाम् ।

na buddhibhedaṁ janayedajñānāṁ karmasaṅginām

जोषयेत्सर्वकर्माणि विद्वान्युक्तः समाचरन् ॥ ३-२६ ॥

joṣayetsarvakarmāṇi vidvānyuktaḥ samācaran (3-26)

The wise should not unsettle the faith of the ignorant who perform work being attached to it—rather he should urge all towards devotion to work, while performing his own duties diligently. (3.26)

— ॐ —

प्रकृतेः क्रियमाणानि गुणैः कर्माणि सर्वशः ।

prakṛteḥ kriyamāṇāni guṇaiḥ karmāṇi sarvaśaḥ

अहङ्कारविमूढात्मा कर्ताहमिति मन्यते ॥ ३-२७ ॥

ahaṅkāravimūḍhātmā kartāhamiti manyate (3-27)

In truth all Karmas are performed impelled by the *Gunas* of Prakriti; it is a deluded being whose mind, deceived by his ego, believes that 'I am the doer.' (3.27)

— ॐ —

तत्त्ववित्तु महाबाहो गुणकर्मविभागयोः ।

tattvavittu mahābāho guṇakarmavibhāgayoḥ

गुणा गुणेषु वर्तन्त इति मत्वा न सज्जते ॥ ३-२८ ॥

guṇā guṇeṣu vartanta iti matvā na sajjate (3-28)

But he who understands the nature of things—who is insightful into the truth of the *Gunas* and their functional divisions, who knows that all *Gunas* are merely playing-out in accordance with their respective nature—he does not get ensnared in the performance of karmas, O mighty-armed. (3.28)

— ॐ —

प्रकृतेर्गुणसम्मूढाः सज्जन्ते गुणकर्मसु ।
prakṛterguṇasammūḍhāḥ sajjante guṇakarmasu
तानकृत्स्नविदो मन्दान्कृत्स्नविन्न विचालयेत् ॥ ३-२९ ॥
tānakṛtsnavido mandānkṛtsnavinna vicālayet (3-29)

Deluded by the constituents of Prakriti, people get attached to the senses and their functions; still the wise should not unsettle these dull-witted people of imperfect understanding. (3.29)

— ॐ —

मयि सर्वाणि कर्माणि संन्यस्याध्यात्मचेतसा ।
mayi sarvāṇi karmāṇi saṁnyasyādhyātmacetasā
निराशीर्निर्ममो भूत्वा युध्यस्व विगतज्वरः ॥ ३-३० ॥
nirāśīrnirmamo bhūtvā yudhyasva vigatajvaraḥ (3-30)

So renouncing all action in Me—and with your mind resting on the Self; and giving up all desires and ideas of ownership; and cured of your mental febrility—arise and fight. (3.30)

— ॐ —

ये मे मतमिदं नित्यमनुतिष्ठन्ति मानवाः ।
ye me matamidaṁ nityamanutiṣṭhanti mānavāḥ
श्रद्धावन्तोऽनसूयन्तो मुच्यन्ते तेऽपि कर्मभिः ॥ ३-३१ ॥
śraddhāvanto'nasūyanto mucyante te'pi karmabhiḥ (3-31)

Even those who endeavor and strive genuinely—who, without caviling, faithfully practice this teaching of mine with diligence—stand freed of the bondages of Karma. (3.31)

— ॐ —

ये त्वेतदभ्यसूयन्तो नानुतिष्ठन्ति मे मतम् ।
ye tvetadabhyasūyanto nānutiṣṭhanti me matam
सर्वज्ञानविमूढांस्तान्विद्धि नष्टानचेतसः ॥ ३-३२ ॥
sarvajñānavimūḍhāṁstānviddhi naṣṭānacetasaḥ (3-32)

But those who quibble and find trivial faults in this teaching—and thus fail to practice it—take such fools, bereft of all knowledge, to be doomed. (3.32)

— ॐ —

सदृशं चेष्टते स्वस्याः प्रकृतेर्ज्ञानवानपि ।
sadṛśaṁ ceṣṭate svasyāḥ prakṛterjñānavānapi
प्रकृतिं यान्ति भूतानि निग्रहः किं करिष्यति ॥ ३-३३ ॥
prakṛtiṁ yānti bhūtāni nigrahaḥ kiṁ kariṣyati (3-33)

Beings follow the dictates of their nature—even the wise act in accordance with their innate disposition—of what use is restraint then? (3.33)

— ॐ —

इन्द्रियस्येन्द्रियस्यार्थे रागद्वेषौ व्यवस्थितौ ।
indriyasyendriyasyārthe rāgadveṣau vyavasthitau
तयोर्न वशमागच्छेत्तौ ह्यस्य परिपन्थिनौ ॥ ३-३४ ॥
tayorna vaśamāgacchettau hyasya paripanthinau (3-34)

In respect of each of the sense-organs, the inclination for attraction and repulsion towards sense-objects is fixed by nature. But rather than coming under their sway, one should instead rise above them—for they are impediments in one's way. (3.34)

— ॐ —

श्रेयान्स्वधर्मो विगुणः परधर्मात्स्वनुष्ठितात् ।
śreyānsvadharmo viguṇaḥ paradharmātsvanuṣṭhitāt
स्वधर्मे निधनं श्रेयः परधर्मो भयावहः ॥ ३-३५ ॥
svadharme nidhanaṁ śreyaḥ paradharmo bhayāvahaḥ (3-35)

It is better to perform one's natural prescribed duty—even though tinged with faults—than to imitate another's duty that's perceived to be perfect. Even death in the cause of one's inborn Dharma is better—while following the Dharma of others is fraught with fear." (3.35)

अर्जुन उवाच --
arjuna uvāca --

अथ केन प्रयुक्तोऽयं पापं चरति पूरुषः ।
atha kena prayukto'yaṁ pāpaṁ carati pūruṣaḥ
अनिच्छन्नपि वार्ष्णेय बलादिव नियोजितः ॥ ३-३६ ॥
anicchannapi vārṣṇeya balādiva niyojitaḥ (3-36)

Arjuna said: "Impelled by what, O Varshneya, does man commit sin—involuntarily, in-spite of himself, as if propelled by some force?" (3.36)

श्रीभगवानुवाच --
śrībhagavānuvāca --

काम एष क्रोध एष रजोगुणसमुद्भवः ।
kāma eṣa krodha eṣa rajoguṇasamudbhavaḥ
महाशनो महापाप्मा विद्ध्येनमिह वैरिणम् ॥ ३-३७ ॥
mahāśano mahāpāpmā viddhyenamiha vairiṇam (3-37)

Shri Bhagwāna said: "It is ire and desire—begotten of the elements of Rājas, insatiable and grossly wicked—which are to be regarded as the culprits here: the veritable foes. (3.37)

— ॐ —

धूमेनाव्रियते वह्निर्यथादर्शो मलेन च ।
dhūmenāvriyate vahniryathādarśo malena ca
यथोल्बेनावृतो गर्भस्तथा तेनेदमावृतम् ॥ ३-३८ ॥
yatholbenāvṛto garbhastathā tenedamāvṛtam (3-38)

Even as fire is enveloped by smoke, and as a mirror is covered with dust, and as the fetus by amnion—even so knowledge gets beclouded by ire and desire. (3.38)

— ॐ —

आवृतं ज्ञानमेतेन ज्ञानिनो नित्यवैरिणा ।
āvṛtaṁ jñānametena jñānino nityavairiṇā
कामरूपेण कौन्तेय दुष्पूरेणानलेन च ॥ ३-३९ ॥
kāmarūpeṇa kaunteya duṣpūreṇānalena ca (3-39)

O Kuntī-son, wisdom is obscured by this eternal enemy of the wise in the form of lust—which is of inordinate appetite, just like the fire. (3.39)

— ॐ —

इन्द्रियाणि मनो बुद्धिरस्याधिष्ठानमुच्यते ।
indriyāṇi mano buddhirasyādhiṣṭhānamucyate
एतैर्विमोहयत्येष ज्ञानमावृत्य देहिनम् ॥ ३-४० ॥
etairvimohayatyeṣa jñānamāvṛtya dehinam (3-40)

The senses, the mind, and the intellect: these are declared to be its seat; covering wisdom through these, Lust is deluding all embodied beings. (3.40)

— ॐ —

तस्मात्त्वमिन्द्रियाण्यादौ नियम्य भरतर्षभ ।

tasmāttvamindriyāṇyādau niyamya bharatarṣabha

पाप्मानं प्रजहि ह्येनं ज्ञानविज्ञाननाशनम् ॥ ३-४१ ॥

pāpmānaṁ prajahi hyenaṁ jñānavijñānanāśanam (3-41)

Therefore, at the very outset, control the sense-organs, O Bhārata, and obliterate this very sinful thing which destroys knowledge and realization. (3.41)

— ॐ —

इन्द्रियाणि पराण्याहुरिन्द्रियेभ्यः परं मनः ।

indriyāṇi parāṇyāhurindriyebhyaḥ paraṁ manaḥ

मनसस्तु परा बुद्धिर्यो बुद्धेः परतस्तु सः ॥ ३-४२ ॥

manasastu parā buddhiryo buddheḥ paratastu saḥ (3-42)

The sense-organs are said to be higher-up to the sense-objects, and superior to the sense-organs is the mind, and higher still is the intellect—but what is infinitely higher is the Self. (3.42)

— ॐ —

एवं बुद्धेः परं बुद्ध्वा संस्तभ्यात्मानमात्मना ।

evaṁ buddheḥ paraṁ buddhvā saṁstabhyātmānamātmanā

जहि शत्रुं महाबाहो कामरूपं दुरासदम् ॥ ३-४३ ॥

jahi śatruṁ mahābāho kāmarūpaṁ durāsadam (3-43)

Therefore realizing That—which is the highest, beyond the intellect—and subduing the mind through That Self, kill the enemy in the form of desire which is so difficult to subdue, O mighty-armed." (3.43)

ॐ तत्सदिति श्रीमद्भगवद्गीतासूपनिषत्सु

om tatsaditi śrīmadbhagavadgītāsūpaniṣatsu

ब्रह्मविद्यायां योगशास्त्रे श्रीकृष्णार्जुनसंवादे

brahmavidyāyāṁ yogaśāstre śrīkṛṣṇārjunasaṁvāde

कर्मयोगो नाम तृतीयोऽध्यायः ॥

karmayogo nāma tṛtīyo'dhyāyaḥ .

In this Yogic Scripture on the Science of Brahama—the Shrimada-Bhāgvada-Gītā Upanishad—hereby ends the dialogue between Shrī Krishna and Arjuna entitled:
Karma Yoga, Canto III

चतुर्थोऽध्यायः - ज्ञानकर्मसंन्यासयोगः

caturtho'dhyāyaḥ - jñānakarmasaṁnyāsayogaḥ

:: Canto – IV ::

- The Path of Knowledge -

श्रीभगवानुवाच --
śrībhagavānuvāca --

इमं विवस्वते योगं प्रोक्तवानहमव्ययम् ।
imaṁ vivasvate yogaṁ proktavānahamavyayam
विवस्वान्मनवे प्राह मनुरिक्ष्वाकवेऽब्रवीत् ॥४-१॥
vivasvānmanave prāha manurikṣvākave'bravīt (4-1)

Shri Bhagwāna said: "This eternal Yoga I taught to Vivasvat; Vivasvat taught it to Manu; and Manu taught it to Ikshvāku. (4.1)

— ॐ —

एवं परम्पराप्राप्तमिमं राजर्षयो विदुः ।
evaṁ paramparāprāptamimaṁ rājarṣayo viduḥ
स कालेनेह महता योगो नष्टः परन्तप ॥४-२॥
sa kāleneha mahatā yogo naṣṭaḥ parantapa (4-2)

Thus handed down the lineage traditionally, this Yoga remained known to the Rāja-Rishīs; but then through a great lapse of time, O Arjuna, it became lost to the world. (4.2)

— ॐ —

स एवायं मया तेऽद्य योगः प्रोक्तः पुरातनः ।
sa evāyaṁ mayā te'dya yogaḥ proktaḥ purātanaḥ
भक्तोऽसि मे सखा चेति रहस्यं ह्येतदुत्तमम् ॥४-३॥
bhakto'si me sakhā ceti rahasyaṁ hyetaduttamam (4-3)

I have this day imparted to you that very ancient Yoga—you being my dear devotee and friend; know this to be supremely secret." (4.3)

अर्जुन उवाच --
arjuna uvāca --

अपरं भवतो जन्म परं जन्म विवस्वतः ।
aparaṁ bhavato janma paraṁ janma vivasvataḥ
कथमेतद्विजानीयां त्वमादौ प्रोक्तवानिति ॥४-४॥
kathametadvijānīyāṁ tvamādau proktavāniti (4-4)

Arjuna said: "Later is your birth, whereas the birth of Vivasvat dates back to remote antiquity; then how am I to understand that it was you indeed who taught it at the beginning?" (4.4)

श्रीभगवानुवाच --
śrībhagavānuvāca --

बहूनि मे व्यतीतानि जन्मानि तव चार्जुन ।
bahūni me vyatītāni janmāni tava cārjuna
तान्यहं वेद सर्वाणि न त्वं वेत्थ परन्तप ॥४-५॥
tānyahaṁ veda sarvāṇi na tvaṁ vettha parantapa (4-5)

Shri Bhagwāna said: "Many a lives have I lived, O Arjuna—you too as well; I know them all but you remember them not, O chastiser of foes. (4.5)

— ॐ —

अजोऽपि सन्नव्ययात्मा भूतानामीश्वरोऽपि सन् ।
ajo'pi sannavyayātmā bhūtānāmīśvaro'pi san
प्रकृतिं स्वामधिष्ठाय सम्भवाम्यात्ममायया ॥४-६॥
prakṛtiṁ svāmadhiṣṭhāya sambhavāmyātmamāyayā (4-6)

Though I am birthless, immutable, and the Lord of all beings, yet I become manifest resorting to My Yoga-Māyā—the inscrutable wonderful power of Mine. (4.6)

— ॐ —

यदा यदा हि धर्मस्य ग्लानिर्भवति भारत ।
yadā yadā hi dharmasya glānirbhavati bhārata
अभ्युत्थानमधर्मस्य तदात्मानं सृजाम्यहम् ॥४-७॥
abhyutthānamadharmasya tadātmānaṁ sṛjāmyaham (4-7)

Whenever Dharma is on a decline, O Bhārata, and whenever Adharma (unrighteousness) is on an ascent, then I body myself forth in this world. (4.7)

— ॐ —

परित्राणाय साधूनां विनाशाय च दुष्कृताम् ।
paritrāṇāya sādhūnāṁ vināśāya ca duṣkṛtām
धर्मसंस्थापनार्थाय सम्भवामि युगे युगे ॥४-८॥
dharmasaṁsthāpanārthāya sambhavāmi yuge yuge (4-8)

For the protection of the righteous, and for the destruction of the evil, and for the establishment of Dharma upon earth, I take advent from age to age. (4.8)

— ॐ —

जन्म कर्म च मे दिव्यमेवं यो वेत्ति तत्त्वतः ।
janma karma ca me divyamevaṁ yo vetti tattvataḥ
त्यक्त्वा देहं पुनर्जन्म नैति मामेति सोऽर्जुन ॥४-९॥
tyaktvā dehaṁ punarjanma naiti māmeti so'rjuna (4-9)

One who truly realizes the essence of my unearthly divine birth and actions, he is not reborn after casting off the body—attaining to Me instead. (4.9)

— ॐ —

वीतरागभयक्रोधा मन्मया मामुपाश्रिताः ।
vītarāgabhayakrodhā manmayā māmupāśritāḥ
बहवो ज्ञानतपसा पूता मद्भावमागताः ॥४-१०॥
bahavo jñānatapasā pūtā madbhāvamāgatāḥ (4-10)

Free from fear, attachments, anger; with their minds intent upon Me; depending on no other; purified by the penance of wisdom—many a beings of yore have attained to My Being. (4.10)

— ॐ —

ये यथा मां प्रपद्यन्ते तांस्तथैव भजाम्यहम् ।
ye yathā māṁ prapadyante tāṁstathaiva bhajāmyaham
मम वर्त्मानुवर्तन्ते मनुष्याः पार्थ सर्वशः ॥४-११॥
mama vartmānuvartante manuṣyāḥ pārtha sarvaśaḥ (4-11)

By whatsoever means men worship Me, I reciprocate likewise and accept them on similar terms. In all ways, O Pārtha, all beings tread on paths that eventually lead just to Me. (4.11)

— ॐ —

काङ्क्षन्तः कर्मणां सिद्धिं यजन्त इह देवताः ।
kāṅkṣantaḥ karmaṇāṁ siddhiṁ yajanta iha devatāḥ
क्षिप्रं हि मानुषे लोके सिद्धिर्भवति कर्मजा ॥४-१२॥
kṣipraṁ hi mānuṣe loke siddhirbhavati karmajā (4-12)

But people who seek the fruits of work, worship rather the gods of the world—for in this world of men, the fruit that's born of action is found to come quicker. (4.12)

— ॐ —

चातुर्वर्ण्यं मया सृष्टं गुणकर्मविभागशः ।

cāturvarṇyaṁ mayā sṛṣṭaṁ guṇakarmavibhāgaśaḥ

तस्य कर्तारमपि मां विद्ध्यकर्तारमव्ययम् ॥४-१३॥

tasya kartāramapi māṁ viddhyakartāramavyayam (4-13)

The four Varnas (class-partitions of society) were created by Me to harmonize the differences in aptitude and works predominant amongst humans; though the author of everything, know Me—the immutable Lord of creation—to be truly a non-doer. (4.13)

— ॐ —

न मां कर्माणि लिम्पन्ति न मे कर्मफले स्पृहा ।

na māṁ karmāṇi limpanti na me karmaphale spṛhā

इति मां योऽभिजानाति कर्मभिर्न स बध्यते ॥४-१४॥

iti māṁ yo'bhijānāti karmabhirna sa badhyate (4-14)

Karmas taint me not, nor have I a desire for their fruit; he who knows me to be so, does not get bound by Karma either. (4.14)

— ॐ —

एवं ज्ञात्वा कृतं कर्म पूर्वैरपि मुमुक्षुभिः ।

evaṁ jñātvā kṛtaṁ karma pūrvairapi mumukṣubhiḥ

कुरु कर्मैव तस्मात्त्वं पूर्वैः पूर्वतरं कृतम् ॥४-१५॥

kuru karmaiva tasmāttvaṁ pūrvaiḥ pūrvataraṁ kṛtam (4-15)

Guided by this understanding, seekers since ancient times have performed Karma and attained to liberation. Therefore, just as performed by your ancestors of yore, you too should perform Karmas in that way. (4.15)

— ॐ —

किं कर्म किमकर्मेति कवयोऽप्यत्र मोहिताः ।

kiṁ karma kimakarmeti kavayo'pyatra mohitāḥ

तत्ते कर्म प्रवक्ष्यामि यज्ज्ञात्वा मोक्ष्यसेऽशुभात् ॥४-१६॥

tatte karma pravakṣyāmi yajjñātvā mokṣyase'śubhāt (4-16)

But what is action and what inaction—as to that even the wise appear befuddled; therefore let me explain to you the science of Karma—knowing which you shall be freed from Karma's ills. (4.16)

— ॐ —

कर्मणो ह्यपि बोद्धव्यं बोद्धव्यं च विकर्मणः ।
karmaṇo hyapi boddhavyaṁ boddhavyaṁ ca vikarmaṇaḥ
अकर्मणश्च बोद्धव्यं गहना कर्मणो गतिः ॥४-१७॥
akarmaṇaśca boddhavyaṁ gahanā karmaṇo gatiḥ (4-17)

The truth of prescribed action must be known, and so should the conception of inaction; and even so, the essence of prohibited action must be clearly discerned—for deep and mystifying is the course of Karma. (4.17)

— ॐ —

कर्मण्यकर्म यः पश्येदकर्मणि च कर्म यः ।
karmaṇyakarma yaḥ paśyedakarmaṇi ca karma yaḥ
स बुद्धिमान्मनुष्येषु स युक्तः कृत्स्नकर्मकृत् ॥४-१८॥
sa buddhimānmanuṣyeṣu sa yuktaḥ kṛtsnakarmakṛt (4-18)

He who knows Karma at its essence—who can discern the inaction inherent in action, and also action within inaction—he is wise amongst men and he a Yogī: the poised performer of work. (4.18)

— ॐ —

यस्य सर्वे समारम्भाः कामसङ्कल्पवर्जिताः ।
yasya sarve samārambhāḥ kāmasaṅkalpavarjitāḥ
ज्ञानाग्निदग्धकर्माणं तमाहुः पण्डितं बुधाः ॥४-१९॥
jñānāgnidagdhakarmāṇaṁ tamāhuḥ paṇḍitaṁ budhāḥ (4-19)

Whose undertakings are completely free of the hankerings after desires, whose actions have been burnt up in the wisdom's fire—him the wise call a *Pundit*. (4.19)

— ॐ —

त्यक्त्वा कर्मफलासङ्गं नित्यतृप्तो निराश्रयः ।
tyaktvā karmaphalāsaṅgaṁ nityatṛpto nirāśrayaḥ
कर्मण्यभिप्रवृत्तोऽपि नैव किञ्चित्करोति सः ॥४-२०॥
karmaṇyabhipravṛtto'pi naiva kiñcitkaroti saḥ (4-20)

Giving up attachment to work and its fruit, ever content and without any recourse [except God]—such a one does not really do anything even though physically engaged in work. (4.20)

— ॐ —

निराशीर्यतचित्तात्मा त्यक्तसर्वपरिग्रहः ।
nirāśīryatacittātmā tyaktasarvaparigrahaḥ
शारीरं केवलं कर्म कुर्वन्नाप्नोति किल्बिषम् ॥४-२१॥
śārīraṁ kevalaṁ karma kurvannāpnoti kilbiṣam (4-21)

Controlled in body and mind, bereft of desires, free of cravings, and with all possessions relinquished—he performs actions merely through the instrument of the body, remaining altogether unsullied of those actions. (4.21)

— ॐ —

यदृच्छालाभसन्तुष्टो द्वन्द्वातीतो विमत्सरः ।
yadṛcchālābhasantuṣṭo dvandvātīto vimatsaraḥ
समः सिद्धावसिद्धौ च कृत्वापि न निबध्यते ॥४-२२॥
samaḥ siddhāvasiddhau ca kṛtvāpi na nibadhyate (4-22)

Content with what chance may bring, transcending the pairs of opposites, free of jealousy, unperturbed in success and failure—he remains unfettered of Karma's bondages even though fully engaged in work. (4.22)

— ॐ —

गतसङ्गस्य मुक्तस्य ज्ञानावस्थितचेतसः ।
gatasaṅgasya muktasya jñānāvasthitacetasaḥ
यज्ञायाचरतः कर्म समग्रं प्रविलीयते ॥४-२३॥
yajñāyācarataḥ karma samagraṁ pravilīyate (4-23)

Free of attachments, with no identification with the body, with his intellect established in wisdom, he whose works are performed only as a sacrifice (Yajna) unto the Lord—all his Karmas entirely melt away from him. (4.23)

— ॐ —

ब्रह्मार्पणं ब्रह्म हविर्ब्रह्माग्नौ ब्रह्मणा हुतम् ।
brahmārpaṇaṁ brahma havirbrahmāgnau brahmaṇā hutam
ब्रह्मैव तेन गन्तव्यं ब्रह्मकर्मसमाधिना ॥४-२४॥
brahmaiva tena gantavyaṁ brahmakarmasamādhinā (4-24)

In that Yajna, all and everything is Brahama—be it the ladle, the fire, or the oblation. Into the fire which is Brahama, by the means which is Brahama, and with Brahama alone as the doer and the receiver—it is offered by one who perceives only Brahama everywhere, in each and every aspect of creation. (4.24)

— ॐ —

दैवमेवापरे यज्ञं योगिनः पर्युपासते ।
daivamevāpare yajñaṁ yoginaḥ paryupāsate
ब्रह्माग्नावपरे यज्ञं यज्ञेनैवोपजुह्वति ॥४-२५॥
brahmāgnāvapare yajñaṁ yajñenaivopajuhvati (4-25)

So this way some Yogīs perform Yajna by offering all in the fire of the all-pervading Brahama. Then there are some who perform this Yajna in the form of ritualistic worship to particular gods. (4.25)

— ॐ —

श्रोत्रादीनीन्द्रियाण्यन्ये संयमाग्निषु जुह्वति ।
śrotrādīnīndriyāṇyanye saṁyamāgniṣu juhvati
शब्दादीन्विषयानन्य इन्द्रियाग्निषु जुह्वति ॥४-२६॥
śabdādīnviṣayānanya indriyāgniṣu juhvati (4-26)

Others still offer as sacrifice the sense-organs of hearing etc., into the fire of self-control; and some offer the sense-objects—like sounds etc.,—into the fire of the sense-organs. (4.26)

— ॐ —

सर्वाणीन्द्रियकर्माणि प्राणकर्माणि चापरे ।
sarvāṇīndriyakarmāṇi prāṇakarmāṇi cāpare
आत्मसंयमयोगाग्नौ जुह्वति ज्ञानदीपिते ॥४-२७॥
ātmasaṁyamayogāgnau juhvati jñānadīpite (4-27)

Some others sacrifice all the functions of the senses and Prānas into the fire of the Yoga-of-self-control—ignited by the light of wisdom. (4.27)

— ॐ —

द्रव्ययज्ञास्तपोयज्ञा योगयज्ञास्तथापरे ।
dravyayajñāstapoyajñā yogayajñāstathāpare
स्वाध्यायज्ञानयज्ञाश्च यतयः संशितव्रताः ॥४-२८॥
svādhyāyajñānayajñāśca yatayaḥ saṁśitavratāḥ (4-28)

There are those who perform Yajna with material gifts, some who offer Yajna in the shape of penances, and some who perform it through the practice of Yoga; and others who perform Yajna in the shape of wisdom through the study of sacred texts while observing austere vows. (4.28)

— ॐ —

अपाने जुह्वति प्राणं प्राणेऽपानं तथापरे ।
apāne juhvati prāṇaṁ prāṇe'pānaṁ tathāpare
प्राणापानगती रुद्ध्वा प्राणायामपरायणाः ॥४-२९॥
prāṇāpānagatī ruddhvā prāṇāyāmaparāyaṇāḥ (4-29)

There are others still—given to the practice of Prāṇāyāma—who offer as sacrifice the outgoing vital breath into the incoming, as also the incoming breath into the outgoing—having controlled the activity of the incoming and outgoing breaths. (4.29)

— ॐ —

अपरे नियताहाराः प्राणान्प्राणेषु जुह्वति ।
apare niyatāhārāḥ prāṇānprāṇeṣu juhvati
सर्वेऽप्येते यज्ञविदो यज्ञक्षपितकल्मषाः ॥४-३०॥
sarve'pyete yajñavido yajñakṣapitakalmaṣāḥ (4-30)

Others again—having regulated their diet etc.,—offer as sacrifice the function of the senses into the sense itself. All these Yogīs are indeed the knowers of sacrificial worship, and they have their sins consumed through such Yajnas. (4.30)

— ॐ —

यज्ञशिष्टामृतभुजो यान्ति ब्रह्म सनातनम् ।
yajñaśiṣṭāmṛtabhujo yānti brahma sanātanam
नायं लोकोऽस्त्ययज्ञस्य कुतोऽन्यः कुरुसत्तम ॥४-३१॥
nāyaṁ loko'styayajñasya kuto'nyaḥ kurusattama (4-31)

Yogīs who enjoy the remnant nectar—left over from performance of Yajna—they are able to attain to the eternal Brahama. And as to others, O best of Kurūs, even this world here is not for a man bereft of Yajna—much less the afterworld. (4.31)

— ॐ —

एवं बहुविधा यज्ञा वितता ब्रह्मणो मुखे ।
evaṁ bahuvidhā yajñā vitatā brahmaṇo mukhe
कर्मजान्विद्धि तान्सर्वानेवं ज्ञात्वा विमोक्ष्यसे ॥४-३२॥
karmajānviddhi tānsarvānevaṁ jñātvā vimokṣyase (4-32)

Thus various kinds of Yajna are prescribed by the Vedas—know them all to be born of Karma. Knowing thus the essence of Karma, you shall stand freed from the ensnarements that are inherent in Karma. (4.32)

— ॐ —

श्रेयान्द्रव्यमयाद्यज्ञाज्ज्ञानयज्ञः परन्तप ।
śreyāndravyamayādyajñājjñānayajñaḥ parantapa
सर्वं कर्माखिलं पार्थ ज्ञाने परिसमाप्यते ॥४-३३॥
sarvaṁ karmākhilaṁ pārtha jñāne parisamāpyate (4-33)

Know that a Yajna performed mentally is far superior to a Yajna performed through materials, O Pārtha—for all actions, without exception, are comprised in knowledge. (4.33)

— ॐ —

तद्विद्धि प्रणिपातेन परिप्रश्नेन सेवया ।
tadviddhi praṇipātena paripraśnena sevayā
उपदेक्ष्यन्ति ते ज्ञानं ज्ञानिनस्तत्त्वदर्शिनः ॥४-३४॥
upadekṣyanti te jñānaṁ jñāninastattvadarśinaḥ (4-34)

Acquire that Knowledge through humility, inquiry and service. The wise—realized knowers of truth—will instruct you in that wisdom. (4.34)

— ॐ —

यज्ज्ञात्वा न पुनर्मोहमेवं यास्यसि पाण्डव ।
yajjñātvā na punarmohamevaṁ yāsyasi pāṇḍava
येन भूतान्यशेषेण द्रक्ष्यस्यात्मन्यथो मयि ॥४-३५॥
yena bhūtānyaśeṣeṇa drakṣyasyātmanyatho mayi (4-35)

Having acquired that Wisdom you shall persist deluded no more, O Pāndava, and in its light you will see all being within your Self—and then in Me, the Supreme-Self. (4.35)

— ॐ —

अपि चेदसि पापेभ्यः सर्वेभ्यः पापकृत्तमः ।
api cedasi pāpebhyaḥ sarvebhyaḥ pāpakṛttamaḥ
सर्वं ज्ञानप्लवेनैव वृजिनं सन्तरिष्यसि ॥४-३६॥
sarvaṁ jñānaplavenaiva vṛjinaṁ santariṣyasi (4-36)

Assuredly you will cross all sins through the raft of Knowledge—even if you be the most sinful of all sinners. (4.36)

— ॐ —

यथैधांसि समिद्धोऽग्निर्भस्मसात्कुरुतेऽर्जुन ।
yathaidhāṁsi samiddho'gnirbhasmasātkurute'rjuna
ज्ञानाग्निः सर्वकर्माणि भस्मसात्कुरुते तथा ॥४-३७॥
jñānāgniḥ sarvakarmāṇi bhasmasātkurute tathā (4-37)

Just as the blazing fire reduces all fuel to ashes, even so the fire of Knowledge burns all Karmas to naught, O Arjuna. (4.37)

— ॐ —

न हि ज्ञानेन सदृशं पवित्रमिह विद्यते ।
na hi jñānena sadṛśaṁ pavitramiha vidyate
तत्स्वयं योगसंसिद्धः कालेनात्मनि विन्दति ॥४-३८॥
tatsvayaṁ yogasaṁsiddhaḥ kālenātmani vindati (4-38)

Indeed there is nothing more purgatorial than Knowledge; and one who is perfected in Yoga attains it naturally within himself over time, as a matter of course. (4.38)

— ॐ —

श्रद्धावाँल्लभते ज्ञानं तत्परः संयतेन्द्रियः ।
śraddhāvāṁllabhate jñānaṁ tatparaḥ saṁyatendriyaḥ
ज्ञानं लब्ध्वा परां शान्तिमचिरेणाधिगच्छति ॥४-३९॥
jñānaṁ labdhvā parāṁ śāntimacireṇādhigacchati (4-39)

A man full of faith, zeal, and self-control, attains Knowledge; and once that is gained, he forthwith achieves supreme peace. (4.39)

— ॐ —

अज्ञश्चाश्रद्दधानश्च संशयात्मा विनश्यति ।
ajñaścāśraddadhānaśca saṁśayātmā vinaśyati
नायं लोकोऽस्ति न परो न सुखं संशयात्मनः ॥४-४०॥
nāyaṁ loko'sti na paro na sukhaṁ saṁśayātmanaḥ (4-40)

But one who is ignorant and wanting in faith, who is possessed of doubts—ends up getting ruined. For a doubtful mortal, there is neither the world, nor the world beyond, nor any happiness either. (4.40)

— ॐ —

योगसंन्यस्तकर्माणं ज्ञानसञ्छिन्नसंशयम् ।
yogasaṁnyastakarmāṇaṁ jñānasañchinnasaṁśayam
आत्मवन्तं न कर्माणि निबध्नन्ति धनञ्जय ॥४-४१॥
ātmavantaṁ na karmāṇi nibadhnanti dhanañjaya (4-41)

O Dhananjaya, unto one intent on the path of Karma-Yoga—who has renounced all actions to the Lord, whose doubts have been destroyed through Knowledge, who abides self-possessed—Karmas ensnare no more. (4.41)

— ॐ —

तस्मादज्ञानसम्भूतं हृत्स्थं ज्ञानासिनात्मनः ।
tasmādajñānasambhūtaṁ hṛtsthaṁ jñānāsinātmanaḥ
छित्त्वैनं संशयं योगमातिष्ठोत्तिष्ठ भारत ॥४-४२॥
chittvainaṁ saṁśayaṁ yogamātiṣṭhottiṣṭha bhārata (4-42)

So, with the sword of Knowledge decimate all doubts that originate in Nescience—ignorance of the Self; and then established in the Karma-Yoga of even-mindedness, rise up and fight, O Bhārata." (4.42)

ॐ तत्सदिति श्रीमद्भगवद्गीतासूपनिषत्सु
om tatsaditi śrīmadbhagavadgītāsūpaniṣatsu
ब्रह्मविद्यायां योगशास्त्रे श्रीकृष्णार्जुनसंवादे
brahmavidyāyāṁ yogaśāstre śrīkṛṣṇārjunasaṁvāde
ज्ञानकर्मसंन्यासयोगो नाम चतुर्थोऽध्यायः ॥
jñānakarmasaṁnyāsayogo nāma caturtho'dhyāyaḥ

In this Yogic Scripture on the Science of Brahama—the Shrimada-Bhāgvada-Gītā Upanishad—hereby ends the dialogue between Shrī Krishna and Arjuna entitled:
Jnāna-Karma-Sanyāsa Yoga, Canto IV

पञ्चमोऽध्यायः - संन्यासयोगः

pañcamo'dhyāyaḥ - saṁnyāsayogaḥ

:: Canto – V ::

- Renunciation of Action -

अर्जुन उवाच --
arjuna uvāca --

संन्यासं कर्मणां कृष्ण पुनर्योगं च शंससि ।
saṁnyāsaṁ karmaṇāṁ kṛṣṇa punaryogaṁ ca śaṁsasi
यच्छ्रेय एतयोरेकं तन्मे ब्रूहि सुनिश्चितम् ॥५-१॥
yacchreya etayorekaṁ tanme brūhi suniścitam (5-1)

Arjuna said: "O Krishna, on the one hand you extol renunciation of action, but then again you exhort me towards action as well; pray tell me decidedly the one thing which is conducive to my good." (5.1)

श्रीभगवानुवाच --
śrībhagavānuvāca --

संन्यासः कर्मयोगश्च निःश्रेयसकरावुभौ ।
saṁnyāsaḥ karmayogaśca niḥśreyasakarāvubhau
तयोस्तु कर्मसंन्यासात्कर्मयोगो विशिष्यते ॥५-२॥
tayostu karmasaṁnyāsātkarmayogo viśiṣyate (5-2)

Shri Bhagwāna said: "Sanyāsa—the complete renunciation of action; and Karma-Yoga—the physical performance of duty but renouncing it mentally: they are both good and lead to emancipation. Of the two however, the path of Karma-Yoga—being easier to practice—is deemed superior. (5.2)

— ॐ —

ज्ञेयः स नित्यसंन्यासी यो न द्वेष्टि न काङ्क्षति ।
jñeyaḥ sa nityasaṁnyāsī yo na dveṣṭi na kāṅkṣati
निर्द्वन्द्वो हि महाबाहो सुखं बन्धात्प्रमुच्यते ॥५-३॥
nirdvandvo hi mahābāho sukhaṁ bandhātpramucyate (5-3)

The Karma-Yogī, free of dualities, who neither hates nor desires, should be held to be a complete renunciant even though fully engaged in action, O mighty-armed; because one who is free of the pairs of opposites, stands freed of Karma's bondages as well. (5.3)

— ॐ —

साङ्ख्ययोगौ पृथग्बालाः प्रवदन्ति न पण्डिताः ।
sāṅkhyayogau pṛthagbālāḥ pravadanti na paṇḍitāḥ
एकमप्यास्थितः सम्यगुभयोर्विन्दते फलम् ॥५-४॥
ekamapyāsthitaḥ samyagubhayorvindate phalam (5-4)

It is the ignorant who perceives Sānkhya-Yoga and Karma-Yoga as leading to different outcomes—but not so the wise. Firmly established in even one, one obtains the fruit of both. (5.4)

— ॐ —

यत्साङ्ख्यैः प्राप्यते स्थानं तद्योगैरपि गम्यते ।
yatsāṅkhyaiḥ prāpyate sthānaṁ tadyogairapi gamyate
एकं साङ्ख्यं च योगं च यः पश्यति स पश्यति ॥५-५॥
ekaṁ sāṅkhyaṁ ca yogaṁ ca yaḥ paśyati sa paśyati (5-5)

That sovereign state which is reached by the Sānkhya-Yogī, is attained by the Karma-Yogī as well. He who sees the Path of Knowledge and the Path of Selfless-Action to be one and the same, he truly sees. (5.5)

— ॐ —

संन्यासस्तु महाबाहो दुःखमाप्तुमयोगतः ।
saṁnyāsastu mahābāho duḥkhamāptumayogataḥ
योगयुक्तो मुनिर्ब्रह्म नचिरेणाधिगच्छति ॥५-६॥
yogayukto munirbrahma nacireṇādhigacchati (5-6)

But renunciation of action is difficult to attain without performance of selfless action, O mighty-armed; whereas the sage who is devoted to selfless action is able to attain to Brahama more speedily. (5.6)

— ॐ —

योगयुक्तो विशुद्धात्मा विजितात्मा जितेन्द्रियः ।
yogayukto viśuddhātmā vijitātmā jitendriyaḥ
सर्वभूतात्मभूतात्मा कुर्वन्नपि न लिप्यते ॥५-७॥
sarvabhūtātmabhūtātmā kurvannapi na lipyate (5-7)

The Karma-Yogī—who has conquered the mind and mastered the senses, whose heart is pure, who has identified one's Self with the Self of all—remains untainted even though fully engaged in work. (5.7)

— ॐ —

नैव किञ्चित्करोमीति युक्तो मन्येत तत्त्ववित् ।
naiva kiñcitkaromīti yukto manyeta tattvavit
पश्यञ्शृण्वन्स्पृशञ्जिघ्रन्नश्नन्गच्छन्स्वपञ्श्वसन् ॥५-८॥
paśyañśṛṇvanspṛśañjighrannaśnangacchansvapañśvasan (5-8)
प्रलपन्विसृजन्गृह्णन्नुन्मिषन्निमिषन्नपि ।
pralapanvisṛjangṛhṇannunmiṣannimiṣannapi
इन्द्रियाणीन्द्रियार्थेषु वर्तन्त इति धारयन् ॥५-९॥
indriyāṇīndriyārtheṣu vartanta iti dhārayan (5-9)

The Yogī who knows the nature of reality, ever avers, 'I am not the doer'—even though seeing, hearing, touching, smelling, feeding, walking, sleeping, breathing, speaking, excreting, grasping, blinking etc.,—maintaining that it is the sense-organs alone, moving amidst the sense-objects, which react and enact. (5.8-5.9)

— ॐ —

ब्रह्मण्याधाय कर्माणि सङ्गं त्यक्त्वा करोति यः ।
brahmaṇyādhāya karmāṇi saṅgaṁ tyaktvā karoti yaḥ
लिप्यते न स पापेन पद्मपत्रमिवाम्भसा ॥५-१०॥
lipyate na sa pāpena padmapatramivāmbhasā (5-10)

One who, giving up attachment, performs all actions dedicating them unto the Lord, always remains untainted by sin—in the same way as the lotus-leaf remains untouched by water. (5.10)

— ॐ —

कायेन मनसा बुद्ध्या केवलैरिन्द्रियैरपि ।
kāyena manasā buddhyā kevalairindriyairapi
योगिनः कर्म कुर्वन्ति सङ्गं त्यक्त्वात्मशुद्धये ॥५-११॥
yoginaḥ karma kurvanti saṅgaṁ tyaktvātmaśuddhaye (5-11)

Completely giving up attachments, the Karma-Yogī simply carries out duties—through the instrument of the body, mind, intellect and organs—only with a view towards self-purification. (5.11)

— ॐ —

युक्तः कर्मफलं त्यक्त्वा शान्तिमाप्नोति नैष्ठिकीम् ।
yuktaḥ karmaphalaṁ tyaktvā śāntimāpnoti naiṣṭhikīm
अयुक्तः कामकारेण फले सक्तो निबध्यते ॥५-१२॥
ayuktaḥ kāmakāreṇa phale sakto nibadhyate (5-12)

That harmonious one—integral in Yoga, giving up fruits of action—attains everlasting peace; whereas the unharmonious person—working under the sway of desires, hankering after fruits—gets ensnared. (5.12)

— ॐ —

सर्वकर्माणि मनसा संन्यस्यास्ते सुखं वशी ।
sarvakarmāṇi manasā saṁnyasyāste sukhaṁ vaśī
नवद्वारे पुरे देही नैव कुर्वन्न कारयन् ॥५-१३॥
navadvāre pure dehī naiva kurvanna kārayan (5-13)

The self-controlled one, mentally renouncing all actions, rests at ease and in peace—like an embodied soul, living merely as an indweller abiding within the city of nine-gates (the body)—neither acting nor causing to act. (5.13)

— ॐ —

न कर्तृत्वं न कर्माणि लोकस्य सृजति प्रभुः ।
na kartṛtvaṁ na karmāṇi lokasya sṛjati prabhuḥ
न कर्मफलसंयोगं स्वभावस्तु प्रवर्तते ॥५-१४॥
na karmaphalasaṁyogaṁ svabhāvastu pravartate (5-14)

God creates for this world neither the doership, nor the doings, nor either the union with the fruits of doings—it is only Nature which enacts, reacts and performs in its natural course. (5.14)

— ॐ —

नादत्ते कस्यचित्पापं न चैव सुकृतं विभुः ।
nādatte kasyacitpāpaṁ na caiva sukṛtaṁ vibhuḥ
अज्ञानेनावृतं ज्ञानं तेन मुह्यन्ति जन्तवः ॥५-१५॥
ajñānenāvṛtaṁ jñānaṁ tena muhyanti jantavaḥ (5-15)

The Lord-God—present everywhere and the same to all—is never really involved with the sins or virtues of any beings. But because Truth remains clouded in Ignorance, the embodied beings of the world persist bewildered. (5.15)

— ॐ —

ज्ञानेन तु तदज्ञानं येषां नाशितमात्मनः ।
jñānena tu tadajñānaṁ yeṣāṁ nāśitamātmanaḥ
तेषामादित्यवज्ज्ञानं प्रकाशयति तत्परम् ॥५-१६॥
teṣāmādityavajjñānaṁ prakāśayati tatparam (5-16)

But when Nescience is destroyed in the light of the Knowledge of the Self, then the mind, shining like the sun, reveals everything—right up to that Supreme-Being. (5.16)

— ॐ —

तद्बुद्धयस्तदात्मानस्तन्निष्ठास्तत्परायणाः ।
tadbuddhayastadātmānastanniṣṭhāstatparāyaṇāḥ
गच्छन्त्यपुनरावृत्तिं ज्ञाननिर्धूतकल्मषाः ॥५-१७॥
gacchantyapunarāvṛttiṁ jñānanirdhūtakalmaṣāḥ (5-17)

With his sins winnowed away through knowledge he—who is decided upon Him, who has his heart and mind fixed upon Him, who is devoted to Him, who has Him alone as his ultimate refuge—reaches that Supreme-Abode wherefrom there is no return to this world of sorrows. (5.17)

— ॐ —

विद्याविनयसम्पन्ने ब्राह्मणे गवि हस्तिनि ।
vidyāvinayasampanne brāhmaṇe gavi hastini
शुनि चैव श्वपाके च पण्डिताः समदर्शिनः ॥५-१८॥
śuni caiva śvapāke ca paṇḍitāḥ samadarśinaḥ (5-18)

The wise looks upon all beings with an equable eye—whether it be a Brahmin endowed with humility and learning, or a pariah, or a cow, or an elephant, or a dog. (5.18)

— ॐ —

इहैव तैर्जितः सर्गो येषां साम्ये स्थितं मनः ।
ihaiva tairjitaḥ sargo yeṣāṁ sāmye sthitaṁ manaḥ
निर्दोषं हि समं ब्रह्म तस्माद् ब्रह्मणि ते स्थिताः ॥५-१९॥
nirdoṣaṁ hi samaṁ brahma tasmād brahmaṇi te sthitāḥ (5-19)

Even this here mortal plane stands conquered by those whose minds stand established in sameness and equanimity. The Absolute Being is untouched by evil and is the same to all—hence they stand established in That Brahama. (5.19)

— ॐ —

न प्रहृष्येत्प्रियं प्राप्य नोद्विजेत्प्राप्य चाप्रियम् ।

na prahṛṣyetpriyaṁ prāpya nodvijetprāpya cāpriyam

स्थिरबुद्धिरसम्मूढो ब्रह्मविद् ब्रह्मणि स्थितः ॥५-२०॥

sthirabuddhirasammūḍho brahmavid brahmaṇi sthitaḥ (5-20)

The Knower of Brahama—firm of mind, free of doubts, who lives established in Brahama—is not elated upon obtaining the sweet, nor gets perturbed upon begetting the bitter. (5.20)

— ॐ —

बाह्यस्पर्शेष्वसक्तात्मा विन्दत्यात्मनि यत्सुखम् ।

bāhyasparśeṣvasaktātmā vindatyātmani yatsukham

स ब्रह्मयोगयुक्तात्मा सुखमक्षयमश्नुते ॥५-२१॥

sa brahmayogayuktātmā sukhamakṣayamaśnute (5-21)

One whose mind remains unattached to the external objects of senses, attains to the inner Sāttvika joy which is inherent in the Self. Such a Yogī—with his mind completely identified with Brahama, through absorption in it—forever enjoys undecaying bliss. (5.21)

— ॐ —

ये हि संस्पर्शजा भोगा दुःखयोनय एव ते ।

ye hi saṁsparśajā bhogā duḥkhayonaya eva te

आद्यन्तवन्तः कौन्तेय न तेषु रमते बुधः ॥५-२२॥

ādyantavantaḥ kaunteya na teṣu ramate budhaḥ (5-22)

Pleasures born of sense-contacts are the very founts of miseries, O Kuntī-son; they have a beginning and an end, and the wise never really rejoices in such ephemeral delights. (5.22)

— ॐ —

शक्नोतीहैव यः सोढुं प्राक्शरीरविमोक्षणात् ।

śaknotīhaiva yaḥ soḍhuṁ prākśarīravimokṣaṇāt

कामक्रोधोद्भवं वेगं स युक्तः स सुखी नरः ॥५-२३॥

kāmakrodhodbhavaṁ vegaṁ sa yuktaḥ sa sukhī naraḥ (5-23)

He who is able to withstand the urges of lust and anger in this very life, before the body drops off, he alone is said to be poised, he alone poised for everlasting happiness. (5.23)

— ॐ —

योऽन्तःसुखोऽन्तरारामस्तथान्तर्ज्योतिरेव यः ।

yo'ntaḥsukho'ntarārāmastathāntarjyotireva yaḥ

स योगी ब्रह्मनिर्वाणं ब्रह्मभूतोऽधिगच्छति ॥५-२४॥

sa yogī brahmanirvāṇaṁ brahmabhūto'dhigacchati (5-24)

He who is content within the Self, who partakes of the joy of the Self, who is illumined with the inner light—that Yogī fixed on Brahama, attains mergence in Brahama: who is all peace. (5.24)

— ॐ —

लभन्ते ब्रह्मनिर्वाणमृषयः क्षीणकल्मषाः ।

labhante brahmanirvāṇamṛṣayaḥ kṣīṇakalmaṣāḥ

छिन्नद्वैधा यतात्मानः सर्वभूतहिते रताः ॥५-२५॥

chinnadvaidhā yatātmānaḥ sarvabhūtahite ratāḥ (5-25)

The sage whose sins have been purged, whose doubts have been dispelled, whose disciplined mind is firmly established in the Lord, who persists devoted to the welfare of all beings—attains to Brahama: the ocean of bliss. (5.25)

— ॐ —

कामक्रोधवियुक्तानां यतीनां यतचेतसाम् ।

kāmakrodhaviyuktānāṁ yatīnāṁ yatacetasām

अभितो ब्रह्मनिर्वाणं वर्तते विदितात्मनाम् ॥५-२६॥

abhito brahmanirvāṇaṁ vartate viditātmanām (5-26)

The sage who is free of desire and ire, who has subdued his mind, who has realized the Self, verily attains Nirvāna—a forever mergence in Brahama, the all-pervading existence replete with bliss and consciousness. (5.26)

— ॐ —

स्पर्शान्कृत्वा बहिर्बाह्यांश्चक्षुश्चैवान्तरे भ्रुवोः ।

sparśānkṛtvā bahirbāhyāṁścakṣuścaivāntare bhruvoḥ

प्राणापानौ समौ कृत्वा नासाभ्यन्तरचारिणौ ॥५-२७॥

prāṇāpānau samau kṛtvā nāsābhyantaracāriṇau (5-27)

यतेन्द्रियमनोबुद्धिर्मुनिर्मोक्षपरायणः ।

yatendriyamanobuddhirmunirmokṣaparāyaṇaḥ

विगतेच्छाभयक्रोधो यः सदा मुक्त एव सः ॥५-२८॥

vigatecchābhayakrodho yaḥ sadā mukta eva saḥ (5-28)

Shutting out the external sense-objects; with the gaze fixed upon the space between the eye-brows; regulating the outgoing and incoming breaths moving through the nostrils; with the senses, mind and intellect well restrained; free of fear, ire, desire—the contemplative sage, who has freedom alone as his highest goal, becomes indeed ever free. (5.27-5.28)

— ॐ —

भोक्तारं यज्ञतपसां सर्वलोकमहेश्वरम् ।
bhoktāraṁ yajñatapasāṁ sarvalokamaheśvaram
सुहृदं सर्वभूतानां ज्ञात्वा मां शान्तिमृच्छति ॥५-२९॥
suhṛdaṁ sarvabhūtānāṁ jñātvā māṁ śāntimṛcchati (5-29)

Knowing Me—the final partaker of all sacrifices and austerities, the great Lord of the world, the selfless friend of all—My devotee attains abiding peace." (5.29)

ॐ तत्सदिति श्रीमद्भगवद्गीतासूपनिषत्सु
om tatsaditi śrīmadbhagavadgītāsūpaniṣatsu
ब्रह्मविद्यायां योगशास्त्रे श्रीकृष्णार्जुनसंवादे
brahmavidyāyāṁ yogaśāstre śrīkṛṣṇārjunasaṁvāde
संन्यासयोगो नाम पञ्चमोऽध्यायः ॥
saṁnyāsayogo nāma pañcamo'dhyāyaḥ .

In this Yogic Scripture on the Science of Brahama—the Shrimada-Bhāgvada-Gītā Upanishad—
hereby ends the dialogue between Shrī Krishna and Arjuna entitled:
Sanyāsa Yoga, Canto V

षष्ठोऽध्यायः - ध्यानयोगः

ṣaṣṭho'dhyāyaḥ - dhyānayogaḥ

:: Canto – VI ::

- The Path of Meditation -

श्रीभगवानुवाच --
śrībhagavānuvāca --

अनाश्रितः कर्मफलं कार्यं कर्म करोति यः ।
anāśritaḥ karmaphalaṁ kāryaṁ karma karoti yaḥ
स संन्यासी च योगी च न निरग्निर्न चाक्रियः ॥ ६-१ ॥
sa saṁnyāsī ca yogī ca na niragnirna cākriyaḥ (6-1)

Shri Bhagwāna said: "He alone is said to be a Sanyāsī—and a Yogī—who performs his prescribed duties without caring for the fruits—and not necessarily he who has outwardly given up actions and renounced the sacred fire. (6.1)

— ॐ —

यं संन्यासमिति प्राहुर्योगं तं विद्धि पाण्डव ।
yaṁ saṁnyāsamiti prāhuryogaṁ taṁ viddhi pāṇḍava
न ह्यसंन्यस्तसङ्कल्पो योगी भवति कश्चन ॥ ६-२ ॥
na hyasaṁnyastasaṅkalpo yogī bhavati kaścana (6-2)

That which is extolled as Sanyāsa—know it to be not different from Yoga, O Pāndava, for he who is a perfect Karma-Yogī, has arrived to that state having, alike the Sanyāsī, renounced it all—only in his case it's the fruits of work and desires. (6.2)

— ॐ —

आरुरुक्षोर्मुनेर्योगं कर्म कारणमुच्यते ।
ārurukṣormuneryogaṁ karma kāraṇamucyate
योगारूढस्य तस्यैव शमः कारणमुच्यते ॥ ६-३ ॥
yogārūḍhasya tasyaiva śamaḥ kāraṇamucyate (6-3)

Unto a contemplative soul who desires to Yoga, action is said to be the means; and it's only for him—after he has attained to Yoga—that inaction is prescribed as the eventual remedy, but only towards the end. (6.3)

— ॐ —

यदा हि नेन्द्रियार्थेषु न कर्मस्वनुषज्जते ।
yadā hi nendriyārtheṣu na karmasvanuṣajjate
सर्वसङ्कल्पसंन्यासी योगारूढस्तदोच्यते ॥६-४॥
sarvasaṅkalpasaṁnyāsī yogārūḍhastadocyate (6-4)

When one naturally forsakes desires—when one is no more attached to the sense-objects or to the actions—then one is said to have attained to Yoga. (6.4)

— ॐ —

उद्धरेदात्मनात्मानं नात्मानमवसादयेत् ।
uddharedātmanātmānaṁ nātmānamavasādayet
आत्मैव ह्यात्मनो बन्धुरात्मैव रिपुरात्मनः ॥६-५॥
ātmaiva hyātmano bandhurātmaiva ripurātmanaḥ (6-5)

Through the self, one should always assay to raise himself higher—never allowing to himself to be degraded lower. Verily the self alone is one's best friend, and the self alone one's worst foe. (6.5)

— ॐ —

बन्धुरात्मात्मनस्तस्य येनात्मैवात्मना जितः ।
bandhurātmātmanastasya yenātmaivātmanā jitaḥ
अनात्मनस्तु शत्रुत्वे वर्तेतात्मैव शत्रुवत् ॥६-६॥
anātmanastu śatrutve vartetātmaiva śatruvat (6-6)

To one who has conquered the self by his self—the self has served as one's friend; whereas unto the uncontrolled man, the self itself becomes adverse—like an adversary. (6.6)

— ॐ —

जितात्मनः प्रशान्तस्य परमात्मा समाहितः ।
jitātmanaḥ praśāntasya paramātmā samāhitaḥ
शीतोष्णसुखदुःखेषु तथा मानापमानयोः ॥६-७॥
śītoṣṇasukhaduḥkheṣu tathā mānāpamānayoḥ (6-7)

Unto the self-controlled, the self always abides poised and serene—be there joys or adversity, honor or dishonor, heat or cold. (6.7)

— ॐ —

ज्ञानविज्ञानतृप्तात्मा कूटस्थो विजितेन्द्रियः ।
jñānavijñānatṛptātmā kūṭastho vijitendriyaḥ
युक्त इत्युच्यते योगी समलोष्टाश्मकाञ्चनः ॥ ६-८ ॥
yukta ityucyate yogī samaloṣṭāśmakāñcanaḥ (6-8)

He whose self is satisfied through knowledge and realization, who is unwavering and has the senses under control—he is held to be a Yogī firm in his steadfastness: to whom a clod of earth, a stone and gold are all of equal worth. (6.8)

— ॐ —

सुहृन्मित्रार्युदासीनमध्यस्थद्वेष्यबन्धुषु ।
suhṛnmitrāryudāsīnamadhyasthadveṣyabandhuṣu
साधुष्वपि च पापेषु समबुद्धिर्विशिष्यते ॥ ६-९ ॥
sādhuṣvapi ca pāpeṣu samabuddhirviśiṣyate (6-9)

Particularly distinguished is that Yogī who looks with equanimity upon all—be they well-wisher, friend, relative or foe, be they neutral or intermediary, be they inimical, or virtuous, or sinful. (6.9)

— ॐ —

योगी युञ्जीत सततमात्मानं रहसि स्थितः ।
yogī yuñjīta satatamātmānaṁ rahasi sthitaḥ
एकाकी यतचित्तात्मा निराशीरपरिग्रहः ॥ ६-१० ॥
ekākī yatacittātmā nirāśīraparigrahaḥ (6-10)

The Yogī—with his body and the mind subdued; and freed of desires; and having recourse to nothing [but the Param-Ātmā]; and dwelling alone in solitude—should constantly engage his mind in meditation. (6.10)

— ॐ —

शुचौ देशे प्रतिष्ठाप्य स्थिरमासनमात्मनः ।
śucau deśe pratiṣṭhāpya sthiramāsanamātmanaḥ
नात्युच्छ्रितं नातिनीचं चैलाजिनकुशोत्तरम् ॥ ६-११ ॥
nātyucchritaṁ nātinīcaṁ cailājinakuśottaram (6-11)
तत्रैकाग्रं मनः कृत्वा यतचित्तेन्द्रियक्रियः ।
tatraikāgraṁ manaḥ kṛtvā yatacittendriyakriyaḥ
उपविश्यासने युञ्ज्याद्योगमात्मविशुद्धये ॥ ६-१२ ॥
upaviśyāsane yuñjyādyogamātmaviśuddhaye (6-12)

In a clean spot; occupying his seat upon a mat of layers made of Kuṣha grass, deerskin and cloth set one upon the other; fixing the seat firmly, neither too high nor too low; with the activities of the mind and senses controlled; and concentrating the mind—one should steadily practice Yoga towards self-purification. (6.11-6.12)

— ॐ —

समं कायशिरोग्रीवं धारयन्नचलं स्थिरः ।
samaṁ kāyaśirogrīvaṁ dhārayannacalaṁ sthiraḥ
सम्प्रेक्ष्य नासिकाग्रं स्वं दिशश्चानवलोकयन् ॥ ६-१३ ॥
samprekṣya nāsikāgraṁ svaṁ diśaścānavalokayan (6-13)
प्रशान्तात्मा विगतभीर्ब्रह्मचारिव्रते स्थितः ।
praśāntātmā vigatabhīrbrahmacārivrate sthitaḥ
मनः संयम्य मच्चित्तो युक्त आसीत मत्परः ॥ ६-१४ ॥
manaḥ saṁyamya maccitto yukta āsīta matparaḥ (6-14)

Holding the trunk head and neck upright and steady; remaining firm; fixing the gaze on the tip of the nose without looking in other directions; tranquil in thought; fearless; firm in the vow of chastity; with the mind restrained and fixed upon Me, the Lord-God—the Yogī should sit vigilantly absorbed, having Me alone as the supreme end. (6.13-6.14)

— ॐ —

युञ्जन्नेवं सदात्मानं योगी नियतमानसः ।
yuñjannevaṁ sadātmānaṁ yogī niyatamānasaḥ
शान्तिं निर्वाणपरमां मत्संस्थामधिगच्छति ॥ ६-१५ ॥
śāntiṁ nirvāṇaparamāṁ matsaṁsthāmadhigacchati (6-15)

In this way constantly concentrating the mind upon Me, the Yogī of disciplined mind attains to that peace which culminates in a final beatitude—that of becoming one in Me. (6.15)

— ॐ —

नात्यश्नतस्तु योगोऽस्ति न चैकान्तमनश्नतः ।
nātyaśnatastu yogo'sti na caikāntamanaśnataḥ
न चातिस्वप्नशीलस्य जाग्रतो नैव चार्जुन ॥ ६-१६ ॥
na cātisvapnaśīlasya jāgrato naiva cārjuna (6-16)

O Arjuna, this Yoga is not attained by one who eats overly, or nothing at all, or by one given to much too sleep, or one who persists ceaselessly awake. (6.16)

— ॐ —

युक्ताहारविहारस्य युक्तचेष्टस्य कर्मसु ।

yuktāhāravihārasya yuktaceṣṭasya karmasu

युक्तस्वप्नावबोधस्य योगो भवति दुःखहा ॥६-१७॥

yuktasvapnāvabodhasya yogo bhavati duḥkhahā (6-17)

One with a well-balanced disposition—who's moderate in eating, moving around, working, sleeping, waking—achieves success in Yoga, which is the destroyer of all miseries. (6.17)

— ॐ —

यदा विनियतं चित्तमात्मन्येवावतिष्ठते ।

yadā viniyataṁ cittamātmanyevāvatiṣṭhate

निःस्पृहः सर्वकामेभ्यो युक्त इत्युच्यते तदा ॥६-१८॥

niḥspṛhaḥ sarvakāmebhyo yukta ityucyate tadā (6-18)

Thoroughly purged of the cravings for sense-enjoyments, when the disciplined mind gets firmly riveted upon the Self alone, then that person is said to be established in Yoga. (6.18)

— ॐ —

यथा दीपो निवातस्थो नेङ्गते सोपमा स्मृता ।

yathā dīpo nivātastho neṅgate sopamā smṛtā

योगिनो यतचित्तस्य युञ्जतो योगमात्मनः ॥६-१९॥

yogino yatacittasya yuñjato yogamātmanaḥ (6-19)

The controlled mind of a Yogī who is practicing meditation on the Self, has its perfect epitome in the flame of a lamp—placed in a windless place—and which does not flicker. (6.19)

— ॐ —

यत्रोपरमते चित्तं निरुद्धं योगसेवया ।

yatroparamate cittaṁ niruddhaṁ yogasevayā

यत्र चैवात्मनात्मानं पश्यन्नात्मनि तुष्यति ॥६-२०॥

yatra caivātmanātmānaṁ paśyannātmani tuṣyati (6-20)

That state in which the mind, subdued through the practice of Yoga, becomes completely settled; the state in which the self rejoices only within the Self—having acquired the sublimity of mind purified by reasoning; (6.20)

— ॐ —

सुखमात्यन्तिकं यत्तद् बुद्धिग्राह्यमतीन्द्रियम् ।
sukhamātyantikaṁ yattad buddhigrāhyamatīndriyam
वेत्ति यत्र न चैवायं स्थितश्चलति तत्त्वतः ॥६-२१॥
vetti yatra na caivāyaṁ sthitaścalati tattvataḥ (6-21)

that state—in which one realizes the absolute, transcendent bliss experienced through pure intellect; established in which state one never wavers from the Truth, the Reality, the Essence; (6.21)

— ॐ —

यं लब्ध्वा चापरं लाभं मन्यते नाधिकं ततः ।
yaṁ labdhvā cāparaṁ lābhaṁ manyate nādhikaṁ tataḥ
यस्मिन्स्थितो न दुःखेन गुरुणापि विचाल्यते ॥६-२२॥
yasminsthito na duḥkhena guruṇāpi vicālyate (6-22)

that state—attaining which one discovers no other acquisition which could be greater than that; established in which state one is not moved even by the heaviest of sorrows— (6.22)

— ॐ —

तं विद्याद् दुःखसंयोगवियोगं योगसंज्ञितम् ।
taṁ vidyād duḥkhasaṁyogaviyogaṁ yogasaṁjñitam
स निश्चयेन योक्तव्यो योगोऽनिर्विण्णचेतसा ॥६-२३॥
sa niścayena yoktavyo yogo'nirviṇṇacetasā (6-23)

—verily that state is designated as Yoga—untouched by any contact with pain. That Yoga should be practiced resolutely, unwearied in spirit. (6.23)

— ॐ —

सङ्कल्पप्रभवान्कामांस्त्यक्त्वा सर्वानशेषतः ।
saṅkalpaprabhavānkāmāṁstyaktvā sarvānaśeṣataḥ
मनसैवेन्द्रियग्रामं विनियम्य समन्ततः ॥६-२४॥
manasaivendriyagrāmaṁ viniyamya samantataḥ (6-24)

शनैः शनैरुपरमेद् बुद्ध्या धृतिगृहीतया ।
śanaiḥ śanairuparamed buddhyā dhṛtigṛhītayā
आत्मसंस्थं मनः कृत्वा न किञ्चिदपि चिन्तयेत् ॥६-२५॥
ātmasaṁsthaṁ manaḥ kṛtvā na kiñcidapi cintayet (6-25)

Abandoning all desires born of fancy; and controlling well the senses from all sides by the mind alone; let one withdraw by degrees. Establishing the mind in the Self gradually—by an intellect regulated through concentration—one should think of nothing else but the Ātmā. (6.24-6.25)

— ॐ —

यतो यतो निश्चरति मनश्चञ्चलमस्थिरम् ।
yato yato niścarati manaścañcalamasthiram
ततस्ततो नियम्यैतदात्मन्येव वशं नयेत् ॥ ६-२६ ॥
tatastato niyamyaitadātmanyeva vaśaṁ nayet (6-26)

And wheresoever the unsteady restless mind tries to wander to, from that very object it should be restrained and brought back—to be held completely under the control of the Self alone. (6.26)

— ॐ —

प्रशान्तमनसं ह्येनं योगिनं सुखमुत्तमम् ।
praśāntamanasaṁ hyenaṁ yoginaṁ sukhamuttamam
उपैति शान्तरजसं ब्रह्मभूतमकल्मषम् ॥ ६-२७ ॥
upaiti śāntarajasaṁ brahmabhūtamakalmaṣam (6-27)

Unto the Yogī whose infatuation has subsided, whose mind abides perfectly still, who is free of sin, who remains tenacious in his practice of identifying himself with Brahama—supreme happiness comes of its own accord. (6.27)

— ॐ —

युञ्जन्नेवं सदात्मानं योगी विगतकल्मषः ।
yuñjannevaṁ sadātmānaṁ yogī vigatakalmaṣaḥ
सुखेन ब्रह्मसंस्पर्शमत्यन्तं सुखमश्नुते ॥ ६-२८ ॥
sukhena brahmasaṁsparśamatyantaṁ sukhamaśnute (6-28)

The Yogī, entirely free from taint, constantly controlling the mind in this way—attains with natural ease that Infinite-Bliss which is inherent in the state of oneness in Brahama. (6.28)

— ॐ —

सर्वभूतस्थमात्मानं सर्वभूतानि चात्मनि ।

sarvabhūtasthamātmānaṁ sarvabhūtāni cātmani

ईक्षते योगयुक्तात्मा सर्वत्र समदर्शनः ॥६-२९॥

īkṣate yogayuktātmā sarvatra samadarśanaḥ (6-29)

The Yogī who is united in identity with the Infinite all pervading Brahama, perceives the Self in all beings—and all beings in the Self. (6.29)

— ॐ —

यो मां पश्यति सर्वत्र सर्वं च मयि पश्यति ।

yo māṁ paśyati sarvatra sarvaṁ ca mayi paśyati

तस्याहं न प्रणश्यामि स च मे न प्रणश्यति ॥६-३०॥

tasyāhaṁ na praṇaśyāmi sa ca me na praṇaśyati (6-30)

He who sees Me present everywhere, who sees all things abiding in Me—he never loses sight of Me; nor I of him. (6.30)

— ॐ —

सर्वभूतस्थितं यो मां भजत्येकत्वमास्थितः ।

sarvabhūtasthitaṁ yo māṁ bhajatyekatvamāsthitaḥ

सर्वथा वर्तमानोऽपि स योगी मयि वर्तते ॥६-३१॥

sarvathā vartamāno'pi sa yogī mayi vartate (6-31)

He who worships Me as dwelling in all beings in a sense of Oneness, he is a Yogī—and he ever abides in Me, whatever his mode of life. (6.31)

— ॐ —

आत्मौपम्येन सर्वत्र समं पश्यति योऽर्जुन ।

ātmaupamyena sarvatra samaṁ paśyati yo'rjuna

सुखं वा यदि वा दुःखं स योगी परमो मतः ॥६-३२॥

sukhaṁ vā yadi vā duḥkhaṁ sa yogī paramo mataḥ (6-32)

He who looks upon the joys and sorrows in all creatures as identical to his own—that Yogī, O Arjuna, is deemed the highest." (6.32)

अर्जुन उवाच --
arjuna uvāca --

योऽयं योगस्त्वया प्रोक्तः साम्येन मधुसूदन ।
yo'yaṁ yogastvayā proktaḥ sāmyena madhusūdana
एतस्याहं न पश्यामि चञ्चलत्वात्स्थितिं स्थिराम् ॥ ६-३३ ॥
etasyāhaṁ na paśyāmi cañcalatvātsthitiṁ sthirām (6-33)

Arjuna said: "This Yoga of equanimity which you have just spoken of, O Madhusūdana, I do not perceive it to be durable—owing to the restlessness of the mind. (6.33)

— ॐ —

चञ्चलं हि मनः कृष्ण प्रमाथि बलवद् दृढम् ।
cañcalaṁ hi manaḥ kṛṣṇa pramāthi balavad dṛḍham
तस्याहं निग्रहं मन्ये वायोरिव सुदुष्करम् ॥ ६-३४ ॥
tasyāhaṁ nigrahaṁ manye vāyoriva suduṣkaram (6-34)

The mind is restless, unyielding, and most obstinate and perverse, O Krishna, I consider it exceedingly difficult to curb—just like the wind itself." (6.34)

श्रीभगवानुवाच --
śrībhagavānuvāca --

असंशयं महाबाहो मनो दुर्निग्रहं चलम् ।
asaṁśayaṁ mahābāho mano durnigrahaṁ calam
अभ्यासेन तु कौन्तेय वैराग्येण च गृह्यते ॥ ६-३५ ॥
abhyāsena tu kaunteya vairāgyeṇa ca gṛhyate (6-35)

Shri Bhagwāna said: "Undoubtedly the mind is turbulent and quite difficult to subdue, O mighty-armed, but through repeated practice and the exercise of dispassion, it can be so controlled. (6.35)

— ॐ —

असंयतात्मना योगो दुष्प्राप इति मे मतिः ।
asaṁyatātmanā yogo duṣprāpa iti me matiḥ
वश्यात्मना तु यतता शक्योऽवाप्तुमुपायतः ॥ ६-३६ ॥
vaśyātmanā tu yatatā śakyo'vāptumupāyataḥ (6-36)

I consider Yoga to be difficult of attainment by those of untamed minds; but it becomes attainable once the mind has been subdued through constant practice following the prescribed discipline." (6.36)

अर्जुन उवाच --
arjuna uvāca --

अयतिः श्रद्धयोपेतो योगाच्चलितमानसः ।
ayatiḥ śraddhayopeto yogāccalitamānasaḥ
अप्राप्य योगसंसिद्धिं कां गतिं कृष्ण गच्छति ॥ ६-३७ ॥
aprāpya yogasaṁsiddhiṁ kāṁ gatiṁ kṛṣṇa gacchati (6-37)

Arjuna said: "O Krishna, what becomes of him who, though endowed with faith, strives not; or whose mind wanders away from Yoga? He who thus fails to attain the fruition of Yoga, where goes he? What becomes of him? (6.37)

— ॐ —

कच्चिन्नोभयविभ्रष्टश्छिन्नाभ्रमिव नश्यति ।
kaccinnobhayavibhraṣṭaśchinnābhramiva naśyati
अप्रतिष्ठो महाबाहो विमूढो ब्रह्मणः पथि ॥ ६-३८ ॥
apratiṣṭho mahābāho vimūḍho brahmaṇaḥ pathi (6-38)

Fallen from both—deprived of realization and enjoyments too, a loser bereft of both—does he not, O mighty-armed, perish like a solitary cloud, having become deluded in the path of Brahama? (6.38)

— ॐ —

एतन्मे संशयं कृष्ण छेत्तुमर्हस्यशेषतः ।
etanme saṁśayaṁ kṛṣṇa chettumarhasyaśeṣataḥ
त्वदन्यः संशयस्यास्य छेत्ता न ह्युपपद्यते ॥ ६-३९ ॥
tvadanyaḥ saṁśayasyāsya chettā na hyupapadyate (6-39)

You should dispel this uncertainty in its entirety, O Krishna, for other than Thee I see no one else who can remove this doubt of mine." (6.39)

श्रीभगवानुवाच --
śrībhagavānuvāca --

पार्थ नैवेह नामुत्र विनाशस्तस्य विद्यते ।
pārtha naiveha nāmutra vināśastasya vidyate
न हि कल्याणकृत्कश्चिद् दुर्गतिं तात गच्छति ॥ ६-४० ॥
na hi kalyāṇakṛtkaścid durgatiṁ tāta gacchati (6-40)

Shri Bhagwāna said: "No, there is no destruction of him, O Pārtha—either here, or in the hereafter; the doer of good never comes by ill, my friend." (6.40)

— ॐ —

प्राप्य पुण्यकृतां लोकानुषित्वा शाश्वतीः समाः ।
prāpya puṇyakṛtāṁ lokānuṣitvā śāśvatīḥ samāḥ
शुचीनां श्रीमतां गेहे योगभ्रष्टोऽभिजायते ॥ ६-४१ ॥
śucīnāṁ śrīmatāṁ gehe yogabhraṣṭo'bhijāyate (6-41)

He who has strayed from Yoga, obtains upon death the holy abodes of the virtuous; and then having dwelt there for many ages, he is born yet again on earth—into a prosperous pious family. (6.41)

— ॐ —

अथवा योगिनामेव कुले भवति धीमताम् ।
athavā yogināmeva kule bhavati dhīmatām
एतद्धि दुर्लभतरं लोके जन्म यदीदृशम् ॥ ६-४२ ॥
etaddhi durlabhataraṁ loke janma yadīdṛśam (6-42)

Or he is even reborn in the household of an enlightened Yogī; certainly such births are indeed rare in the world. (6.42)

— ॐ —

तत्र तं बुद्धिसंयोगं लभते पौर्वदेहिकम् ।
tatra taṁ buddhisaṁyogaṁ labhate paurvadehikam
यतते च ततो भूयः संसिद्धौ कुरुनन्दन ॥ ६-४३ ॥
yatate ca tato bhūyaḥ saṁsiddhau kurunandana (6-43)

In that birth he involuntarily regains the latencies of even-mindedness accumulated in his previous births, O descendent of Kurū; and through that, he strives even harder for perfection. (6.43)

— ॐ —

पूर्वाभ्यासेन तेनैव ह्रियते ह्यवशोऽपि सः ।
pūrvābhyāsena tenaiva hriyate hyavaśo'pi saḥ
जिज्ञासुरपि योगस्य शब्दब्रह्मातिवर्तते ॥ ६-४४ ॥
jijñāsurapi yogasya śabdabrahmātivartate (6-44)

By that very practice which he acquired in his previous births, he becomes irresistibly drawn; and even though a mere inquiry into Yoga, he is able to transcend and soon go beyond—beyond the writs, beyond the rituals. (6.44)

— ॐ —

प्रयत्नाद्यतमानस्तु योगी संशुद्धकिल्बिषः ।
prayatnādyatamānastu yogī saṁśuddhakilbiṣaḥ
अनेकजन्मसंसिद्धस्ततो याति परां गतिम् ॥ ६-४५ ॥
anekajanmasaṁsiddhastato yāti parāṁ gatim (6-45)

And forthwith through a sedulous practice that Yogī—who has attained the culmination of endeavors perfected over many prior births—directly attains the supreme goal once he has become thoroughly purged of sin. (6.45)

— ॐ —

तपस्विभ्योऽधिको योगी ज्ञानिभ्योऽपि मतोऽधिकः ।
tapasvibhyo'dhiko yogī jñānibhyo'pi mato'dhikaḥ
कर्मिभ्यश्चाधिको योगी तस्माद्योगी भवार्जुन ॥ ६-४६ ॥
karmibhyaścādhiko yogī tasmādyogī bhavārjuna (6-46)

A Yogī is held superior to ascetic—higher even to those versed in the sacred lore, greater still than those who are devoted to action; therefore, O Arjuna, do thou be a Yogī. (6.46)

— ॐ —

योगिनामपि सर्वेषां मद्गतेनान्तरात्मना ।
yogināmapi sarveṣāṁ madgatenāntarātmanā
श्रद्धावान्भजते यो मां स मे युक्ततमो मतः ॥ ६-४७ ॥
śraddhāvānbhajate yo māṁ sa me yuktatamo mataḥ (6-47)

Of all the Yogīs again, he who, possessed of faith, devoutly worships Me—with his mind intent completely upon Me—he is deemed to be the highest." (6.47)

ॐ तत्सदिति श्रीमद्भगवद्गीतासूपनिषत्सु
om tatsaditi śrīmadbhagavadgītāsūpaniṣatsu
ब्रह्मविद्यायां योगशास्त्रे श्रीकृष्णार्जुनसंवादे
brahmavidyāyāṁ yogaśāstre śrīkṛṣṇārjunasaṁvāde
ध्यानयोगो नाम षष्ठोऽध्यायः ॥
dhyānayogo nāma ṣaṣṭho'dhyāyaḥ

In this Yogic Scripture on the Science of Brahama—the Shrimada-Bhāgvada-Gītā Upanishad—
hereby ends the dialogue between Shrī Krishna and Arjuna entitled:
Dhyāna Yoga, Canto VI

सप्तमोऽध्यायः - ज्ञानविज्ञानयोगः

saptamo'dhyāyaḥ - jñānavijñānayogaḥ

:: Canto – VII ::

- The Path of Knowledge and Realization -

श्रीभगवानुवाच --
śrībhagavānuvāca --

मय्यासक्तमनाः पार्थ योगं युञ्जन्मदाश्रयः ।
mayyāsaktamanāḥ pārtha yogaṁ yuñjanmadāśrayaḥ
असंशयं समग्रं मां यथा ज्ञास्यसि तच्छृणु ॥७-१॥
asaṁśayaṁ samagraṁ māṁ yathā jñāsyasi tacchṛṇu (7-1)

Shri Bhagwāna said: "As to how—with absolute dependence on Me, and with your mind intent, and practicing Yoga—you will know Me in entirety, free of doubts, now listen, O Pārtha. (7.1)

— ॐ —

ज्ञानं तेऽहं सविज्ञानमिदं वक्ष्याम्यशेषतः ।
jñānaṁ te'haṁ savijñānamidaṁ vakṣyāmyaśeṣataḥ
यज्ज्ञात्वा नेह भूयोऽन्यज्ज्ञातव्यमवशिष्यते ॥७-२॥
yajjñātvā neha bhūyo'nyajjñātavyamavaśiṣyate (7-2)

I shall impart to you without reserve that very knowledge, that very realization, knowing which there remains nothing more to be known in this world. (7.2)

— ॐ —

मनुष्याणां सहस्रेषु कश्चिद्यतति सिद्धये ।
manuṣyāṇāṁ sahasreṣu kaścidyatati siddhaye
यततामपि सिद्धानां कश्चिन्मां वेत्ति तत्त्वतः ॥७-३॥
yatatāmapi siddhānāṁ kaścinmāṁ vetti tattvataḥ (7-3)

Perhaps one in a thousand strives for perfection; and of those that strive, hardly one attains it; and amongst those that reach the ideal—it's a rare soul who knows Me in essence. (7.3)

— ॐ —

भूमिरापोऽनलो वायुः खं मनो बुद्धिरेव च ।
bhūmirāpo'nalo vāyuḥ khaṁ mano buddhireva ca
अहङ्कार इतीयं मे भिन्ना प्रकृतिरष्टधा ॥७-४॥
ahaṅkāra itīyaṁ me bhinnā prakṛtiraṣṭadhā (7-4)

Earth, water, fire, air, aether, mind, intellect and egoism—this comprises My eight-fold Prakriti (Nature). (7.4)

— ॐ —

अपरेयमितस्त्वन्यां प्रकृतिं विद्धि मे पराम् ।
apareyamitastvanyāṁ prakṛtiṁ viddhi me parām
जीवभूतां महाबाहो ययेदं धार्यते जगत् ॥७-५॥
jīvabhūtāṁ mahābāho yayedaṁ dhāryate jagat (7-5)

This is My lower Nature—the material. Different from that, O mighty-armed, know My higher Prakriti—in the form of Jīva, the individual soul; and in this duality of my Prakriti, the world is held existent. (7.5)

— ॐ —

एतद्योनीनि भूतानि सर्वाणीत्युपधारय ।
etadyonīni bhūtāni sarvāṇītyupadhāraya
अहं कृत्स्नस्य जगतः प्रभवः प्रलयस्तथा ॥७-६॥
ahaṁ kṛtsnasya jagataḥ prabhavaḥ pralayastathā (7-6)

Know, O Arjuna, that all beings have evolved from this twofold nature of Mine. I am the origin of this whole creation, and into Me again everything submerges in the end. (7.6)

— ॐ —

मत्तः परतरं नान्यत्किञ्चिदस्ति धनञ्जय ।
mattaḥ parataraṁ nānyatkiñcidasti dhanañjaya
मयि सर्वमिदं प्रोतं सूत्रे मणिगणा इव ॥७-७॥
mayi sarvamidaṁ protaṁ sūtre maṇigaṇā iva (7-7)

Besides and beyond Me, O Dhananjaya, there exists nothing else. Within Me alone is this universe strung—like gems threaded on a string. (7.7)

— ॐ —

रसोऽहमप्सु कौन्तेय प्रभास्मि शशिसूर्ययोः ।
raso'hamapsu kaunteya prabhāsmi śaśisūryayoḥ
प्रणवः सर्ववेदेषु शब्दः खे पौरुषं नृषु ॥ ७-८ ॥
praṇavaḥ sarvavedeṣu śabdaḥ khe pauruṣaṁ nṛṣu (7-8)

Hearken, O Kuntī-son, I am all: in water, I am its sapidity; I am the radiance in the sun and moon; I am the sacred syllable Om of the Vedas; and I am the sound in aether, and the endeavor in men. (7.8)

— ॐ —

पुण्यो गन्धः पृथिव्यां च तेजश्चास्मि विभावसौ ।
puṇyo gandhaḥ pṛthivyāṁ ca tejaścāsmi vibhāvasau
जीवनं सर्वभूतेषु तपश्चास्मि तपस्विषु ॥ ७-९ ॥
jīvanaṁ sarvabhūteṣu tapaścāsmi tapasviṣu (7-9)

I am the pure odor of the earth; and the brightness of the fire; and I am the life in all beings; and of the ascetics—I am their austerity. (7.9)

— ॐ —

बीजं मां सर्वभूतानां विद्धि पार्थ सनातनम् ।
bījaṁ māṁ sarvabhūtānāṁ viddhi pārtha sanātanam
बुद्धिर्बुद्धिमतामस्मि तेजस्तेजस्विनामहम् ॥ ७-१० ॥
buddhirbuddhimatāmasmi tejastejasvināmaham (7-10)

O Pārtha, know Me to be the eternal seed of all beings; I am the intelligence of the intelligent—and the glory of the glorious. (7.10)

— ॐ —

बलं बलवतां चाहं कामरागविवर्जितम् ।
balaṁ balavatāṁ cāhaṁ kāmarāgavivarjitam
धर्माविरुद्धो भूतेषु कामोऽस्मि भरतर्षभ ॥ ७-११ ॥
dharmāviruddho bhūteṣu kāmo'smi bharatarṣabha (7-11)

I am that strength of the strong which is free of passion and attachment; and O Bhārata, in beings I am that concupiscence which is unopposed to virtue and scriptural injunctions. (7.11)

— ॐ —

ये चैव सात्त्विका भावा राजसास्तामसाश्च ये ।
ye caiva sāttvikā bhāvā rājasāstāmasāśca ye
मत्त एवेति तान्विद्धि न त्वहं तेषु ते मयि ॥७-१२॥
matta eveti tānviddhi na tvahaṁ teṣu te mayi (7-12)

All these three—the Sattvika, Rājasika, and Tāmasika states—know these to be born of Me; I am not in them, though they abide in Me. (7.12)

— ॐ —

त्रिभिर्गुणमयैर्भावैरेभिः सर्वमिदं जगत् ।
tribhirguṇamayairbhāvairebhiḥ sarvamidaṁ jagat
मोहितं नाभिजानाति मामेभ्यः परमव्ययम् ॥७-१३॥
mohitaṁ nābhijānāti māmebhyaḥ paramavyayam (7-13)

Deluded by the three *Gunas* of Nature this whole creation fails to recognize Me—who am the immutable Primal Cause which is beyond the three. (7.13)

— ॐ —

दैवी ह्येषा गुणमयी मम माया दुरत्यया ।
daivī hyeṣā guṇamayī mama māyā duratyayā
मामेव ये प्रपद्यन्ते मायामेतां तरन्ति ते ॥७-१४॥
māmeva ye prapadyante māyāmetāṁ taranti te (7-14)

This most enchanting Māyā of mine, constituted of the *Gunas*, is indeed most difficult to overcome; only those who take refuge in Me are able to get across Māyā. (7.14)

— ॐ —

न मां दुष्कृतिनो मूढाः प्रपद्यन्ते नराधमाः ।
na māṁ duṣkṛtino mūḍhāḥ prapadyante narādhamāḥ
माययापहृतज्ञाना आसुरं भावमाश्रिताः ॥७-१५॥
māyayāpahṛtajñānā āsuraṁ bhāvamāśritāḥ (7-15)

Wretches among men, the wicked and the ignorant, do not take refuge in Me—betaking themselves to their demoniacal nature, and being deprived of their discrimination and discernment by dint of Māyā. (7.15)

— ॐ —

चतुर्विधा भजन्ते मां जनाः सुकृतिनोऽर्जुन ।

caturvidhā bhajante māṁ janāḥ sukṛtino'rjuna

आर्तो जिज्ञासुरर्थार्थी ज्ञानी च भरतर्षभ ॥७-१६॥

ārto jijñāsurarthārthī jñānī ca bharatarṣabha (7-16)

Four kinds of people who have done virtuous deeds worship Me, O Arjuna: the afflicted, the inquisitive, the seekers after worldly possessions, and the wise. (7.16)

— ॐ —

तेषां ज्ञानी नित्ययुक्त एकभक्तिर्विशिष्यते ।

teṣāṁ jñānī nityayukta ekabhaktirviśiṣyate

प्रियो हि ज्ञानिनोऽत्यर्थमहं स च मम प्रियः ॥७-१७॥

priyo hi jñānino'tyarthamahaṁ sa ca mama priyaḥ (7-17)

Of these the wise—who remains ever established in Me with a single-minded devotion—stands out. To that seer, I am indeed most dear—and indeed, he is most dear to me. (7.17)

— ॐ —

उदाराः सर्व एवैते ज्ञानी त्वात्मैव मे मतम् ।

udārāḥ sarva evaite jñānī tvātmaiva me matam

आस्थितः स हि युक्तात्मा मामेवानुत्तमां गतिम् ॥७-१८॥

āsthitaḥ sa hi yuktātmā māmevānuttamāṁ gatim (7-18)

All these four seekers are indeed noble, but the man of realization I regard as my very own Self; for with his mind and intellect fixed upon Me, that devotee has taken refuge in Me alone as the supreme end. (7.18)

— ॐ —

बहूनां जन्मनामन्ते ज्ञानवान्मां प्रपद्यते ।

bahūnāṁ janmanāmante jñānavānmāṁ prapadyate

वासुदेवः सर्वमिति स महात्मा सुदुर्लभः ॥७-१९॥

vāsudevaḥ sarvamiti sa mahātmā sudurlabhaḥ (7-19)

In the very last of all births, O Arjuna, the man of realization takes direct refuge in Me: when he comes by the knowledge that all which exists in existence is just only Me: Vāsudeva. Aye, such a saint is exceedingly rare. (7.19)

— ॐ —

कामैस्तैस्तैर्हृतज्ञानाः प्रपद्यन्तेऽन्यदेवताः ।
kāmaistaistairhṛtajñānāḥ prapadyante'nyadevatāḥ
तं तं नियममास्थाय प्रकृत्या नियताः स्वया ॥७-२०॥
taṁ taṁ niyamamāsthāya prakṛtyā niyatāḥ svayā (7-20)

Deprived of discrimination, owing to their diverse desires, people get drawn to various gods—in accordance with their inner nature—and they worship them adopting the norms peculiar to that deity. (7.20)

— ॐ —

यो यो यां यां तनुं भक्तः श्रद्धयार्चितुमिच्छति ।
yo yo yāṁ yāṁ tanuṁ bhaktaḥ śraddhayārcitumicchati
तस्य तस्याचलां श्रद्धां तामेव विदधाम्यहम् ॥७-२१॥
tasya tasyācalāṁ śraddhāṁ tāmeva vidadhāmyaham (7-21)

And whichever particular divinity a devotee chooses to worship with faith—I stabilize his belief in that very form. (7.21)

— ॐ —

स तया श्रद्धया युक्तस्तस्याराधनमीहते ।
sa tayā śraddhayā yuktastasyārādhanamīhate
लभते च ततः कामान्मयैव विहितान्हि तान् ॥७-२२॥
labhate ca tataḥ kāmānmayaiva vihitānhi tān (7-22)

Endowed with that faith he worships that very specific deity; and he obtains through that deity all the objectives of his desires—which have indeed been granted only by Me. (7.22)

— ॐ —

अन्तवत्तु फलं तेषां तद्भवत्यल्पमेधसाम् ।
antavattu phalaṁ teṣāṁ tadbhavatyalpamedhasām
देवान्देवयजो यान्ति मद्भक्ता यान्ति मामपि ॥७-२३॥
devāndevayajo yānti madbhaktā yānti māmapi (7-23)

However this fruit—gained by these people of limited understanding—is found to be perishable; the worshippers of gods go to the gods—whereas my devotees come directly to Me. (7.23)

— ॐ —

अव्यक्तं व्यक्तिमापन्नं मन्यन्ते मामबुद्धयः ।
avyaktaṁ vyaktimāpannaṁ manyante māmabuddhayaḥ
परं भावमजानन्तो ममाव्ययमनुत्तमम् ॥ ७-२४ ॥
paraṁ bhāvamajānanto mamāvyayamanuttamam (7-24)

Not knowing of my unsurpassable, immutable, undecaying nature, the ignorant regard Me—the Lord-God, the embodiment of Existence, Knowledge and Bliss, the Supreme Spirit beyond the reach of the mind and senses—to have come into being as an ordinary mortal. (7.24)

— ॐ —

नाहं प्रकाशः सर्वस्य योगमायासमावृतः ।
nāhaṁ prakāśaḥ sarvasya yogamāyāsamāvṛtaḥ
मूढोऽयं नाभिजानाति लोको मामजमव्ययम् ॥ ७-२५ ॥
mūḍho'yaṁ nābhijānāti loko māmajamavyayam (7-25)

Veiled by my Yoga-Māyā—my divine potency—I do not become apparent to all; the ignorant world does not know Me—who am the unborn, immutable Absolute. (7.25)

— ॐ —

वेदाहं समतीतानि वर्तमानानि चार्जुन ।
vedāhaṁ samatītāni vartamānāni cārjuna
भविष्याणि च भूतानि मां तु वेद न कश्चन ॥ ७-२६ ॥
bhaviṣyāṇi ca bhūtāni māṁ tu veda na kaścana (7-26)

O Arjuna, I know all beings—from past and present and those yet to come—but no one knows Me for who I truly am. (7.26)

— ॐ —

इच्छाद्वेषसमुत्थेन द्वन्द्वमोहेन भारत ।
icchādveṣasamutthena dvandvamohena bhārata
सर्वभूतानि सम्मोहं सर्गे यान्ति परन्तप ॥ ७-२७ ॥
sarvabhūtāni sammohaṁ sarge yānti parantapa (7-27)

O valiant one, through delusion—in the form of pairs of opposites that are born of desire and aversion—all beings are held prey to my Māyā from their very births. (7.27)

— ॐ —

येषां त्वन्तगतं पापं जनानां पुण्यकर्मणाम् ।

yeṣāṁ tvantagataṁ pāpaṁ janānāṁ puṇyakarmaṇām

ते द्वन्द्वमोहनिर्मुक्ता भजन्ते मां दृढव्रताः ॥७-२८॥

te dvandvamohanirmuktā bhajante māṁ dṛḍhavratāḥ (7-28)

But those of virtuous deeds, whose sins past and present have come to an end, they are freed from this delusion of dualities—and they go on to worship Me with a firmness of vow. (7.28)

— ॐ —

जरामरणमोक्षाय मामाश्रित्य यतन्ति ये ।

jarāmaraṇamokṣāya māmāśritya yatanti ye

ते ब्रह्म तद्विदुः कृत्स्नमध्यात्मं कर्म चाखिलम् ॥७-२९॥

te brahma tadviduḥ kṛtsnamadhyātmaṁ karma cākhilam (7-29)

Those who strive for deliverance from the cycle of death and decay, they take refuge in Me, and they find of Brahama, and of the embodied soul, and of this entire bailiwick of Karma. (7.29)

— ॐ —

साधिभूताधिदैवं मां साधियज्ञं च ये विदुः ।

sādhibhūtādhidaivaṁ māṁ sādhiyajñaṁ ca ye viduḥ

प्रयाणकालेऽपि च मां ते विदुर्युक्तचेतसः ॥७-३०॥

prayāṇakāle'pi ca māṁ te viduryuktacetasaḥ (7-30)

They who know My integral Being—comprising of *Adhibhūta* (the field of Matter), and *Adhidaiva* (the all-pervading Brahama), and *Adhiyajṅa* (the indwelling soul in all)—and who have fixed their mind firmly upon Me with that understanding, they directly realize My Being when the body falls away." (7.30)

ॐ तत्सदिति श्रीमद्भगवद्गीतासूपनिषत्सु

om tatsaditi śrīmadbhagavadgītāsūpaniṣatsu

ब्रह्मविद्यायां योगशास्त्रे श्रीकृष्णार्जुनसंवादे

brahmavidyāyāṁ yogaśāstre śrīkṛṣṇārjunasaṁvāde

ज्ञानविज्ञानयोगो नाम सप्तमोऽध्यायः ॥

jñānavijñānayogo nāma saptamo'dhyāyaḥ

In this Yogic Scripture on the Science of Brahama—the Shrimada-Bhāgvada-Gītā Upanishad—
hereby ends the dialogue between Shrī Krishna and Arjuna entitled:
Jnana-Vijnana Yoga, Canto VII

अष्टमोऽध्यायः - अक्षरब्रह्मयोगः

aṣṭamo'dhyāyaḥ - akṣarabrahmayogaḥ

:: Canto – VIII ::

- Path to the Supreme Spirit -

अर्जुन उवाच --
arjuna uvāca --

किं तद् ब्रह्म किमध्यात्मं किं कर्म पुरुषोत्तम ।
kiṁ tad brahma kimadhyātmaṁ kiṁ karma puruṣottama
अधिभूतं च किं प्रोक्तमधिदैवं किमुच्यते ॥८-१॥
adhibhūtaṁ ca kiṁ proktamadhidaivaṁ kimucyate (8-1)

Arjuna said: "O Krishna, what is this Brahama, and what is *Adhyātma*? What is Karma and what *Adhibhūta*? And what is said to be this *Adhidaiva*? (8.1)

— ॐ —

अधियज्ञः कथं कोऽत्र देहेऽस्मिन्मधुसूदन ।
adhiyajñaḥ kathaṁ ko'tra dehe'sminmadhusūdana
प्रयाणकाले च कथं ज्ञेयोऽसि नियतात्मभिः ॥८-२॥
prayāṇakāle ca kathaṁ jñeyo'si niyatātmabhiḥ (8-2)

Who is the *Adhiyajna*? How it dwells within the body? And how at the time of death, are You to be known by the self-restrained, O Madhu-Sudan?" (8.2)

श्रीभगवानुवाच --
śrībhagavānuvāca --

अक्षरं ब्रह्म परमं स्वभावोऽध्यात्ममुच्यते ।
akṣaraṁ brahma paramaṁ svabhāvo'dhyātmamucyate
भूतभावोद्भवकरो विसर्गः कर्मसंज्ञितः ॥८-३॥
bhūtabhāvodbhavakaro visargaḥ karmasaṁjñitaḥ (8-3)

Shri Bhagwāna said: "The supreme indestructible all-pervading unmanifest Being is called Brahama; and His manifestation as the embodied soul—one's own Self—is called the *Adhyātma*; and the offering (as like unto the sacrificial Yajna fire), which brings about the existence and sustenance of beings, is called Karma. (8.3)

— ॐ —

अधिभूतं क्षरो भावः पुरुषश्चाधिदैवतम् ।
adhibhūtaṁ kṣaro bhāvaḥ puruṣaścādhidaivatam
अधियज्ञोऽहमेवात्र देहे देहभृतां वर ॥८-४॥
adhiyajño'hamevātra dehe dehabhṛtāṁ vara (8-4)

All perishable entities are the *Adhibhuta*. The shining Purusha—the Cosmic Being—is the *Adhidaiva*. And I myself—dwelling as the inner witness in all embodied beings—am called the *Adhiyajna*, O best of embodied beings! (8.4)

— ॐ —

अन्तकाले च मामेव स्मरन्मुक्त्वा कलेवरम् ।
antakāle ca māmeva smaranmuktvā kalevaram
यः प्रयाति स मद्भावं याति नास्त्यत्र संशयः ॥८-५॥
yaḥ prayāti sa madbhāvaṁ yāti nāstyatra saṁśayaḥ (8-5)

He who, at the end time, remembers just Me when dropping away this body, he attains to my Being—of this let there be no doubt. (8.5)

— ॐ —

यं यं वापि स्मरन्भावं त्यजत्यन्ते कलेवरम् ।
yaṁ yaṁ vāpi smaranbhāvaṁ tyajatyante kalevaram
तं तमेवैति कौन्तेय सदा तद्भावभावितः ॥८-६॥
taṁ tamevaiti kaunteya sadā tadbhāvabhāvitaḥ (8-6)

Which whatever thing one thinks of at the time of death, O Kuntī-son, that alone he attains upon leaving the body—being constantly absorbed in its thought. (8.6)

— ॐ —

तस्मात्सर्वेषु कालेषु मामनुस्मर युध्य च ।
tasmātsarveṣu kāleṣu māmanusmara yudhya ca
मय्यर्पितमनोबुद्धिर्मामेवैष्यस्यसंशयः ॥८-७॥
mayyarpitamanobuddhirmāmevaiṣyasyasaṁśayaḥ (8-7)

Therefore remember Me at all times and then fight, O Arjuna; with the mind and intellect thus set upon Me, you will attain to Me alone—let there be no doubt on that. (8.7)

— ॐ —

अभ्यासयोगयुक्तेन चेतसा नान्यगामिना ।
abhyāsayogayuktena cetasā nānyagāminā
परमं पुरुषं दिव्यं याति पार्थानुचिन्तयन् ॥८-८॥
paramaṁ puruṣaṁ divyaṁ yāti pārthānucintayan (8-8)

With a mind that has taken to the path of diligent practice, he who does not stray away to anything else—but remains constantly engaged in contemplation upon the divine Effulgent-One—he attains to that Being, O Pārtha. (8.8)

— ॐ —

कविं पुराणमनुशासितार मणोरणीयंसमनुस्मरेद्यः ।
kaviṁ purāṇamanuśāsitāra maṇoraṇīyaṁsamanusmaredyaḥ
सर्वस्य धातारमचिन्त्यरूपमादित्यवर्णं तमसः परस्तात् ॥८-९॥
sarvasya dhātāramacintyarūpamādityavarṇaṁ tamasaḥ parastāt (8-9)

प्रयाणकाले मनसाऽचलेन भक्त्या युक्तो योगबलेन चैव ।
prayāṇakāle manasā'calena bhaktyā yukto yogabalena caiva
भ्रुवोर्मध्ये प्राणमावेश्य सम्यक् स तं परं पुरुषमुपैति दिव्यम् ॥८-१०॥
bhruvormadhye prāṇamāveśya samyak
sa taṁ paraṁ puruṣamupaiti divyam (8-10)

Endowed with devotion; and thinking of the Divine *Purusha*—ancient-most, the ruler of all, subtler than the subtlest, the sustainer of all, of inconceivable form, resplendent like the sun, beyond the darkness of ignorance—and having, by the power of Yoga, properly held the Prāna (life-breath) in the space between the eyebrows—he who, at the time of death, meditates with a steady mind upon the all-knowing Primordial Being, verily attains to Him. (8.9-8.10)

— ॐ —

यदक्षरं वेदविदो वदन्ति विशन्ति यद्यतयो वीतरागाः ।
yadakṣaraṁ vedavido vadanti viśanti yadyatayo vītarāgāḥ
यदिच्छन्तो ब्रह्मचर्यं चरन्ति तत्ते पदं सङ्ग्रहेण प्रवक्ष्ये ॥८-११॥
yadicchanto brahmacaryaṁ caranti
tatte padaṁ saṅgraheṇa pravakṣye (8-11)

That Imperishable-One—whom the knowers of the Vedas extol—desiring whom the celibates ever practice Brahmachārya—into Whom the aspirants, bereft of desires, eventually ascend—of that Supreme-Absolute I shall now speak to you in brief. (8.11)

— ॐ —

सर्वद्वाराणि संयम्य मनो हृदि निरुध्य च ।
sarvadvārāṇi saṁyamya mano hṛdi nirudhya ca
मूर्ध्न्याधायात्मनः प्राणमास्थितो योगधारणाम् ॥८-१२॥
mūrdhnyādhāyātmanaḥ prāṇamāsthito yogadhāraṇām (8-12)
ओमित्येकाक्षरं ब्रह्म व्याहरन्मामनुस्मरन् ।
omityekākṣaraṁ brahma vyāharanmāmanusmaran
यः प्रयाति त्यजन्देहं स याति परमां गतिम् ॥८-१३॥
yaḥ prayāti tyajandehaṁ sa yāti paramāṁ gatim (8-13)

Controlling all the sense-organs; and restraining the mind upon the heart; and fixing the life-breath in the head; and remaining confined to absorption in Yoga; and repeating the monosyllable OM (ॐ), which is Brahama; and dwelling upon Me, the Lord-God—he who leaves the body thusly, attains the supreme-most goal. (8.12-8.13)

— ॐ —

अनन्यचेताः सततं यो मां स्मरति नित्यशः ।
ananyacetāḥ satataṁ yo māṁ smarati nityaśaḥ
तस्याहं सुलभः पार्थ नित्ययुक्तस्य योगिनः ॥८-१४॥
tasyāhaṁ sulabhaḥ pārtha nityayuktasya yoginaḥ (8-14)

Unto the ever-restrained Yogī who continually dwells upon Me everyday—with his mind intent on nothing else—I am very easy of access, O Pārtha. (8.14)

— ॐ —

मामुपेत्य पुनर्जन्म दुःखालयमशाश्वतम् ।
māmupetya punarjanma duḥkhālayamaśāśvatam
नाप्नुवन्ति महात्मानः संसिद्धिं परमां गताः ॥८-१५॥
nāpnuvanti mahātmānaḥ saṁsiddhiṁ paramāṁ gatāḥ (8-15)

Exalted souls, having attained Me, are no more subjected to the rounds of deaths and rebirths in this dreadful world—which is transient and an abode of sorrows—for they have already attained the highest perfection possible. (8.15)

— ॐ —

आब्रह्मभुवनाल्लोकाः पुनरावर्तिनोऽर्जुन ।
ābrahmabhuvanāllokāḥ punarāvartino'rjuna
मामुपेत्य तु कौन्तेय पुनर्जन्म न विद्यते ॥८-१६॥
māmupetya tu kaunteya punarjanma na vidyate (8-16)

All the worlds, from the Brahammā-Loka downwards, are subject to reoccurrence, O Arjuna; but after attaining Me, there is no more birth or death, O Kuntī-son. (8.16)

— ॐ —

सहस्रयुगपर्यन्तमहर्यद् ब्रह्मणो विदुः ।
sahasrayugaparyantamaharyad brahmaṇo viduḥ
रात्रिं युगसहस्रान्तां तेऽहोरात्रविदो जनाः ॥८-१७॥
rātriṁ yugasahasrāntāṁ te'horātravido janāḥ (8-17)

Those who know of Brahammā's Day—which lasts a thousand Yugas, as also the Night of equal duration—they are said to be the true knowers of the Day and Night. (8.17)

— ॐ —

अव्यक्ताद् व्यक्तयः सर्वाः प्रभवन्त्यहरागमे ।
avyaktād vyaktayaḥ sarvāḥ prabhavantyaharāgame
रात्र्यागमे प्रलीयन्ते तत्रैवाव्यक्तसंज्ञके ॥८-१८॥
rātryāgame pralīyante tatraivāvyaktasaṁjñake (8-18)

At the coming of the cosmic dawn, all manifest beings emerge from the Unmanifest; and at the approach of the cosmic night, everything is absorbed once again into that same mist called the Unmanifest. (8.18)

— ॐ —

भूतग्रामः स एवायं भूत्वा भूत्वा प्रलीयते ।
bhūtagrāmaḥ sa evāyaṁ bhūtvā bhūtvā pralīyate
रात्र्यागमेऽवशः पार्थ प्रभवत्यहरागमे ॥८-१९॥
rātryāgame'vaśaḥ pārtha prabhavatyaharāgame (8-19)

Verily this multitude of beings, being born again and again, submerges into the Unmanifest at the approach of the Cosmic-Night, O Pārtha; and then everything re-emerges at the commencement of the Cosmic-Day—in spite of itself. (8.19)

— ॐ —

परस्तस्मात्तु भावोऽन्योऽव्यक्तोऽव्यक्तात्सनातनः ।

parastasmāttu bhāvo'nyo'vyakto'vyaktātsanātanaḥ

यः स सर्वेषु भूतेषु नश्यत्सु न विनश्यति ॥८-२०॥

yaḥ sa sarveṣu bhūteṣu naśyatsu na vinaśyati (8-20)

Behind all manifestations is the Absolute—not a void but the Supreme Consciousness which is as yet unmanifest. That is the divine Being who prevails ever eternal—even when everything else has disappeared. (8.20)

— ॐ —

अव्यक्तोऽक्षर इत्युक्तस्तमाहुः परमां गतिम् ।

avyakto'kṣara ityuktastamāhuḥ paramāṁ gatim

यं प्राप्य न निवर्तन्ते तद्धाम परमं मम ॥८-२१॥

yaṁ prāpya na nivartante taddhāma paramaṁ mama (8-21)

That Unmanifest—which is imperishable, which is the absolute, attaining to which one never returns—that One is stated to be the supreme goal. That is My domicile, My abode. That is Me. (8.21)

— ॐ —

पुरुषः स परः पार्थ भक्त्या लभ्यस्त्वनन्यया ।

puruṣaḥ sa paraḥ pārtha bhaktyā labhyastvananyayā

यस्यान्तःस्थानि भूतानि येन सर्वमिदं ततम् ॥८-२२॥

yasyāntaḥsthāni bhūtāni yena sarvamidaṁ tatam (8-22)

That eternal supreme Being—in whom all beings abide, and by whom all this stands pervaded—is attainable only through a one-pointed devotion, O Pārtha. (8.22)

— ॐ —

यत्र काले त्वनावृत्तिमावृत्तिं चैव योगिनः ।

yatra kāle tvanāvṛttimāvṛttiṁ caiva yoginaḥ

प्रयाता यान्ति तं कालं वक्ष्यामि भरतर्षभ ॥८-२३॥

prayātā yānti taṁ kālaṁ vakṣyāmi bharatarṣabha (8-23)

The time at which departing from hence, the Yogīs attain to a state of return or no-return, of that I shall now speak to you, O best of Bhāratas. (8.23)

— ॐ —

अग्निर्ज्योतिरहः शुक्लः षण्मासा उत्तरायणम् ।
agnirjyotirahaḥ śuklaḥ ṣaṇmāsā uttarāyaṇam
तत्र प्रयाता गच्छन्ति ब्रह्म ब्रह्मविदो जनाः ॥८-२४॥
tatra prayātā gacchanti brahma brahmavido janāḥ (8-24)

The path on which exist the effulgent fire-god, and the deity presiding over the daylight, as also the bright fortnight and the six months of the northern course of sun—departing by that path, the knower of Brahama attains to Brahama. (8.24)

— ॐ —

धूमो रात्रिस्तथा कृष्णः षण्मासा दक्षिणायनम् ।
dhūmo rātristathā kṛṣṇaḥ ṣaṇmāsā dakṣiṇāyanam
तत्र चान्द्रमसं ज्योतिर्योगी प्राप्य निवर्तते ॥८-२५॥
tatra cāndramasaṁ jyotiryogī prāpya nivartate (8-25)

The path on which abide the gods presiding over the smoke and night, as also the dark half of month, and the six months of the southern course of sun—taking to that path, the Yogī reaches the lunar sphere; and returns thence. (8.25)

— ॐ —

शुक्लकृष्णे गती ह्येते जगतः शाश्वते मते ।
śuklakṛṣṇe gatī hyete jagataḥ śāśvate mate
एकया यात्यनावृत्तिमन्ययावर्तते पुनः ॥८-२६॥
ekayā yātyanāvṛttimanyayāvartate punaḥ (8-26)

These two paths of the world—the Bright and the Dark—are considered to be eternal: going by one, one returns not; and going by the other, one returns. (8.26)

— ॐ —

नैते सृती पार्थ जानन्योगी मुह्यति कश्चन ।
naite sṛtī pārtha jānanyogī muhyati kaścana
तस्मात्सर्वेषु कालेषु योगयुक्तो भवार्जुन ॥८-२७॥
tasmātsarveṣu kāleṣu yogayukto bhavārjuna (8-27)

Knowing the mystery of these two paths, O Pārtha, a Yogī persist deluded no more; therefore at all times, do thou remain steadfast in Yoga, O Arjuna. (8.27)

— ॐ —

वेदेषु यज्ञेषु तपःसु चैव दानेषु यत्पुण्यफलं प्रदिष्टम् ।
vedeṣu yajñeṣu tapaḥsu caiva dāneṣu yatpuṇyaphalaṁ pradiṣṭam
अत्येति तत्सर्वमिदं विदित्वा योगी परं स्थानमुपैति चाद्यम् ॥८-२८॥
atyeti tatsarvamidaṁ viditvā yogī paraṁ sthānamupaiti cādyam (8-28)

Whatever good results are declared for the study of the Vedas, and for the performance of Yajnas, and for austerities and charities: all of these the Yogī, who knows the above, undoubtedly achieves—nay, verily transcends—attaining the primordial Supreme Abode." (8.28)

ॐ तत्सदिति श्रीमद्भगवद्गीतासूपनिषत्सु
om tatsaditi śrīmadbhagavadgītāsūpaniṣatsu
ब्रह्मविद्यायां योगशास्त्रे श्रीकृष्णार्जुनसंवादे
brahmavidyāyāṁ yogaśāstre śrīkṛṣṇārjunasaṁvāde
अक्षरब्रह्मयोगो नामाष्टमोऽध्यायः ॥
akṣarabrahmayogo nāmāṣṭamo'dhyāyaḥ

In this Yogic Scripture on the Science of Brahama—the Shrimada-Bhāgvada-Gītā Upanishad—hereby ends the dialogue between Shrī Krishna and Arjuna entitled: Akshara-Brahama Yoga, Canto VIII

नवमोऽध्यायः - राजविद्याराजगुह्ययोगः

navamo'dhyāyaḥ - rājavidyārājaguhyayogaḥ

:: Canto – IX ::

- The Path of Royal-Knowledge Royal-Science -

श्रीभगवानुवाच --
śrībhagavānuvāca –

इदं तु ते गुह्यतमं प्रवक्ष्याम्यनसूयवे ।
idaṁ tu te guhyatamaṁ pravakṣyāmyanasūyave
ज्ञानं विज्ञानसहितं यज्ज्ञात्वा मोक्ष्यसेऽशुभात् ॥९-१॥
jñānaṁ vijñānasahitaṁ yajjñātvā mokṣyase'śubhāt (9-1)

Shri Bhagwāna said: "To you who are innocent of carping, I shall reveal that very special secret knowledge—coupled with realization—knowing which you will be freed from all ills. (9.1)

— ॐ —

राजविद्या राजगुह्यं पवित्रमिदमुत्तमम् ।
rājavidyā rājaguhyaṁ pavitramidamuttamam
प्रत्यक्षावगमं धर्म्यं सुसुखं कर्तुमव्ययम् ॥९-२॥
pratyakṣāvagamaṁ dharmyaṁ susukhaṁ kartumavyayam (9-2)

This is a sovereign science of paramount secrecy, supremely holy and most excellent, replete with virtue, easy of practice, experienced directly—and imperishable in its results. (9.2)

— ॐ —

अश्रद्दधानाः पुरुषा धर्मस्यास्य परन्तप ।
aśraddadhānāḥ puruṣā dharmasyāsya parantapa
अप्राप्य मां निवर्तन्ते मृत्युसंसारवर्त्मनि ॥९-३॥
aprāpya māṁ nivartante mṛtyusaṁsāravartmani (9-3)

Those that lack faith in this Teaching, they continue to revolve in this birth-death cycle of the mortals, without attaining Me. (9.3)

— ॐ —

मया ततमिदं सर्वं जगदव्यक्तमूर्तिना ।
mayā tatamidaṁ sarvaṁ jagadavyaktamūrtinā
मत्स्थानि सर्वभूतानि न चाहं तेष्ववस्थितः ॥९-४॥
matsthāni sarvabhūtāni na cāhaṁ teṣvavasthitaḥ (9-4)

Know that this entire universe is pervaded by Me in my unmanifest aspect. All beings abide situated in Me—but I am not in them. (9.4)

— ॐ —

न च मत्स्थानि भूतानि पश्य मे योगमैश्वरम् ।
na ca matsthāni bhūtāni paśya me yogamaiśvaram
भूतभृन्न च भूतस्थो ममात्मा भूतभावनः ॥९-५॥
bhūtabhṛnna ca bhūtastho mamātmā bhūtabhāvanaḥ (9-5)

Nor are the beings in Me—behold this wonderful divine mystery of mine; although the creator and sustainer of all, yet My Self is not in these beings. (9.5)

— ॐ —

यथाकाशस्थितो नित्यं वायुः सर्वत्रगो महान् ।
yathākāśasthito nityaṁ vāyuḥ sarvatrago mahān
तथा सर्वाणि भूतानि मत्स्थानीत्युपधारय ॥९-६॥
tathā sarvāṇi bhūtāni matsthānītyupadhāraya (9-6)

Just as this immense air—although moving everywhere—still exists abiding in space, even so all these moving creatures ever exist abiding in Me, rooted in my consciousness. (9.6)

— ॐ —

सर्वभूतानि कौन्तेय प्रकृतिं यान्ति मामिकाम् ।
sarvabhūtāni kaunteya prakṛtiṁ yānti māmikām
कल्पक्षये पुनस्तानि कल्पादौ विसृजाम्यहम् ॥९-७॥
kalpakṣaye punastāni kalpādau visṛjāmyaham (9-7)

At the time of final dissolution, all beings submerge into my Prakriti; and at the start of a new creation, I project them forth once again, O Kuntī-son. (9.7)

— ॐ —

प्रकृतिं स्वामवष्टभ्य विसृजामि पुनः पुनः ।

prakṛtiṁ svāmavaṣṭabhya visṛjāmi punaḥ punaḥ

भूतग्राममिमं कृत्स्नमवशं प्रकृतेर्वशात् ॥९-८॥

bhūtagrāmamimaṁ kṛtsnamavaśaṁ prakṛtervaśāt (9-8)

Presiding over my Nature, again and again do I send forth these multitudes of beings—bound powerless, driven by the dictates of nature. (9.8)

— ॐ —

न च मां तानि कर्माणि निबध्नन्ति धनञ्जय ।

na ca māṁ tāni karmāṇi nibadhnanti dhanañjaya

उदासीनवदासीनमसक्तं तेषु कर्मसु ॥९-९॥

udāsīnavadāsīnamasaktaṁ teṣu karmasu (9-9)

O Arjuna, know that all this Karma (of Creation) does not ensnare Me—who remain unattached to it all, like one indifferent. (9.9)

— ॐ —

मयाध्यक्षेण प्रकृतिः सूयते सचराचरम् ।

mayādhyakṣeṇa prakṛtiḥ sūyate sacarācaram

हेतुनानेन कौन्तेय जगद्विपरिवर्तते ॥९-१०॥

hetunānena kaunteya jagadviparivartate (9-10)

Under my aegis, O Kuntī-son, this Prakriti brings forth the entire creation comprising of the sentient and insentient beings; and powered by its unremitting functioning, the wheel of the world is thus set mechanically revolving. (9.10)

— ॐ —

अवजानन्ति मां मूढा मानुषीं तनुमाश्रितम् ।

avajānanti māṁ mūḍhā mānuṣīṁ tanumāśritam

परं भावमजानन्तो मम भूतमहेश्वरम् ॥९-११॥

paraṁ bhāvamajānanto mama bhūtamaheśvaram (9-11)

Out of ignorance, some deride Me—the Creator, who has taken up a human form; they fail to perceive my higher nature: as the great Lord of all beings. (9.11)

— ॐ —

मोघाशा मोघकर्माणो मोघज्ञाना विचेतसः ।
moghāśā moghakarmāṇo moghajñānā vicetasaḥ
राक्षसीमासुरीं चैव प्रकृतिं मोहिनीं श्रिताः ॥९-१२॥
rākṣasīmāsurīṁ caiva prakṛtiṁ mohinīṁ śritāḥ (9-12)

Of vain hopes, futile actions, and conceited knowledge, such beings exhibit that part of their nature which stems from ignorance and is demoniacal and fiendish. (9.12)

— ॐ —

महात्मानस्तु मां पार्थ दैवीं प्रकृतिमाश्रिताः ।
mahātmānastu māṁ pārtha daivīṁ prakṛtimāśritāḥ
भजन्त्यनन्यमनसो ज्ञात्वा भूतादिमव्ययम् ॥९-१३॥
bhajantyananyamanaso jñātvā bhūtādimavyayam (9-13)

But taking to their divine nature, O Pārtha, the noble souls worship Me with a one-pointed unceasing devotion—knowing Me to be the eternal, imperishable, primal cause of all beings and things. (9.13)

— ॐ —

सततं कीर्तयन्तो मां यतन्तश्च दृढव्रताः ।
satataṁ kīrtayanto māṁ yatantaśca dṛḍhavratāḥ
नमस्यन्तश्च मां भक्त्या नित्ययुक्ता उपासते ॥९-१४॥
namasyantaśca māṁ bhaktyā nityayuktā upāsate (9-14)

Chanting My names and glories, striving for realization through austerities, venerating Me, and united to Me through meditation—such ardent devotees of Mine remain ever engaged in worshipping Me with a single one-pointed devotion. (9.14)

— ॐ —

ज्ञानयज्ञेन चाप्यन्ये यजन्तो मामुपासते ।
jñānayajñena cāpyanye yajanto māmupāsate
एकत्वेन पृथक्त्वेन बहुधा विश्वतोमुखम् ॥९-१५॥
ekatvena pṛthaktvena bahudhā viśvatomukham (9-15)

Others, who follow the path of knowledge, betake themselves to Me through the Yajna of Knowledge—worshipping Me in My Absolute-Formless aspect—as identical with themselves. Still others worship Me in my aspect having manifold bodily forms—which are many and diverse: (9.15)

— ॐ —

अहं क्रतुरहं यज्ञः स्वधाहमहमौषधम् ।
ahaṁ kraturahaṁ yajñaḥ svadhāhamahamauṣadham
मन्त्रोऽहमहमेवाज्यमहमग्निरहं हुतम् ॥९-१६॥
mantro'hamahamevājyamahamagniraham hutam (9-16)

For I am the Vedic ritual; and I am the Yajna sacrifice; and I am the offering to the departed; and I am the herbage and the food-grains; and I am the sacred Mantra; and I am the sacred fire; and I am the oblation of clarified butter that's poured into that fire—and also the act of pouring that oblation. (9.16)

— ॐ —

पिताहमस्य जगतो माता धाता पितामहः ।
pitāhamasya jagato mātā dhātā pitāmahaḥ
वेद्यं पवित्रमोङ्कार ऋक्साम यजुरेव च ॥९-१७॥
vedyaṁ pavitramoṅkāra ṛksāma yajureva ca (9-17)

I am the father of all—and their mother; and I am the sustainer and ruler of the worlds and the ancient grandsire. I am that which needs be known; I am the sanctifier, the sacred Om, and also the Vedas—*Rika, Yajura, Sāma*. (9.17)

— ॐ —

गतिर्भर्ता प्रभुः साक्षी निवासः शरणं सुहृत् ।
gatirbhartā prabhuḥ sākṣī nivāsaḥ śaraṇaṁ suhṛt
प्रभवः प्रलयः स्थानं निधानं बीजमव्ययम् ॥९-१८॥
prabhavaḥ pralayaḥ sthānaṁ nidhānaṁ bījamavyayam (9-18)

I am the goal, the sustainer, the Lord-God, the witness, the abode, the refuge, the friend; I am the start, middle and end; I am the sustenance, the repository, and the eternal seed of life. (9.18)

— ॐ —

तपाम्यहमहं वर्षं निगृह्णाम्युत्सृजामि च ।
tapāmyahamahaṁ varṣaṁ nigṛhṇāmyutsṛjāmi ca
अमृतं चैव मृत्युश्च सदसच्चाहमर्जुन ॥९-१९॥
amṛtaṁ caiva mṛtyuśca sadasaccāhamarjuna (9-19)

I radiate heat as the sun; and I restrain and unleash the rains; and I am the ambrosia of Immortality O Arjuna; and even so, I am Death. I am the Absolute-Being—manifest and unmanifest as well. (9.19)

— ॐ —

त्रैविद्या मां सोमपाः पूतपापा

traividyā māṁ somapāḥ pūtapāpā

यज्ञैरिष्ट्वा स्वर्गतिं प्रार्थयन्ते ।

yajñairiṣṭvā svargatiṁ prārthayante

ते पुण्यमासाद्य सुरेन्द्रलोक-

te puṇyamāsādya surendraloka-

मश्नन्ति दिव्यान्दिवि देवभोगान् ॥९-२०॥

maśnanti divyāndivi devabhogān (9-20)

The knowers of Vedas—purged of sins by partaking of the nectar of Soma, and worshipping Me through Yajnas—pray for obtaining heaven; and having attained that meritorious sphere of Indra, they enjoy in heaven all the celestial pleasures of gods. (9.20)

— ॐ —

ते तं भुक्त्वा स्वर्गलोकं विशालं क्षीणे पुण्ये मर्त्यलोकं विशन्ति ।

te taṁ bhuktvā svargalokaṁ viśālaṁ kṣīṇe puṇye martyalokaṁ viśanti

एवं त्रयीधर्ममनुप्रपन्ना गतागतं कामकामा लभन्ते ॥९-२१॥

evaṁ trayīdharmamanuprapannā gatāgataṁ kāmakāmā labhante (9-21)

And having enjoyed those vast heavenly realms, they again return to this world of mortals—upon their merits becoming exhausted. Thus those who take recourse to the rituals of Vedas, desiring worldly enjoyments—they repeatedly come and go. (9.21)

— ॐ —

अनन्याश्चिन्तयन्तो मां ये जनाः पर्युपासते ।

ananyāścintayanto māṁ ye janāḥ paryupāsate

तेषां नित्याभियुक्तानां योगक्षेमं वहाम्यहम् ॥९-२२॥

teṣāṁ nityābhiyuktānāṁ yogakṣemaṁ vahāmyaham (9-22)

But for the devouts who, loving no one else, constantly think of Me, who worship Me through meditation—for such devotees ever united with Me in thoughts and deeds, I myself look after their welfare and attend to all their needs. (9.22)

— ॐ —

येऽप्यन्यदेवता भक्ता यजन्ते श्रद्धयान्विताः ।

ye'pyanyadevatā bhaktā yajante śraddhayānvitāḥ

तेऽपि मामेव कौन्तेय यजन्त्यविधिपूर्वकम् ॥९-२३॥

te'pi māmeva kaunteya yajantyavidhipūrvakam (9-23)

Even such devotees who endowed with faith worship other gods—they too are found to be eventually worshipping just Me, albeit with a misguided approach O Arjuna. (9.23)

— ॐ —

अहं हि सर्वयज्ञानां भोक्ता च प्रभुरेव च ।
aham hi sarvayajñānāṁ bhoktā ca prabhureva ca
न तु मामभिजानन्ति तत्त्वेनातश्च्यवन्ति ते ॥९-२४॥
na tu māmabhijānanti tattvenātaścyavanti te (9-24)

It is I who am the eventual partaker, and the Lord also, of all *Yajnas*; but because these worshipper do not know Me to be the Supreme-One, they are seen to fall down—because they have taken recourse to the impermanent and not the Ultimate. (9.24)

— ॐ —

यान्ति देवव्रता देवान्पितॄन्यान्ति पितृव्रताः ।
yānti devavratā devānpitṝnyānti pitṛvratāḥ
भूतानि यान्ति भूतेज्या यान्ति मद्याजिनोऽपि माम् ॥९-२५॥
bhūtāni yānti bhūtejyā yānti madyājino'pi mām (9-25)

Those who are the votaries of gods, go to gods; they who are the votaries of manes, reach the manes; they who worship the spirits, reach the spirits; and they who worship Me—they reach Me directly, released of everything in between. (9.25)

— ॐ —

पत्रं पुष्पं फलं तोयं यो मे भक्त्या प्रयच्छति ।
patraṁ puṣpaṁ phalaṁ toyaṁ yo me bhaktyā prayacchati
तदहं भक्त्युपहृतमश्नामि प्रयतात्मनः ॥९-२६॥
tadahaṁ bhaktyupahṛtamaśnāmi prayatātmanaḥ (9-26)

Whosoever offers Me with love something—be it a flower, a leaf, a fruit or water—that devout offering of the pure-minded, I forthwith accept. (9.26)

— ॐ —

यत्करोषि यदश्नासि यज्जुहोषि ददासि यत् ।
yatkaroṣi yadaśnāsi yajjuhoṣi dadāsi yat
यत्तपस्यसि कौन्तेय तत्कुरुष्व मदर्पणम् ॥९-२७॥
yattapasyasi kaunteya tatkuruṣva madarpaṇam (9-27)

O Arjuna, whatever you do, whatever you partake, whatever you offer as oblation, whatever you bestow as a gift, whatever austerities you perform—offer all those unto Me first. (9.27)

— ॐ —

शुभाशुभफलैरेवं मोक्ष्यसे कर्मबन्धनैः ।
śubhāśubhaphalairevaṁ mokṣyase karmabandhanaiḥ
संन्यासयोगयुक्तात्मा विमुक्तो मामुपैष्यसि ॥९-२८॥
saṁnyāsayogayuktātmā vimukto māmupaiṣyasi (9-28)

And in this way you will be freed from the bondages of Karma—which take the form of the good and evil accruals resulting from Karma. And thus freed, and with your mind established in the Yoga of renunciation having offered all unto Me—you shall directly attain to Me. (9.28)

— ॐ —

समोऽहं सर्वभूतेषु न मे द्वेष्योऽस्ति न प्रियः ।
samo'haṁ sarvabhūteṣu na me dveṣyo'sti na priyaḥ
ये भजन्ति तु मां भक्त्या मयि ते तेषु चाप्यहम् ॥९-२९॥
ye bhajanti tu māṁ bhaktyā mayi te teṣu cāpyaham (9-29)

Know that I am the same to all beings—there is no one here who's hateful or dear to Me—but, those who worship Me with devotion, they are in Me, and I too am in them. (9.29)

— ॐ —

अपि चेत्सुदुराचारो भजते मामनन्यभाक् ।
api cetsudurācāro bhajate māmananyabhāk
साधुरेव स मन्तव्यः सम्यग्व्यवसितो हि सः ॥९-३०॥
sādhureva sa mantavyaḥ samyagvyavasito hi saḥ (9-30)

Even if the vilest of vile sinners were to worship me devotedly, to the exclusion of all else, he should be regarded to be a good soul—for he has rightly resolved. (9.30)

— ॐ —

क्षिप्रं भवति धर्मात्मा शश्वच्छान्तिं निगच्छति ।
kṣipraṁ bhavati dharmātmā śaśvacchāntiṁ nigacchati
कौन्तेय प्रतिजानीहि न मे भक्तः प्रणश्यति ॥९-३१॥
kaunteya pratijānīhi na me bhaktaḥ praṇaśyati (9-31)

And before long he truly becomes virtuous and attains ever abiding peace. Bear witness to this, O Kuntī-son, know that my devotee will never be destroyed—this is my avowed declaration. (9.31)

— ॐ —

मां हि पार्थ व्यपाश्रित्य येऽपि स्युः पापयोनयः ।
māṁ hi pārtha vyapāśritya ye'pi syuḥ pāpayonayaḥ
स्त्रियो वैश्यास्तथा शूद्रास्तेऽपि यान्ति परां गतिम् ॥९-३२॥
striyo vaiśyāstathā śūdrāste'pi yānti parāṁ gatim (9-32)
किं पुनर्ब्राह्मणाः पुण्या भक्ता राजर्षयस्तथा ।
kiṁ punarbrāhmaṇāḥ puṇyā bhaktā rājarṣayastathā
अनित्यमसुखं लोकमिमं प्राप्य भजस्व माम् ॥९-३३॥
anityamasukhaṁ lokamimaṁ prāpya bhajasva mām (9-33)

Whosoever they may be, O Arjuna—woman, vaishya, shudra, or even those of impious births—they all attain to the supreme state once having taken refuge in Me—what then to say of holy Brahmins and devout royal sages! Therefore, having obtained this human body—which is otherwise ephemeral and void of joys—worship Me unceasingly. (9.32-9.33)

— ॐ —

मन्मना भव मद्भक्तो मद्याजी मां नमस्कुरु ।
manmanā bhava madbhakto madyājī māṁ namaskuru
मामेवैष्यसि युक्त्वैवमात्मानं मत्परायणः ॥९-३४॥
māmevaiṣyasi yuktvaivamātmānaṁ matparāyaṇaḥ (9-34)

Be devoted, and offer obeisance, and fix your mind upon Me; and thus binding yourself to Me, and having only Me as your supreme goal, you shall attain to Me alone." (9.34)

ॐ तत्सदिति श्रीमद्भगवद्गीतासूपनिषत्सु
om tatsaditi śrīmadbhagavadgītāsūpaniṣatsu
ब्रह्मविद्यायां योगशास्त्रे श्रीकृष्णार्जुनसंवादे
brahmavidyāyāṁ yogaśāstre śrīkṛṣṇārjunasaṁvāde
राजविद्याराजगुह्ययोगो नाम नवमोऽध्यायः ॥
rājavidyārājaguhyayogo nāma navamo'dhyāyaḥ

In this Yogic Scripture on the Science of Brahama—the Shrimada-Bhāgvada-Gītā Upanishad—hereby ends the dialogue between Shrī Krishna and Arjuna entitled:
Rāja-Vidyārāja-Guhya Yoga, Canto IX

दशमोऽध्यायः - विभूतियोगः

daśamo'dhyāyaḥ - vibhūtiyogaḥ

:: Canto – X. ::

- Glories of the Divine -

श्रीभगवानुवाच --
śrībhagavānuvāca --

भूय एव महाबाहो श्रृणु मे परमं वचः ।
bhūya eva mahābāho śṛṇu me paramaṁ vacaḥ
यत्तेऽहं प्रीयमाणाय वक्ष्यामि हितकाम्यया ॥१०-१॥
yatte'haṁ prīyamāṇāya vakṣyāmi hitakāmyayā (10-1)

Shri Bhagwāna said: "Hear again, O mighty-armed, the supreme words which I—wishing your welfare—speak to you: who takes delight in hearing them. (10.1)

— ॐ —

न मे विदुः सुरगणाः प्रभवं न महर्षयः ।
na me viduḥ suragaṇāḥ prabhavaṁ na maharṣayaḥ
अहमादिर्हि देवानां महर्षीणां च सर्वशः ॥१०-२॥
ahamādirhi devānāṁ maharṣīṇāṁ ca sarvaśaḥ (10-2)

Neither the gods nor the great Rishis know of my origin—for in every respect I am the Ultimate-Cause of all, even of the gods and the great sages themselves. (10.2)

— ॐ —

यो मामजमनादिं च वेत्ति लोकमहेश्वरम् ।
yo māmajamanādiṁ ca vetti lokamaheśvaram
असम्मूढः स मर्त्येषु सर्वपापैः प्रमुच्यते ॥१०-३॥
asammūḍhaḥ sa martyeṣu sarvapāpaiḥ pramucyate (10-3)

One who lives in the realization that I am the birth-less, beginning-less Lord of Creation, he abides undeluded amongst mortals, freed of all sins. (10.3)

— ॐ —

बुद्धिर्ज्ञानमसम्मोहः क्षमा सत्यं दमः शमः ।
buddhirjñānamasammohaḥ kṣamā satyaṁ damaḥ śamaḥ
सुखं दुःखं भवोऽभावो भयं चाभयमेव च ॥ १०-४॥
sukhaṁ duḥkhaṁ bhavo'bhāvo bhayaṁ cābhayameva ca (10-4)

अहिंसा समता तुष्टिस्तपो दानं यशोऽयशः ।
ahiṁsā samatā tuṣṭistapo dānaṁ yaśo'yaśaḥ
भवन्ति भावा भूतानां मत्त एव पृथग्विधाः ॥ १०-५॥
bhavanti bhāvā bhūtānāṁ matta eva pṛthagvidhāḥ (10-5)

Discrimination, knowledge, non-delusional understanding, forbearance, veracity, self-control, tranquility, happiness and misery, evolution and dissolution, fear and also fearlessness, non-injury, equanimity, contentment, austerity, charity, fame and obloquy—these different dispositions and circumstance of beings are indeed born of Me. (10.4-10.5)

— ॐ —

महर्षयः सप्त पूर्वे चत्वारो मनवस्तथा ।
maharṣayaḥ sapta pūrve catvāro manavastathā
मद्भावा मानसा जाता येषां लोक इमाः प्रजाः ॥ १०-६॥
madbhāvā mānasā jātā yeṣāṁ loka imāḥ prajāḥ (10-6)

The seven great sages, the earlier four (Sanaka, Sanata-Kumār et al), and the Manūs (Svayambhū & others), all were born of My mind, endowed with My essence—and whose progeny are all these beings of the world. (10.6)

— ॐ —

एतां विभूतिं योगं च मम यो वेत्ति तत्त्वतः ।
etāṁ vibhūtiṁ yogaṁ ca mama yo vetti tattvataḥ
सोऽविकम्पेन योगेन युज्यते नात्र संशयः ॥ १०-७॥
so'vikampena yogena yujyate nātra saṁśayaḥ (10-7)

He who knows in essence the glories and divine powers of Mine, attains unflinching Yoga—of this let there be no doubts. (10.7)

— ॐ —

अहं सर्वस्य प्रभवो मत्तः सर्वं प्रवर्तते ।

ahaṁ sarvasya prabhavo mattaḥ sarvaṁ pravartate

इति मत्वा भजन्ते मां बुधा भावसमन्विताः ॥ १०-८ ॥

iti matvā bhajante māṁ budhā bhāvasamanvitāḥ (10-8)

I am the origin of all and everything proceeds out of Me—knowing this, the wise ever worship Me with arrant devotion. (10.8)

— ॐ —

मच्चित्ता मद्गतप्राणा बोधयन्तः परस्परम् ।

maccittā madgataprāṇā bodhayantaḥ parasparam

कथयन्तश्च मां नित्यं तुष्यन्ति च रमन्ति च ॥ १०-९ ॥

kathayantaśca māṁ nityaṁ tuṣyanti ca ramanti ca (10-9)

With their mind and the senses fixed upon Me, conversing and enlightening one another regarding Me—my devotees always abide ever glad, ever content. (10.9)

— ॐ —

तेषां सततयुक्तानां भजतां प्रीतिपूर्वकम् ।

teṣāṁ satatayuktānāṁ bhajatāṁ prītipūrvakam

ददामि बुद्धियोगं तं येन मामुपयान्ति ते ॥ १०-१० ॥

dadāmi buddhiyogaṁ taṁ yena māmupayānti te (10-10)

To such who are thus devoted to Me and worship Me with love, I confer upon them that very Yoga of understanding by which they are able to directly reach Me. (10.10)

— ॐ —

तेषामेवानुकम्पार्थमहमज्ञानजं तमः ।

teṣāmevānukampārthamahamajñānajaṁ tamaḥ

नाशयाम्यात्मभावस्थो ज्ञानदीपेन भास्वता ॥ १०-११ ॥

nāśayāmyātmabhāvastho jñānadīpena bhāsvatā (10-11)

To show them special mercy I—abiding in their intellect—destroy with the shining lamp of knowledge that darkness of the mind which has its origin in Ignorance." (10.11)

अर्जुन उवाच --
arjuna uvāca --

परं ब्रह्म परं धाम पवित्रं परमं भवान् ।
paraṁ brahma paraṁ dhāma pavitraṁ paramaṁ bhavān
पुरुषं शाश्वतं दिव्यमादिदेवमजं विभुम् ॥ १०-१२ ॥
puruṣaṁ śāśvataṁ divyamādidevamajaṁ vibhum (10-12)
आहुस्त्वामृषयः सर्वे देवर्षिर्नारदस्तथा ।
āhustvāmṛṣayaḥ sarve devarṣirnāradastathā
असितो देवलो व्यासः स्वयं चैव ब्रवीषि मे ॥ १०-१३ ॥
asito devalo vyāsaḥ svayaṁ caiva bravīṣi me (10-13)

Arjuna said: "You are the Transcendent-Eternal, the Supreme-Abode, the Holy-Most. All the Rishīs—the blessed Nārada, and sages Asita and Devala and Vyāsa—speak of you as the eternal divine *Purusha*, the primal Deity, unborn and all-pervading; and you too are telling me so from your own lips. (10.12-10.13)

— ॐ —

सर्वमेतदृतं मन्ये यन्मां वदसि केशव ।
sarvametadṛtaṁ manye yanmāṁ vadasi keśava
न हि ते भगवन्व्यक्तिं विदुर्देवा न दानवाः ॥ १०-१४ ॥
na hi te bhagavanvyaktiṁ vidurdevā na dānavāḥ (10-14)

O Keshava, I believe as true all that you say; verily neither the gods nor the demons know of your manifestations, O Lord. (10.14)

— ॐ —

स्वयमेवात्मनात्मानं वेत्थ त्वं पुरुषोत्तम ।
svayamevātmanātmānaṁ vettha tvaṁ puruṣottama
भूतभावन भूतेश देवदेव जगत्पते ॥ १०-१५ ॥
bhūtabhāvana bhūteśa devadeva jagatpate (10-15)

You yourself know yourself by yourself, O Creator of creatures, O Ruler of beings, O God of gods, O Lord of the universe, O supreme Purusha. (10.15)

— ॐ —

वक्तुमर्हस्यशेषेण दिव्या ह्यात्मविभूतयः ।

vaktumarhasyaśeṣeṇa divyā hyātmavibhūtayaḥ

याभिर्विभूतिभिर्लोकानिमांस्त्वं व्याप्य तिष्ठसि ॥ १०-१६ ॥

yābhirvibhūtibhirlokānimāṁstvaṁ vyāpya tiṣṭhasi (10-16)

Verily you alone can fully delineate your divine glories by which—pervading all these worlds—you exist. (10.16)

— ॐ —

कथं विद्यामहं योगिंस्त्वां सदा परिचिन्तयन् ।

kathaṁ vidyāmahaṁ yogiṁstvāṁ sadā paricintayan

केषु केषु च भावेषु चिन्त्योऽसि भगवन्मया ॥ १०-१७ ॥

keṣu keṣu ca bhāveṣu cintyo'si bhagavanmayā (10-17)

Tell me, O Supreme-Yogī, in which way shall I always think of you, know you? In which particular form, O Lord, are you to be meditated upon by me? (10.17)

— ॐ —

विस्तरेणात्मनो योगं विभूतिं च जनार्दन ।

vistareṇātmano yogaṁ vibhūtiṁ ca janārdana

भूयः कथय तृप्तिर्हि शृण्वतो नास्ति मेऽमृतम् ॥ १०-१८ ॥

bhūyaḥ kathaya tṛptirhi śṛṇvato nāsti me'mṛtam (10-18)

Tell me once more in minutia, O Janārdana, of your mystic power and glories! I am never satiated in hearing your ambrosial words—for the more I hear, my thirst remains unabated still." (10.18)

श्रीभगवानुवाच --

śrībhagavānuvāca --

हन्त ते कथयिष्यामि दिव्या ह्यात्मविभूतयः ।

hanta te kathayiṣyāmi divyā hyātmavibhūtayaḥ

प्राधान्यतः कुरुश्रेष्ठ नास्त्यन्तो विस्तरस्य मे ॥ १०-१९ ॥

prādhānyataḥ kuruśreṣṭha nāstyanto vistarasya me (10-19)

Shri Bhagwāna said: "All right, but let me tell you of just of My principal divine glories, O Arjuna, for there is no end to the extent of My manifestations. (10.19)

— ॐ —

अहमात्मा गुडाकेश सर्वभूताशयस्थितः ।
ahamātmā guḍākeśa sarvabhūtāśayasthitaḥ
अहमादिश्च मध्यं च भूतानामन्त एव च ॥ १०-२० ॥
ahamādiśca madhyaṁ ca bhūtānāmanta eva ca (10-20)

Know, O Gudākesha, that I am the universal Self seated in the hearts of all; of all beings, I am the beginning, the middle, and the end. (10.20)

— ॐ —

आदित्यानामहं विष्णुर्ज्योतिषां रविरंशुमान् ।
ādityānāmahaṁ viṣṇurjyotiṣāṁ raviraṁśumān
मरीचिर्मरुतामस्मि नक्षत्राणामहं शशी ॥ १०-२१ ॥
marīcirmarutāmasmi nakṣatrāṇāmahaṁ śaśī (10-21)

Of the twelve sons of Aditi, I am Vishnu; of the luminaries, I am the radiant Sun; of the Marutas, I am Marichi; and of the constellations, I am the Moon. (10.21)

— ॐ —

वेदानां सामवेदोऽस्मि देवानामस्मि वासवः ।
vedānāṁ sāmavedo'smi devānāmasmi vāsavaḥ
इन्द्रियाणां मनश्चास्मि भूतानामस्मि चेतना ॥ १०-२२ ॥
indriyāṇāṁ manaścāsmi bhūtānāmasmi cetanā (10-22)

Of the Vedas, I am the Sāma; amongst the gods, I am Indra; of the senses, I am the mind; and within all beings, I am their consciousness. (10.22)

— ॐ —

रुद्राणां शङ्करश्चास्मि वित्तेशो यक्षरक्षसाम् ।
rudrāṇāṁ śaṅkaraścāsmi vitteśo yakṣarakṣasām
वसूनां पावकश्चास्मि मेरुः शिखरिणामहम् ॥ १०-२३ ॥
vasūnāṁ pāvakaścāsmi meruḥ śikhariṇāmaham (10-23)

Of the Rudras, I am Shankara; and amongst Yakshas and Rākshasas, I am Kubera; of the eight Vāsus, I am the Fire; and among mountains, I am the Merū. (10.23)

— ॐ —

पुरोधसां च मुख्यं मां विद्धि पार्थ बृहस्पतिम् ।
purodhasāṁ ca mukhyaṁ māṁ viddhi pārtha bṛhaspatim
सेनानीनामहं स्कन्दः सरसामस्मि सागरः ॥१०-२४॥
senānīnāmahaṁ skandaḥ sarasāmasmi sāgaraḥ (10-24)

Know, O Pārtha, that I am Brihaspatī—the foremost of the priests; among the warrior-chiefs, I am Skandha; and amongst the bodes of natural reservoirs, I am the ocean. (10.24)

— ॐ —

महर्षीणां भृगुरहं गिरामस्म्येकमक्षरम् ।
maharṣīṇāṁ bhṛgurahaṁ girāmasmyekamakṣaram
यज्ञानां जपयज्ञोऽस्मि स्थावराणां हिमालयः ॥१०-२५॥
yajñānāṁ japayajño'smi sthāvarāṇāṁ himālayaḥ (10-25)

Of the Maha-Rishīs, I am Bhrigū; among words, I am the sacred syllable Om; of the Yajnas, I am the Japa; and amongst the immovables, I am the Himālaya. (10.25)

— ॐ —

अश्वत्थः सर्ववृक्षाणां देवर्षीणां च नारदः ।
aśvatthaḥ sarvavṛkṣāṇāṁ devarṣīṇāṁ ca nāradaḥ
गन्धर्वाणां चित्ररथः सिद्धानां कपिलो मुनिः ॥१०-२६॥
gandharvāṇāṁ citrarathaḥ siddhānāṁ kapilo muniḥ (10-26)

Amongst all trees, I am the Ashvattha; of the celestial sages, I am Nārada; among the Gandharvas—Chitraratha; and amongst Siddhas, I am muni Kapila. (10.26)

— ॐ —

उच्चैःश्रवसमश्वानां विद्धि माममृतोद्भवम् ।
uccaiḥśravasamaśvānāṁ viddhi māmamṛtodbhavam
ऐरावतं गजेन्द्राणां नराणां च नराधिपम् ॥१०-२७॥
airāvataṁ gajendrāṇāṁ narāṇāṁ ca narādhipam (10-27)

Among equids, know me to be the celestial horse Uchaishrava—begotten along with nectar; and know me to be the lordly Airāvata amongst elephants; and amongst humans, know me to be the King. (10.27)

— ॐ —

आयुधानामहं वज्रं धेनूनामस्मि कामधुक् ।
āyudhānāmahaṁ vajraṁ dhenūnāmasmi kāmadhuk
प्रजनश्चास्मि कन्दर्पः सर्पाणामस्मि वासुकिः ॥ १०-२८॥
prajanaścāsmi kandarpaḥ sarpāṇāmasmi vāsukiḥ (10-28)

Of the weapons, I am thunderbolt; and I am the celestial Kāmadhenu amongst cows; I am the productive passion which leads to procreation; and of the poisonous serpents, I am Vāsuki. (10.28)

— ॐ —

अनन्तश्चास्मि नागानां वरुणो यादसामहम् ।
anantaścāsmi nāgānāṁ varuṇo yādasāmaham
पितॄणामर्यमा चास्मि यमः संयमतामहम् ॥ १०-२९॥
pitṝṇāmaryamā cāsmi yamaḥ saṁyamatāmaham (10-29)

Among the non-poisonous Nāgas, I am the serpent-god Ananta; and I am Varuna, the lord of aquatic beings. Among the manes, I am Āryamān; and amongst regulators, I am Yama: Death. (10.29)

— ॐ —

प्रह्लादश्चास्मि दैत्यानां कालः कलयतामहम् ।
prahlādaścāsmi daityānāṁ kālaḥ kalayatāmaham
मृगाणां च मृगेन्द्रोऽहं वैनतेयश्च पक्षिणाम् ॥ १०-३०॥
mṛgāṇāṁ ca mṛgendro'haṁ vainateyaśca pakṣiṇām (10-30)

Among the Daityas, know Me to be the devotee Prahlāda; of the reckoners know Me to be Time; amongst quadrupeds, I am the Lion; and among birds, Garuda. (10.30)

— ॐ —

पवनः पवतामस्मि रामः शस्त्रभृतामहम् ।
pavanaḥ pavatāmasmi rāmaḥ śastrabhṛtāmaham
झषाणां मकरश्चास्मि स्रोतसामस्मि जाह्नवी ॥ १०-३१॥
jhaṣāṇāṁ makaraścāsmi srotasāmasmi jāhnavī (10-31)

I am the wind among those that move fast; among the wielders of arms, I am Rāma. Among fishes, I am the Makara; and among the rivers, I am Gangā. (10.31)

— ॐ —

सर्गाणामादिरन्तश्च मध्यं चैवाहमर्जुन ।

sargāṇāmādirantaśca madhyaṁ caivāhamarjuna

अध्यात्मविद्या विद्यानां वादः प्रवदतामहम् ॥ १०-३२ ॥

adhyātmavidyā vidyānāṁ vādaḥ pravadatāmaham (10-32)

Of creations, I am the beginning, the end, as also the middle, O Arjuna; and of sciences, I am metaphysics—the knowledge of soul; and among disputants, I am the constructive reasoning. (10.32)

— ॐ —

अक्षराणामकारोऽस्मि द्वन्द्वः सामासिकस्य च ।

akṣarāṇāmakāro'smi dvandvaḥ sāmāsikasya ca

अहमेवाक्षयः कालो धाताहं विश्वतोमुखः ॥ १०-३३ ॥

ahamevākṣayaḥ kālo dhātāhaṁ viśvatomukhaḥ (10-33)

Of letters I am the letter 'A'; and of the compounds, I am the Dvandva. I myself am the eternal Existence; and I am the universal dispenser. (10.33)

— ॐ —

मृत्युः सर्वहरश्चाहमुद्भवश्च भविष्यताम् ।

mṛtyuḥ sarvaharaścāhamudbhavaśca bhaviṣyatām

कीर्तिः श्रीर्वाक्च नारीणां स्मृतिर्मेधा धृतिः क्षमा ॥ १०-३४ ॥

kīrtiḥ śrīrvākca nārīṇāṁ smṛtirmedhā dhṛtiḥ kṣamā (10-34)

Of that which devours everything—I am Death; of that which is ever born or ever will—I am the inception. Of women, I am: Kīrti (glory), Shrī (prosperity), Vāk (speech), Smritī (memory), Medhā (intelligence), Dhritī (fortitude) and Kshamā (forgiveness). (10.34)

— ॐ —

बृहत्साम तथा साम्नां गायत्री छन्दसामहम् ।

bṛhatsāma tathā sāmnāṁ gāyatrī chandasāmaham

मासानां मार्गशीर्षोऽहमृतूनां कुसुमाकरः ॥ १०-३५ ॥

māsānāṁ mārgaśīrṣo'hamṛtūnāṁ kusumākaraḥ (10-35)

Of the Vedic lyrics, I am the Brihat-Sāma; of the Vedic metres, I am the Gāyatrī. Of the months, I am Mārgashirsha; and of the seasons, I am the Spring. (10.35)

— ॐ —

द्यूतं छलयतामस्मि तेजस्तेजस्विनामहम् ।
dyūtaṁ chalayatāmasmi tejastejasvināmaham
जयोऽस्मि व्यवसायोऽस्मि सत्त्वं सत्त्ववतामहम् ॥ १०-३६ ॥
jayo'smi vyavasāyo'smi sattvaṁ sattvavatāmaham (10-36)

Amongst deceptions, I am gamble and risk. I am the prowess of the mighty. I am victory, I am endeavor, and I am the goodness of the good. (10.36)

— ॐ —

वृष्णीनां वासुदेवोऽस्मि पाण्डवानां धनञ्जयः ।
vṛṣṇīnāṁ vāsudevo'smi pāṇḍavānāṁ dhanañjayaḥ
मुनीनामप्यहं व्यासः कवीनामुशना कविः ॥ १०-३७ ॥
munīnāmapyahaṁ vyāsaḥ kavīnāmuśanā kaviḥ (10-37)

Of the Vrishnīs, I am Vāsudeva; of the Pāndavas, I am Dhananjaya; of sages I am Vyāsa; and of the great thinkers, I am the seer Ushanas. (10.37)

— ॐ —

दण्डो दमयतामस्मि नीतिरस्मि जिगीषताम् ।
daṇḍo damayatāmasmi nītirasmi jigīṣatām
मौनं चैवास्मि गुह्यानां ज्ञानं ज्ञानवतामहम् ॥ १०-३८ ॥
maunaṁ caivāsmi guhyānāṁ jñānaṁ jñānavatāmaham (10-38)

Of the rulers, I am their subduing prowess. Of those desirous of victory, I am the Nīti (policy). Of things that are secret, I am silence. And I am the knowledge of the wise. (10.38)

— ॐ —

यच्चापि सर्वभूतानां बीजं तदहमर्जुन ।
yaccāpi sarvabhūtānāṁ bījaṁ tadahamarjuna
न तदस्ति विना यत्स्यान्मया भूतं चराचरम् ॥ १०-३९ ॥
na tadasti vinā yatsyānmayā bhūtaṁ carācaram (10-39)

I am, O Arjuna, the seed of all existence. There is no being—moving or unmoving—which exists devoid of Me. (10.39)

— ॐ —

नान्तोऽस्ति मम दिव्यानां विभूतीनां परन्तप ।

nānto'sti mama divyānāṁ vibhūtīnāṁ parantapa

एष तूद्देशतः प्रोक्तो विभूतेर्विस्तरो मया ॥ १०-४० ॥

eṣa tūddeśataḥ prokto vibhūtervistaro mayā (10-40)

There is no end to the extent of my divine glories, O destroyer of foes; and those that I have just indicated here are stated merely in brief. (10.40)

— ॐ —

यद्यद्विभूतिमत्सत्त्वं श्रीमदूर्जितमेव वा ।

yadyadvibhūtimatsattvaṁ śrīmadūrjitameva vā

तत्तदेवावगच्छ त्वं मम तेजोंऽशसम्भवम् ॥ १०-४१ ॥

tattadevāvagaccha tvaṁ mama tejoṁ'śasambhavam (10-41)

Verily whatever there is that—which is glorious, brilliant, and pre-eminent—know that to be born of a tiny fragment of my splendor. (10.41)

— ॐ —

अथवा बहुनैतेन किं ज्ञातेन तवार्जुन ।

athavā bahunaitena kiṁ jñātena tavārjuna

विष्टभ्याहमिदं कृत्स्नमेकांशेन स्थितो जगत् ॥ १०-४२ ॥

viṣṭabhyāhamidaṁ kṛtsnamekāṁśena sthito jagat (10-42)

But of what avail is knowing all this in detail, O Arjuna? Know the essence: I exist pervading and sustaining the entirety of existence—by a mere fraction of my Being." (10.42)

ॐ तत्सदिति श्रीमद्भगवद्गीतासूपनिषत्सु

oṁ tatsaditi śrīmadbhagavadgītāsūpaniṣatsu

ब्रह्मविद्यायां योगशास्त्रे श्रीकृष्णार्जुनसंवादे

brahmavidyāyāṁ yogaśāstre śrīkṛṣṇārjunasaṁvāde

विभूतियोगो नाम दशमोऽध्यायः ॥

vibhūtiyogo nāma daśamo'dhyāyaḥ

In this Yogic Scripture on the Science of Brahama—the Shrimada-Bhāgvada-Gītā Upanishad—hereby ends the dialogue between Shrī Krishna and Arjuna entitled: Vibhūti Yoga, Canto X

एकादशोऽध्यायः - विश्वरूपदर्शनयोगः

ekādaśo'dhyāyaḥ - viśvarūpadarśanayogaḥ

:: Canto – XI ::

- Vision of the Universal Divine Form -

अर्जुन उवाच --
arjuna uvāca --

मदनुग्रहाय परमं गुह्यमध्यात्मसंज्ञितम् ।
madanugrahāya paramaṁ guhyamadhyātmasaṁjñitam
यत्त्वयोक्तं वचस्तेन मोहोऽयं विगतो मम ॥ ११-१ ॥
yattvayoktaṁ vacastena moho'yaṁ vigato mama (11-1)

Arjuna said: "My delusions stand destroyed by these profound words of spiritual wisdom that you have imparted out of kindness to me. (11.1)

— ॐ —

भवाप्ययौ हि भूतानां श्रुतौ विस्तरशो मया ।
bhavāpyayau hi bhūtānāṁ śrutau vistaraśo mayā
त्वत्तः कमलपत्राक्ष माहात्म्यमपि चाव्ययम् ॥ ११-२ ॥
tvattaḥ kamalapatrākṣa māhātmyamapi cāvyayam (11-2)

I have heard from you in detail of the origin and dissolution of beings, O Lotus-eyed, and I myself recognize your inexhaustible glories as well. (11.2)

— ॐ —

एवमेतद्यथात्थ त्वमात्मानं परमेश्वर ।
evametadyathāttha tvamātmānaṁ parameśvara
द्रष्टुमिच्छामि ते रूपमैश्वरं पुरुषोत्तम ॥ ११-३ ॥
draṣṭumicchāmi te rūpamaiśvaraṁ puruṣottama (11-3)

O Supreme Soul, you are precisely what you declare yourself to be; and yet, O Purushottama, I long to see your divine form. (11.3)

— ॐ —

मन्यसे यदि तच्छक्यं मया द्रष्टुमिति प्रभो ।
manyase yadi tacchakyaṁ mayā draṣṭumiti prabho
योगेश्वर ततो मे त्वं दर्शयात्मानमव्ययम् ॥ ११-४ ॥
yogeśvara tato me tvaṁ darśayātmānamavyayam (11-4)

O Lord, if you deem it apt—that this form of yours can be seen by me—then do please reveal yourself to me as the eternal Divine-Being." (11.4)

श्रीभगवानुवाच --
śrībhagavānuvāca --

पश्य मे पार्थ रूपाणि शतशोऽथ सहस्रशः ।
paśya me pārtha rūpāṇi śataśo'tha sahasraśaḥ
नानाविधानि दिव्यानि नानावर्णाकृतीनि च ॥ ११-५ ॥
nānāvidhāni divyāni nānāvarṇākṛtīni ca (11-5)

Shṙi Bhagwāna said: "Behold, O Arjuna, the manifold, multifarious divine body of mine, of various hues and forms, manifested by the hundreds and thousands. (11.5)

— ॐ —

पश्यादित्यान्वसून्रुद्रानश्विनौ मरुतस्तथा ।
paśyādityānvasūnrudrānaśvinau marutastathā
बहून्यदृष्टपूर्वाणि पश्याश्चर्याणि भारत ॥ ११-६ ॥
bahūnyadṛṣṭapūrvāṇi paśyāścaryāṇi bhārata (11-6)

Here see the twelve sons of Āditī, the eight Vasus, the eleven Rudras, the twin Ashvin-Kumāras, the forty-nine Mārutas; and witness the many, many wonderful manifestations which have not ere been witnessed, O Bhārata. (11.6)

— ॐ —

इहैकस्थं जगत्कृत्स्नं पश्याद्य सचराचरम् ।
ihaikasthaṁ jagatkṛtsnaṁ paśyādya sacarācaram
मम देहे गुडाकेश यच्चान्यद् द्रष्टुमिच्छसि ॥ ११-७ ॥
mama dehe guḍākeśa yaccānyad draṣṭumicchasi (11-7)

Behold this very day the entire universe—with all its immovable and movable entities—united here in this body of mine, O Gudākesha, and see whatever else you wish to see. (11.7)

— ॐ —

न तु मां शक्यसे द्रष्टुमनेनैव स्वचक्षुषा ।
na tu māṁ śakyase draṣṭumanenaiva svacakṣuṣā
दिव्यं ददामि ते चक्षुः पश्य मे योगमैश्वरम् ॥ ११-८ ॥
divyaṁ dadāmi te cakṣuḥ paśya me yogamaiśvaram (11-8)

But you will not be able to look at Me with your earthly eyes; therefore, I vouchsafe unto you these ethereal eyes—with which behold now My divine miracle." (11.8)

सञ्जय उवाच --
sañjaya uvāca --

एवमुक्त्वा ततो राजन्महायोगेश्वरो हरिः ।
evamuktvā tato rājanmahāyogeśvaro hariḥ
दर्शयामास पार्थाय परमं रूपमैश्वरम् ॥ ११-९ ॥
darśayāmāsa pārthāya paramaṁ rūpamaiśvaram (11-9)

अनेकवक्त्रनयनमनेकाद्भुतदर्शनम् ।
anekavaktranayanamanekādbhutadarśanam
अनेकदिव्याभरणं दिव्यानेकोद्यतायुधम् ॥ ११-१० ॥
anekadivyābharaṇaṁ divyānekodyatāyudham (11-10)

दिव्यमाल्याम्बरधरं दिव्यगन्धानुलेपनम् ।
divyamālyāmbaradharaṁ divyagandhānulepanam
सर्वाश्चर्यमयं देवमनन्तं विश्वतोमुखम् ॥ ११-११ ॥
sarvāścaryamayaṁ devamanantaṁ viśvatomukham (11-11)

Sanjay said: "O king! Having spoken thusly, Hari, the great Lord of Yoga, forthwith revealed to Arjuna his glorious celestial form—having faces on every side, with innumerous mouths and eyes, of many wonderful vistas, bedecked with myriad divine ornaments, wielding legions of celestial weapons, embellished with supernal garlands and vestments, anointed all over with heavenly fragrances—a figure infinite and resplendent, replete with wonders. (11.9-11.11)

— ॐ —

दिवि सूर्यसहस्रस्य भवेद्युगपदुत्थिता ।
divi sūryasahasrasya bhavedyugapadutthitā
यदि भाः सदृशी सा स्याद्भासस्तस्य महात्मनः ॥ ११-१२ ॥
yadi bhāḥ sadṛśī sā syādbhāsastasya mahātmanaḥ (11-12)

If the effulgence of a thousand suns were to burst forth all at once in the sky, that would pale in comparison to the splendor of that Supreme One. (11.12)

— ॐ —

तत्रैकस्थं जगत्कृत्स्नं प्रविभक्तमनेकधा ।
tatraikasthaṁ jagatkṛtsnaṁ pravibhaktamanekadhā
अपश्यद्देवदेवस्य शरीरे पाण्डवस्तदा ॥ ११-१३ ॥
apaśyaddevadevasya śarīre pāṇḍavastadā (11-13)

United together at one place in the person of that God of gods, Arjuna beheld the entire universe with its manifold divisions all connected together as one. (11.13)

— ॐ —

ततः स विस्मयाविष्टो हृष्टरोमा धनञ्जयः ।
tataḥ sa vismayāviṣṭo hṛṣṭaromā dhanañjayaḥ
प्रणम्य शिरसा देवं कृताञ्जलिरभाषत ॥ ११-१४ ॥
praṇamya śirasā devaṁ kṛtāñjalirabhāṣata (11-14)

Then Dhananjeya—full of wonder and with his hair all abristle—reverently bowed his head to the divine Lord-God, and with folded palms he spoke the following words full of awe: (11.14)

अर्जुन उवाच --
arjuna uvāca --

पश्यामि देवांस्तव देव देहे सर्वांस्तथा भूतविशेषसङ्घान् ।
paśyāmi devāṁstava deva dehe sarvāṁstathā bhūtaviśeṣasaṅghān
ब्रह्माणमीशं कमलासनस्थमृषींश्च सर्वानुरगांश्च दिव्यान् ॥ ११-१५ ॥
brahmāṇamīśaṁ kamalāsanastha-
mṛṣīṁśca sarvānuragāṁśca divyān (11-15)

Arjuna said: "Within Thy body, O Lord-God, I behold all the many gods and hordes of various beings; and here I see Brahammā enthroned upon his lotus-seat; and I also see all the heavenly Nāgas and Rishīs. (11.15)

— ॐ —

अनेकबाहूदरवक्त्रनेत्रं पश्यामि त्वां सर्वतोऽनन्तरूपम् ।
anekabāhūdaravaktranetraṁ paśyāmi tvāṁ sarvato'nantarūpam
नान्तं न मध्यं न पुनस्तवादिं पश्यामि विश्वेश्वर विश्वरूप ॥ ११-१६ ॥
nāntaṁ na madhyaṁ na punastavādiṁ
paśyāmi viśveśvara viśvarūpa (11-16)

O Lord of the universe, I behold Thee—endowed with innumerous arms, torsos, mouths, eyes and possessing infinite forms extending on all sides—but O Thou Being of universal form, I see not the end, nor the middle, nor the origin of Thine. (11.16)

— ॐ —

किरीटिनं गदिनं चक्रिणं च तेजोराशिं सर्वतो दीप्तिमन्तम् ।
kirīṭinaṁ gadinaṁ cakriṇaṁ ca tejorāśiṁ sarvato dīptimantam
पश्यामि त्वां दुर्निरीक्ष्यं समन्ताद् दीप्तानलार्कद्युतिमप्रमेयम् ॥ ११-१७॥
paśyāmi tvāṁ durnirīkṣyaṁ samantād dīptānalārkadyutimaprameyam (11-17)

I behold Thee endowed all around with diadems and maces and discs, a mass of light glowing on every side, blinding like the blazing flames of sun—all of immeasurable extent. (11.17)

— ॐ —

त्वमक्षरं परमं वेदितव्यं त्वमस्य विश्वस्य परं निधानम् ।
tvamakṣaraṁ paramaṁ veditavyaṁ
tvamasya viśvasya paraṁ nidhānam
त्वमव्ययः शाश्वतधर्मगोप्ता सनातनस्त्वं पुरुषो मतो मे ॥ ११-१८॥
tvamavyayaḥ śāśvatadharmagoptā
sanātanastvaṁ puruṣo mato me (11-18)

Thou art the imperishable, the supreme, the only being worthy of being known; Thou art the final sanctuary of the universe; Thou art the protector of the eternal Dharma; I know Thee to be the eternal primeval Being. (11.18)

— ॐ —

अनादिमध्यान्तमनन्तवीर्यमनन्तबाहुं शशिसूर्यनेत्रम् ।
anādimadhyāntamanantavīrya-
manantabāhuṁ śaśisūryanetram
पश्यामि त्वां दीप्तहुताशवक्त्रं स्वतेजसा विश्वमिदं तपन्तम् ॥ ११-१९॥
paśyāmi tvāṁ dīptahutāśavaktraṁ
svatejasā viśvamidaṁ tapantam (11-19)

I see Thou—without a beginning, middle or end, endowed with infinite arms, having the moon and sun for Thy eyes, with blazing fires as Thy mouth—scorching the whole universe with Thy radiance. (11.19)

— ॐ —

द्यावापृथिव्योरिदमन्तरं हि व्याप्तं त्वयैकेन दिशश्च सर्वाः ।
dyāvāpṛthivyoridamantaraṁ hi vyāptaṁ tvayaikena diśaśca sarvāḥ
दृष्ट्वाद्भुतं रूपमुग्रं तवेदं लोकत्रयं प्रव्यथितं महात्मन् ॥ ११-२० ॥
dṛṣṭvādbhutaṁ rūpamugraṁ tavedaṁ
lokatrayaṁ pravyathitaṁ mahātman (11-20)

The space betwixt the heaven and earth, and all the quarters—they are entirely filled just with Thee. Seeing this wonderful terrifying form of Thine, all the three worlds are greatly afflicted, O Supreme Soul. (11.20)

— ॐ —

अमी हि त्वां सुरसङ्घा विशन्ति केचिद्भीताः प्राञ्जलयो गृणन्ति ।
amī hi tvāṁ surasaṅghā viśanti kecidbhītāḥ prāñjalayo gṛṇanti
स्वस्तीत्युक्त्वा महर्षिसिद्धसङ्घाः
svastītyuktvā maharṣisiddhasaṅghāḥ
स्तुवन्ति त्वां स्तुतिभिः पुष्कलाभिः ॥ ११-२१ ॥
stuvanti tvāṁ stutibhiḥ puṣkalābhiḥ (11-21)

Yonder I see hosts of gods ascending towards Thee; and out of fright, some are reciting Thy names and glories with folded palms; and multitudes of Mahā-Rishīs and Siddhas are chanting 'Peace-Peace' and praising Thee with excellent hymns. (11.21)

— ॐ —

रुद्रादित्या वसवो ये च साध्या विश्वेऽश्विनौ मरुतश्चोष्मपाश्च ।
rudrādityā vasavo ye ca sādhyā
viśve'śvinau marutaścoṣmapāśca
गन्धर्वयक्षासुरसिद्धसङ्घा वीक्षन्ते त्वां विस्मिताश्चैव सर्वे ॥ ११-२२ ॥
gandharvayakṣāsurasiddhasaṅghā
vīkṣante tvāṁ vismitāścaiva sarve (11-22)

The Rudras and Ādityas and Vasus, and the Sādhyas and Vishvedevas, and the Ashvin Kumārs, the Mārutas, and the manes, and the Gandharvas, Yakshas, Asuras, and the many, many bands of Siddhas—all of them gaze upon Thee, completely aghast. (11.22)

— ॐ —

रूपं महत्ते बहुवक्त्रनेत्रं महाबाहो बहुबाहूरुपादम् ।
rūpaṁ mahatte bahuvaktranetraṁ mahābāho bahubāhūrupādam
बहूदरं बहुदंष्ट्राकरालं दृष्ट्वा लोकाः प्रव्यथितास्तथाहम् ॥ ११-२३ ॥
bahūdaraṁ bahudaṁṣṭrākarālaṁ dṛṣṭvā lokāḥ pravyathitāstathāham (11-23)

O mighty-armed Lord, seeing this colossal form of Thine—of innumerous mouths and eyes, many arms, thighs, and feet, with many bellies and terrible with fearful tusks—the entire world is awe-struck; and so am I. (11.23)

— ॐ —

नभःस्पृशं दीप्तमनेकवर्णं व्यात्ताननं दीप्तविशालनेत्रम् ।
nabhaḥspṛśaṁ dīptamanekavarṇaṁ
vyāttānanaṁ dīptaviśālanetram
दृष्ट्वा हि त्वां प्रव्यथितान्तरात्मा
dṛṣṭvā hi tvāṁ pravyathitāntarātmā
धृतिं न विन्दामि शमं च विष्णो ॥ ११-२४ ॥
dhṛtiṁ na vindāmi śamaṁ ca viṣṇo (11-24)

O Lord, watching this ferocious form touching the heavens—blazing radiant and embued with infinite hues, mouths open wide and of large flaming eyes—I am frightened to my very core, and I find no peace or fortitude. (11.24)

— ॐ —

दंष्ट्राकरालानि च ते मुखानि दृष्ट्वैव कालानलसन्निभानि ।
daṁṣṭrākarālāni ca te mukhāni dṛṣṭvaiva kālānalasannibhāni
दिशो न जाने न लभे च शर्म प्रसीद देवेश जगन्निवास ॥ ११-२५ ॥
diśo na jāne na labhe ca śarma prasīda deveśa jagannivāsa (11-25)

As I view this dreadful form—fearsome with gaping mouths and grisly teeth and fulgent like the fires of end-times—I am utterly bewildered, and the cardinal points are lost to me, and I find no repose; O celestial being, O abode of the universe, please have mercy! (11.25)

— ॐ —

अमी च त्वां धृतराष्ट्रस्य पुत्राः सर्वे सहैवावनिपालसङ्घैः ।
amī ca tvāṁ dhṛtarāṣṭrasya putrāḥ sarve sahaivāvanipālasaṅghaiḥ
भीष्मो द्रोणः सूतपुत्रस्तथासौ सहास्मदीयैरपि योधमुख्यैः ॥ ११-२६ ॥
bhīṣmo droṇaḥ sūtaputrastathāsau
sahāsmadīyairapi yodhamukhyaiḥ (11-26)

वक्त्राणि ते त्वरमाणा विशन्ति दंष्ट्राकरालानि भयानकानि ।
vaktrāṇi te tvaramāṇā viśanti daṁṣṭrākarālāni bhayānakāni
केचिद्विलग्ना दशनान्तरेषु सन्दृश्यन्ते चूर्णितैरुत्तमाङ्गैः ॥ ११-२७ ॥
kecidvilagnā daśanāntareṣu sandṛśyante cūrṇitairuttamāṅgaiḥ (11-27)

And I see these sons of Dhritarāshtra along with hosts of kings, rushing rashly towards Thee; and also Bhīshma, and Drona and Karna—and with the principal warriors on our side as well—all are being drawn headlong into Thy gruesome jaws, terrible with grisly teeth; and many are the people seen stuck between the teeth—with their heads crushed. (11.26-11.27)

— ॐ —

यथा नदीनां बहवोऽम्बुवेगाः समुद्रमेवाभिमुखा द्रवन्ति ।
yathā nadīnāṁ bahavo'mbuvegāḥ samudramevābhimukhā dravanti
तथा तवामी नरलोकवीरा विशन्ति वक्त्राण्यभिविज्वलन्ति ॥ ११-२८ ॥
tathā tavāmī naralokavīrā viśanti vaktrāṇyabhivijvalanti (11-28)

Just as a myriad streams of rivers rush headlong towards the sea, even so these heroes of the mortal world are hurrying hastily into Thy jaws—which are flaming all around. (11.28)

— ॐ —

यथा प्रदीप्तं ज्वलनं पतङ्गा विशन्ति नाशाय समृद्धवेगाः ।
yathā pradīptaṁ jvalanaṁ pataṅgā viśanti nāśāya samṛddhavegāḥ
तथैव नाशाय विशन्ति लोकास् तवापि वक्त्राणि समृद्धवेगाः ॥ ११-२९ ॥
tathaiva nāśāya viśanti lokāstavāpi vaktrāṇi samṛddhavegāḥ (11-29)

As swarms of moths hurl with great speed into the blazing fire to die—even so, all these people are pouring like torrents into Thy mouths to meet their fiery end. (11.29)

— ॐ —

लेलिह्यसे ग्रसमानः समन्ताल्लोकान्समग्रान्वदनैर्ज्वलद्भिः ।
lelihyase grasamānaḥ samantāllokānsamagrānvadanairjvaladbhiḥ
तेजोभिरापूर्य जगत्समग्रं भासस्तवोग्राः प्रतपन्ति विष्णो ॥ ११-३० ॥
tejobhirāpūrya jagatsamagraṁ bhāsastavogrāḥ pratapanti viṣṇo (11-30)

Severing, lopping, licking at them from every which direction, Thou art devouring these mortals with Thy gargantuan jaws that are aflame with fire. Filling the universe with its blazing radiance, Thy fiery rays are scorching the earth. (11.30)

— ॐ —

आख्याहि मे को भवानुग्ररूपो नमोऽस्तु ते देववर प्रसीद ।
ākhyāhi me ko bhavānugrarūpo namo'stu te devavara prasīda
विज्ञातुमिच्छामि भवन्तमाद्यं न हि प्रजानामि तव प्रवृत्तिम् ॥ ११-३१ ॥
vijñātumicchāmi bhavantamādyaṁ na hi prajānāmi tava pravṛttim (11-31)

Tell me who art Thou of such a fearsome form, O Supreme-God? Salutations to Thee, O please be pleased! I desire to know Thee, O Primeval-Being—because I am not able to know Thee, or to comprehend Thine intent." (11.31)

श्रीभगवानुवाच --
śrībhagavānuvāca --

कालोऽस्मि लोकक्षयकृत्प्रवृद्धो लोकान्समाहर्तुमिह प्रवृत्तः ।
kālo'smi lokakṣayakṛtpravṛddho lokānsamāhartumiha pravṛttaḥ
ऋतेऽपि त्वां न भविष्यन्ति सर्वे येऽवस्थिताः प्रत्यनीकेषु योधाः ॥११-३२॥
ṛte'pi tvāṁ na bhaviṣyanti sarve ye'vasthitāḥ pratyanīkeṣu yodhāḥ (11-32)

Shri Bhagwāna said: "I am the terrible Kāla—Eternal-Time; I am Death—the destroyer of the worlds, and I am out to exterminate all these beings. Even without you, all these warriors—arrayed on both sides of the battle field—shall die. (11.32)

— ॐ —

तस्मात्त्वमुत्तिष्ठ यशो लभस्व जित्वा शत्रून् भुङ्क्ष्व राज्यं समृद्धम् ।
tasmāttvamuttiṣṭha yaśo labhasva jitvā śatrūn bhuṅkṣva rājyaṁ samṛddham
मयैवैते निहताः पूर्वमेव निमित्तमात्रं भव सव्यसाचिन् ॥११-३३॥
mayaivaite nihatāḥ pūrvameva nimittamātraṁ bhava savyasācin (11-33)

Therefore do arise and win glory for yourself and conquering your enemies enjoy the sovereignty of an affluent kingdom on earth. These warriors are already slain by Me, O Arjuna—you shall merely be the instrument of my will. (11.33)

— ॐ —

द्रोणं च भीष्मं च जयद्रथं च कर्णं तथान्यानपि योधवीरान् ।
droṇaṁ ca bhīṣmaṁ ca jayadrathaṁ ca karṇaṁ tathānyānapi yodhavīrān
मया हतांस्त्वं जहि मा व्यथिष्ठा युध्यस्व जेतासि रणे सपत्नान् ॥११-३४॥
mayā hatāṁstvaṁ jahi mā vyathiṣṭhā yudhyasva jetāsi raṇe sapatnān (11-34)

Fight and kill Drona and Bhīshma and Jayadratha and Karna, and all these other mighty warriors—all slayed by Me already. Fear not; fight on, and you shall surely conquer your enemies in this battle." (11.34)

सञ्जय उवाच --
sañjaya uvāca --

एतच्छ्रुत्वा वचनं केशवस्य कृताञ्जलिर्वेपमानः किरीटी ।
etacchrutvā vacanaṁ keśavasya kṛtāñjalirvepamānaḥ kirīṭī
नमस्कृत्वा भूय एवाह कृष्णं सगद्गदं भीतभीतः प्रणम्य ॥११-३५॥
namaskṛtvā bhūya evāha kṛṣṇaṁ sagadgadaṁ bhītabhītaḥ praṇamya (11-35)

Sanjay said: Hearing these words of Keshava, the trembling Arjuna bowed to the Lord with folded hands; and then bowing again and again he spoke with faltering accents the following words, full of fear and awe. (11.35)

अर्जुन उवाच --
arjuna uvāca --

स्थाने हृषीकेश तव प्रकीर्त्या जगत्प्रहृष्यत्यनुरज्यते च ।
sthāne hṛṣīkeśa tava prakīrtyā jagatprahṛṣyatyanurajyate ca
रक्षांसि भीतानि दिशो द्रवन्ति सर्वे नमस्यन्ति च सिद्धसङ्घाः ॥११-३६॥
rakṣāṁsi bhītāni diśo dravanti sarve namasyanti ca siddhasaṅghāḥ (11-36)

Arjuna said: "It is befitting, O Lord, that the world chants your glories and names, and finding joy thereby, is drawn towards you; and that these hosts of perfected beings repeatedly prostrate before you; and that these frightened monsters scuttle away every which way. (11.36)

— ॐ —

कस्माच्च ते न नमेरन्महात्मन् गरीयसे ब्रह्मणोऽप्यादिकर्त्रे ।
kasmācca te na nameranmahātman garīyase brahmaṇo'pyādikartre
अनन्त देवेश जगन्निवास त्वमक्षरं सदसत्तत्परं यत् ॥११-३७॥
ananta deveśa jagannivāsa tvamakṣaraṁ sadasattatparaṁ yat (11-37)

And rightly so, O Supreme-Soul: they offer venerations to you—the primordial cause, the progenitor of Brahammā himself, the highest of the highs! O Infinite-Being, O Lord of the celestials, O abode of the worlds: you are the indestructible principle, the manifest, the unmanifest, and also that which is beyond both. (11.37)

— ॐ —

त्वमादिदेवः पुरुषः पुराणस्त्वमस्य विश्वस्य परं निधानम् ।
tvamādidevaḥ puruṣaḥ purāṇastvamasya viśvasya paraṁ nidhānam
वेत्तासि वेद्यं च परं च धाम त्वया ततं विश्वमनन्तरूप ॥११-३८॥
vettāsi vedyaṁ ca paraṁ ca dhāma tvayā tataṁ viśvamanantarūpa (11-38)

You are the primal being, the ancient most, the supreme repository of the universe; you are the knower, the knowable, and the highest abode. O you of infinite forms, by you alone is the universe fully pervaded. (11.38)

— ॐ —

वायुर्यमोऽग्निर्वरुणः शशाङ्कः प्रजापतिस्त्वं प्रपितामहश्च ।
vāyuryamo'gnirvaruṇaḥ śaśāṅkaḥ prajāpatistvaṁ prapitāmahaśca
नमो नमस्तेऽस्तु सहस्रकृत्वः पुनश्च भूयोऽपि नमो नमस्ते ॥ ११-३९ ॥
namo namaste'stu sahasrakṛtvaḥ punaśca bhūyo'pi namo namaste (11-39)

You are Vāyu—the Wind; Yama—the Death; Agnī—the Fire; Varuna—the Water; Shashānk—the Moon; Prajāpatī—the Creator and the great grandsire. Salutations, a thousand-fold salutations to you, and my repeated salutations to you once again. (11.39)

— ॐ —

नमः पुरस्तादथ पृष्ठतस्ते नमोऽस्तु ते सर्वत एव सर्व ।
namaḥ purastādatha pṛṣṭhataste namo'stu te sarvata eva sarva
अनन्तवीर्यामितविक्रमस्त्वं सर्वं समाप्नोषि ततोऽसि सर्वः ॥ ११-४० ॥
anantavīryāmitavikramastvaṁ sarvaṁ samāpnoṣi tato'si sarvaḥ (11-40)

All salutations to you, from the front and behind, O soul of souls, and my obeisance to you from all sides. O Lord of infinite prowess and immeasurable might, you pervade everywhere; you truly are everything, you indeed are all, my Lord. (11.40)

— ॐ —

सखेति मत्वा प्रसभं यदुक्तं हे कृष्ण हे यादव हे सखेति ।
sakheti matvā prasabhaṁ yaduktaṁ he kṛṣṇa he yādava he sakheti
अजानता महिमानं तवेदं मया प्रमादात्प्रणयेन वापि ॥ ११-४१ ॥
ajānatā mahimānaṁ tavedaṁ mayā pramādātpraṇayena vāpi (11-41)
यच्चावहासार्थमसत्कृतोऽसि विहारशय्यासनभोजनेषु ।
yaccāvahāsārthamasatkṛto'si vihāraśayyāsanabhojaneṣu
एकोऽथवाप्यच्युत तत्समक्षं तत्क्षामये त्वामहमप्रमेयम् ॥ ११-४२ ॥
eko'thavāpyacyuta tatsamakṣaṁ tatkṣāmaye tvāmahamaprameyam (11-42)

Not knowing of this grand divine form of yours, and considering you just to be a friend, I may have in the past unwittingly addressed you—unthinkingly and out of familiarity—calling out depreciative words like 'Hey Krishna! Hey Yādava! Hey fellow!'; and O infallible Achyuta, the ways in which you may have been slighted by me—in jest, while at play, reposing, sitting, or at meals, either alone or in the presence of others—for all of that, O Immeasurable-One, I seek forgiveness from the bottom of my heart. (11.41-11.42)

— ॐ —

पितासि लोकस्य चराचरस्य त्वमस्य पूज्यश्च गुरुर्गरीयान् ।
pitāsi lokasya carācarasya tvamasya pūjyaśca gururgarīyān
न त्वत्समोऽस्त्यभ्यधिकः कुतोऽन्यो लोकत्रयेऽप्यप्रतिमप्रभाव ॥ ११-४३ ॥
na tvatsamo'styabhyadhikaḥ kuto'nyo lokatraye'pyapratimaprabhāva (11-43)

Verily you are the sire of this world of the moving and unmoving; adorable and the great teacher—greater than any superior. In all the three worlds there is none equal to you, let alone greater, O Lord of incomparable might. (11.43)

— ॐ —

तस्मात्प्रणम्य प्रणिधाय कायं प्रसादये त्वामहमीशमीड्यम् ।
tasmātpraṇamya praṇidhāya kāyaṁ prasādaye tvāmahamīśamīḍyam
पितेव पुत्रस्य सखेव सख्युः प्रियः प्रियायार्हसि देव सोढुम् ॥ ११-४४ ॥
piteva putrasya sakheva sakhyuḥ priyaḥ priyāyārhasi deva soḍhum (11-44)

Therefore O Lord, prostrating myself at your feet and bowing low I seek to propitiate you—the ruler of all and worthy of all praises. And even as a father forgives his son, and a friend his friend, and a lover his beloved—even so should you grant me pardon, O Lord. (11.44)

— ॐ —

अदृष्टपूर्वं हृषितोऽस्मि दृष्ट्वा भयेन च प्रव्यथितं मनो मे ।
adṛṣṭapūrvaṁ hṛṣito'smi dṛṣṭvā bhayena ca pravyathitaṁ mano me
तदेव मे दर्शय देव रूपं प्रसीद देवेश जगन्निवास ॥ ११-४५ ॥
tadeva me darśaya deva rūpaṁ prasīda deveśa jagannivāsa (11-45)

Having seen this fascinating form—which has never ever been seen before—I feel transported with awe and joy. But at the same time my mind is agitated with fear, O Lord. Pray reveal to me your divine form—the form of Vishnu with four-arms—O Lord of celestials. O abode of the universe, please do be gracious. (11.45)

— ॐ —

किरीटिनं गदिनं चक्रहस्तं इच्छामि त्वां द्रष्टुमहं तथैव ।
kirīṭinaṁ gadinaṁ cakrahastaṁ icchāmi tvāṁ draṣṭumahaṁ tathaiva
तेनैव रूपेण चतुर्भुजेन सहस्रबाहो भव विश्वमूर्ते ॥ ११-४६ ॥
tenaiva rūpeṇa caturbhujena sahasrabāho bhava viśvamūrte (11-46)

I desire to see Thee in Thy erstwhile form—adorned with a diadem on the head and wielding a mace and discus in Thy hands. Appear to me in Thy four-armed form, O Lord of a thousand arms, O Thou universal being." (11.46)

श्रीभगवानुवाच --
śrībhagavānuvāca --
मया प्रसन्नेन तवार्जुनेदं रूपं परं दर्शितमात्मयोगात् ।
mayā prasannena tavārjunedaṁ rūpaṁ paraṁ darśitamātmayogāt
तेजोमयं विश्वमनन्तमाद्यं यन्मे त्वदन्येन न दृष्टपूर्वम् ॥ ११-४७ ॥
tejomayaṁ viśvamanantamādyaṁ yanme tvadanyena na dṛṣṭapūrvam (11-47)

Shri Bhagwāna said: "O Arjuna! Pleased with you I have shown you, through my power of Yoga, this supreme, resplendent, primeval and infinite cosmic form—which has hitherto never been seen before by anyone other than you. (11.47)

— ॐ —

न वेदयज्ञाध्ययनैर्न दानैर्न च क्रियाभिर्न तपोभिरुग्रैः ।
na vedayajñādhyayanairna dānairna ca kriyābhirna tapobhirugraiḥ
एवंरूपः शक्य अहं नृलोके द्रष्टुं त्वदन्येन कुरुप्रवीर ॥ ११-४८ ॥
evaṁrūpaḥ śakya ahaṁ nṛloke draṣṭuṁ tvadanyena kurupravīra (11-48)

In this world of mortals, I can not be seen in this universal form—neither by the study of Vedas, nor through rituals, charities, or austere penances—O great amongst the hero of Kurūs, it was just only for you. (11.48)

— ॐ —

मा ते व्यथा मा च विमूढभावो दृष्ट्वा रूपं घोरमीदृङ्ममेदम् ।
mā te vyathā mā ca vimūḍhabhāvo dṛṣṭvā rūpaṁ ghoramīdṛṅmamedam
व्यपेतभीः प्रीतमनाः पुनस्त्वं तदेव मे रूपमिदं प्रपश्य ॥ ११-४९ ॥
vyapetabhīḥ prītamanāḥ punastvaṁ tadeva me rūpamidaṁ prapaśya (11-49)

Be no more agitated and deluded perceiving my fearsome form, O Arjuna; behold once again the erstwhile four-armed form of mine—bearing the conch, discus, mace and lotus—and be fearless and of cheerful mind." (11.49)

सञ्जय उवाच --
sañjaya uvāca --

इत्यर्जुनं वासुदेवस्तथोक्त्वा स्वकं रूपं दर्शयामास भूयः ।
ityarjunaṁ vāsudevastathoktvā svakaṁ rūpaṁ darśayāmāsa bhūyaḥ
आश्वासयामास च भीतमेनं भूत्वा पुनः सौम्यवपुर्महात्मा ॥ ११-५० ॥
āśvāsayāmāsa ca bhītamenaṁ bhūtvā punaḥ saumyavapurmahātmā (11-50)

Sanjay said: Speaking thusly to Arjuna, Bhagwāna Vāsudeva showed once again his former form. And in this way, assuming his benign form, the great soul Krishna brought solace to the frightened Arjuna. (11.50)

अर्जुन उवाच --
arjuna uvāca --

दृष्ट्वेदं मानुषं रूपं तव सौम्यं जनार्दन ।
dṛṣṭvedaṁ mānuṣaṁ rūpaṁ tava saumyaṁ janārdana
इदानीमस्मि संवृत्तः सचेताः प्रकृतिं गतः ॥ ११-५१ ॥
idānīmasmi saṁvṛttaḥ sacetāḥ prakṛtiṁ gataḥ (11-51)

Arjuna said: "O Janārdana, seeing this benignant human form of yours, I have once again regained my poise and am now my own self." (11.51)

श्रीभगवानुवाच --
śrībhagavānuvāca --

सुदुर्दर्शमिदं रूपं दृष्टवानसि यन्मम ।
sudurdarśamidaṁ rūpaṁ dṛṣṭavānasi yanmama
देवा अप्यस्य रूपस्य नित्यं दर्शनकाङ्क्षिणः ॥ ११-५२ ॥
devā apyasya rūpasya nityaṁ darśanakāṅkṣiṇaḥ (11-52)

Shri Bhagwāna said: "Exceedingly difficult it is to behold even this form of mine which you now see, O Arjuna; even gods are ever eager to see this image of mine. (11.52)

— ॐ —

नाहं वेदैर्न तपसा न दानेन न चेज्यया ।
nāhaṁ vedairna tapasā na dānena na cejyayā
शक्य एवंविधो द्रष्टुं दृष्टवानसि मां यथा ॥ ११-५३ ॥
śakya evaṁvidho draṣṭuṁ dṛṣṭavānasi māṁ yathā (11-53)

Neither by the study of Vedas, nor by penances, nor again by charity or rituals, can I be seen in this form which you now behold. (11.53)

— ॐ —

भक्त्या त्वनन्यया शक्य अहमेवंविधोऽर्जुन ।
bhaktyā tvananyayā śakya ahamevaṁvidho'rjuna
ज्ञातुं द्रष्टुं च तत्त्वेन प्रवेष्टुं च परन्तप ॥ ११-५४ ॥
jñātuṁ draṣṭuṁ ca tattvena praveṣṭuṁ ca parantapa (11-54)

But through a single-minded devotion, O Arjuna, I can be seen in this form. Aye, by the practice of undivided devotion, one can realize Me, and know My essence, and enter My way. (11.54)

— ॐ —

मत्कर्मकृन्मत्परमो मद्भक्तः सङ्गवर्जितः ।
matkarmakṛnmatparamo madbhaktaḥ saṅgavarjitaḥ
निर्वैरः सर्वभूतेषु यः स मामेति पाण्डव ॥ ११-५५ ॥
nirvairaḥ sarvabhūteṣu yaḥ sa māmeti pāṇḍava (11-55)

He who performs all his duties for My sake, who has only Me as his supreme goal, who is devoted to Me, who has neither attachments nor hostilities towards beings—he verily attains to Me, O Pāndava." (11.55)

ॐ तत्सदिति श्रीमद्भगवद्गीतासूपनिषत्सु
om tatsaditi śrīmadbhagavadgītāsūpaniṣatsu
ब्रह्मविद्यायां योगशास्त्रे श्रीकृष्णार्जुनसंवादे
brahmavidyāyāṁ yogaśāstre śrīkṛṣṇārjunasaṁvāde
विश्वरूपदर्शनयोगो नामैकादशोऽध्यायः ॥
viśvarūpadarśanayogo nāmaikādaśo'dhyāyaḥ

In this Yogic Scripture on the Science of Brahama—the Shrimada-Bhāgvada-Gītā Upanishad—
hereby ends the dialogue between Shrī Krishna and Arjuna entitled:
Viśva-Rūpa-Darśana Yoga, Canto XI

द्वादशोऽध्यायः - भक्तियोगः

dvādaśo'dhyāyaḥ - bhaktiyogaḥ

:: Canto – XII ::

- The Path of Bhakti -

अर्जुन उवाच --
arjuna uvāca --

एवं सततयुक्ता ये भक्तास्त्वां पर्युपासते ।
evaṁ satatayuktā ye bhaktāstvāṁ paryupāsate
ये चाप्यक्षरमव्यक्तं तेषां के योगवित्तमाः ॥१२-१॥
ye cāpyakṣaramavyaktaṁ teṣāṁ ke yogavittamāḥ (12-1)

Arjuna said: "Of devotees who worship you in the manner you just spoke of—with having a manifest form, and those who worship you as the Imperishable-Absolute of unmanifest form—of those two, who is to be considered better versed in Yoga?" (12.1)

श्रीभगवानुवाच --
śrībhagavānuvāca --

मय्यावेश्य मनो ये मां नित्ययुक्ता उपासते ।
mayyāveśya mano ye māṁ nityayuktā upāsate
श्रद्धया परयोपेताः ते मे युक्ततमा मताः ॥१२-२॥
śraddhayā parayopetāḥ te me yuktatamā matāḥ (12-2)

Shri Bhagwāna said: "Ever devoted and endowed with supreme faith, those who fix their minds upon Me as the Lord-God of manifest form, and worship thusly—them I deem to be higher. (12.2)

— ॐ —

ये त्वक्षरमनिर्देश्यमव्यक्तं पर्युपासते ।
ye tvakṣaramanirdeśyamavyaktaṁ paryupāsate
सर्वत्रगमचिन्त्यञ्च कूटस्थमचलन्ध्रुवम् ॥१२-३॥
sarvatragamacintyañca kūṭasthamacalandhruvam (12-3)

सन्नियम्येन्द्रियग्रामं सर्वत्र समबुद्धयः ।
sanniyamyendriyagrāmaṁ sarvatra samabuddhayaḥ
ते प्राप्नुवन्ति मामेव सर्वभूतहिते रताः ॥१२-४॥
te prāpnuvanti māmeva sarvabhūtahite ratāḥ (12-4)

Those who worship the imperishable, indescribable, unmanifest, omnipresent, eternal, immovable, inconceivable, unalterable form of Mine (Brahama)—by controlling well their senses, ever remaining even-minded, devoted to Me as the Ātmā presiding everywhere, and given to all-round welfare of beings everywhere—such too attain just to Me. (12.3-12.4)

— ॐ —

क्लेशोऽधिकतरस्तेषामव्यक्तासक्तचेतसाम् ।
kleśo'dhikatarasteṣāmavyaktāsaktacetasām
अव्यक्ता हि गतिर्दुःखं देहवद्भिरवाप्यते ॥ १२-५ ॥
avyaktā hi gatirduḥkhaṁ dehavadbhiravāpyate (12-5)

However the effort is much harder for those who perform their worship attached to Brahama. The devotion to the Unmanifest is attained only with great difficulty by a soul—having become manifest in bodily form. (12.5)

— ॐ —

ये तु सर्वाणि कर्माणि मयि संन्यस्य मत्पराः ।
ye tu sarvāṇi karmāṇi mayi saṁnyasya matparāḥ
अनन्येनैव योगेन मां ध्यायन्त उपासते ॥ १२-६ ॥
ananyenaiva yogena māṁ dhyāyanta upāsate (12-6)
तेषामहं समुद्धर्ता मृत्युसंसारसागरात् ।
teṣāmahaṁ samuddhartā mṛtyusaṁsārasāgarāt
भवामि नचिरात्पार्थ मय्यावेशितचेतसाम् ॥ १२-७ ॥
bhavāmi nacirātpārtha mayyāveśitacetasām (12-7)

By contrast those who are attached to my manifest form; who, surrendering all action in Me, worship Me with unflinching devotion; who, through meditation, have fixed their minds intently upon Me—them I quickly redeem from this ocean of transmigratory existence which is fraught with miseries of births and deaths. (12.6-12.7)

— ॐ —

मय्येव मन आधत्स्व मयि बुद्धिं निवेशय ।
mayyeva mana ādhatsva mayi buddhiṁ niveśaya
निवसिष्यसि मय्येव अत ऊर्ध्वं न संशयः ॥ १२-८ ॥
nivasiṣyasi mayyeva ata ūrdhvaṁ na saṁśayaḥ (12-8)

Therefore with your mind fixed upon my manifest form, let your intellect rest in Me—and thereafter you shall abide in Me alone—of this there is no doubt. (12.8)

— ॐ —

अथ चित्तं समाधातुं न शक्नोषि मयि स्थिरम् ।
atha cittaṁ samādhātuṁ na śaknoṣi mayi sthiram
अभ्यासयोगेन ततो मामिच्छाप्तुं धनञ्जय ॥ १२-९ ॥
abhyāsayogena tato māmicchāptuṁ dhanañjaya (12-9)

If however you are unable to fix your mind upon Me steadily, then seek to do so by exercising the Yoga of practice, O Dhananjaya. (12.9)

— ॐ —

अभ्यासेऽप्यसमर्थोऽसि मत्कर्मपरमो भव ।
abhyāse'pyasamartho'si matkarmaparamo bhava
मदर्थमपि कर्माणि कुर्वन्सिद्धिमवाप्स्यसि ॥ १२-१० ॥
madarthamapi karmāṇi kurvansiddhimavāpsyasi (12-10)

If unequal even to the pursuit of practice, then be resolved to perform the prescribed rites for my sake; surely you shall attain perfection even by performing actions for Me. (12.10)

— ॐ —

अथैतदप्यशक्तोऽसि कर्तुं मद्योगमाश्रितः ।
athaitadapyaśakto'si kartuṁ madyogamāśritaḥ
सर्वकर्मफलत्यागं ततः कुरु यतात्मवान् ॥ १२-११ ॥
sarvakarmaphalatyāgaṁ tataḥ kuru yatātmavān (12-11)

And if you are unable to do even that, then simply take refuge in Me, and being self-controlled, renounce the fruits of all actions in Me. (12.11)

— ॐ —

श्रेयो हि ज्ञानमभ्यासाज्ज्ञानाद्ध्यानं विशिष्यते ।
śreyo hi jñānamabhyāsājjñānāddhyānaṁ viśiṣyate
ध्यानात्कर्मफलत्यागस्त्यागाच्छान्तिरनन्तरम् ॥ १२-१२ ॥
dhyānātkarmaphalatyāgastyāgācchāntiranantaram (12-12)

Compared to mere Practice, Knowledge is far superior; and Meditation is superior even to that. And superior to Meditation is Renunciation of the fruit of actions; and from such Renunciation, there arises immediate peace. (12.12)

— ॐ —

अद्वेष्टा सर्वभूतानां मैत्रः करुण एव च ।
adveṣṭā sarvabhūtānāṁ maitraḥ karuṇa eva ca
निर्ममो निरहङ्कारः समदुःखसुखः क्षमी ॥ १२-१३ ॥
nirmamo nirahaṅkāraḥ samaduḥkhasukhaḥ kṣamī (12-13)
सन्तुष्टः सततं योगी यतात्मा दृढनिश्चयः ।
santuṣṭaḥ satataṁ yogī yatātmā dṛḍhaniścayaḥ
मय्यर्पितमनोबुद्धिर्यो मद्भक्तः स मे प्रियः ॥ १२-१४ ॥
mayyarpitamanobuddhiryo madbhaktaḥ sa me priyaḥ (12-14)

He who is friendly and compassionate to all, non-envious, free of the feelings of 'I' and 'mine', balanced in joy and sorrow, forgiving by nature, ever-content, contemplative, self-controlled and of firm resolve, mentally established in Me, who has surrendered his mind and reason to Me—such a devotee of mine is very dear to Me. (12.13-12.14)

— ॐ —

यस्मान्नोद्विजते लोको लोकान्नोद्विजते च यः ।
yasmānnodvijate loko lokānnodvijate ca yaḥ
हर्षामर्षभयोद्वेगैर्मुक्तो यः स च मे प्रियः ॥ १२-१५ ॥
harṣāmarṣabhayodvegairmukto yaḥ sa ca me priyaḥ (12-15)

From whom the world gets no troubles and who gets no troubles from the world; who is free from elation, jealousy, fear, anxiety—such a devotee of mine is dear to Me. (12.15)

— ॐ —

अनपेक्षः शुचिर्दक्ष उदासीनो गतव्यथः ।
anapekṣaḥ śucirdakṣa udāsīno gatavyathaḥ
सर्वारम्भपरित्यागी यो मद्भक्तः स मे प्रियः ॥ १२-१६ ॥
sarvārambhaparityāgī yo madbhaktaḥ sa me priyaḥ (12-16)

Independent, immaculate, adroit, aloof, and untroubled, who renounces the sense of doership in undertakings—such a devotee of mine is dear to Me. (12.16)

— ॐ —

यो न हृष्यति न द्वेष्टि न शोचति न काङ्क्षति ।
yo na hṛṣyati na dveṣṭi na śocati na kāṅkṣati
शुभाशुभपरित्यागी भक्तिमान्यः स मे प्रियः ॥ १२-१७ ॥
śubhāśubhaparityāgī bhaktimānyaḥ sa me priyaḥ (12-17)

He who neither rejoices nor detests, nor grieves, nor desires; having renounced both good and evil who is full of devotion—such a devotee is dear to Me. (12.17)

— ॐ —

समः शत्रौ च मित्रे च तथा मानापमानयोः ।
samaḥ śatrau ca mitre ca tathā mānāpamānayoḥ
शीतोष्णसुखदुःखेषु समः सङ्गविवर्जितः ॥१२-१८॥
śītoṣṇasukhaduḥkheṣu samaḥ saṅgavivarjitaḥ (12-18)
तुल्यनिन्दास्तुतिर्मौनी सन्तुष्टो येन केनचित् ।
tulyanindāstutirmaunī santuṣṭo yena kenacit
अनिकेतः स्थिरमतिर्भक्तिमान्मे प्रियो नरः ॥१२-१९॥
aniketaḥ sthiramatirbhaktimānme priyo naraḥ (12-19)

Free of attachments; alike to friend and foe; the same in honor and disgrace; equanimous in joy, sorrow, heat, cold and such pairs of dualities; reticent; he who takes praise and reproach alike; who is content with any available means of subsistence; who entertains no sense of ownership or attachment with respect to the dwelling place; who is given to contemplation; and is of unflinching steady mind—such a devotee of mine is dear to Me. (12.18-12.19)

— ॐ —

ये तु धर्म्यामृतमिदं यथोक्तं पर्युपासते ।
ye tu dharmyāmṛtamidaṁ yathoktaṁ paryupāsate
श्रद्दधाना मत्परमा भक्तास्तेऽतीव मे प्रियाः ॥१२-२०॥
śraddadhānā matparamā bhaktāste'tīva me priyāḥ (12-20)

Having Me as their supreme goal, these devotees of mine who practice with faith this nectar-like teaching, this ambrosial Dharma which I have just taught—are very dear to Me." (12.20)

ॐ तत्सदिति श्रीमद्भगवद्गीतासूपनिषत्सु
om tatsaditi śrīmadbhagavadgītāsūpaniṣatsu
ब्रह्मविद्यायां योगशास्त्रे श्रीकृष्णार्जुनसंवादे
brahmavidyāyāṁ yogaśāstre śrīkṛṣṇārjunasaṁvāde
भक्तियोगो नाम द्वादशोऽध्यायः ॥
bhaktiyogo nāma dvādaśo'dhyāyaḥ

In this Yogic Scripture on the Science of Brahama—the Shrimada-Bhāgvada-Gītā Upanishad—
hereby ends the dialogue between Shrī Krishna and Arjuna entitled:
Bhakti Yoga, Canto XII

त्रयोदशोऽध्यायः - क्षेत्रक्षेत्रज्ञविभागयोगः

trayodaśo'dhyāyaḥ - kṣetrakṣetrajñavibhāgayogaḥ

:: Canto – XIII ::

- Of the Body and the Embodied-Soul –

श्रीभगवानुवाच --
śrībhagavānuvāca --

इदं शरीरं कौन्तेय क्षेत्रमित्यभिधीयते ।
idaṁ śarīraṁ kaunteya kṣetramityabhidhīyate
एतद्यो वेत्ति तं प्राहुः क्षेत्रज्ञ इति तद्विदः ॥ १३-१ ॥
etadyo vetti taṁ prāhuḥ kṣetrajña iti tadvidaḥ (13-1)

Shri Bhagwāna said: "Sages who have discerned the truth of these matters, O Kuntī-son, have declared this body to be the *Kshetra*—the domicile; and *Kshetrajna* is the name given to the indweller who dwells within—he who is conscious of the body. (13.1)

— ॐ —

क्षेत्रज्ञं चापि मां विद्धि सर्वक्षेत्रेषु भारत ।
kṣetrajñaṁ cāpi māṁ viddhi sarvakṣetreṣu bhārata
क्षेत्रक्षेत्रज्ञयोर्ज्ञानं यत्तज्ज्ञानं मतं मम ॥ १३-२ ॥
kṣetrakṣetrajñayorjñānaṁ yattajjñānaṁ mataṁ mama (13-2)

Know the *Kshetrajna* (the embodied-soul) in all bodies to be none other than Me, O scion of Bhārata. The knowledge of the *Kshetra* and the *Kshetrajna* is what I regard to be true knowledge. (13.2)

— ॐ —

तत्क्षेत्रं यच्च यादृक्क यद्विकारि यतश्च यत् ।
tatkṣetraṁ yacca yādṛkca yadvikāri yataśca yat
स च यो यत्प्रभावश्च तत्समासेन मे शृणु ॥ १३-३ ॥
sa ca yo yatprabhāvaśca tatsamāsena me śṛṇu (13-3)

What that *Kshetra* is, and what its nature, and what its modifications, and whence it arises, and what its forms; and also this other entity—the *Kshetrajna*—what it is and what its abilities—hear of all that in brief from me. (13.3)

— ॐ —

ऋषिभिर्बहुधा गीतं छन्दोभिर्विविधैः पृथक् ।
ṛṣibhirbahudhā gītaṁ chandobhirvividhaiḥ pṛthak
ब्रह्मसूत्रपदैश्चैव हेतुमद्भिर्विनिश्चितैः ॥ १३-४ ॥
brahmasūtrapadaiścaiva hetumadbhirviniścitaiḥ (13-4)

The knowledge of this has been sung variously by many sages and expounded in manifold different ways through diverse Vedic Hymns on Brahama—and also in the conclusive reasoned texts of the Brahama-Sutras. (13.4)

— ॐ —

महाभूतान्यहङ्कारो बुद्धिरव्यक्तमेव च ।
mahābhūtānyahaṅkāro buddhiravyaktameva ca
इन्द्रियाणि दशैकं च पञ्च चेन्द्रियगोचराः ॥ १३-५ ॥
indriyāṇi daśaikaṁ ca pañca cendriyagocarāḥ (13-5)
इच्छा द्वेषः सुखं दुःखं सङ्घातश्चेतना धृतिः ।
icchā dveṣaḥ sukhaṁ duḥkhaṁ saṅghātaścetanā dhṛtiḥ
एतत्क्षेत्रं समासेन सविकारमुदाहृतम् ॥ १३-६ ॥
etatkṣetraṁ samāsena savikāramudāhṛtam (13-6)

The five great elements, the egoism, the intellect, and the Unmanifest; the ten sense-organs along with the controller and the five sense-objects; and also desire, aversion, happiness, misery, intelligence, and patience—thus has the *Kshetra* been described in brief, together with its modifications. (13.5-13.6)

— ॐ —

अमानित्वमदम्भित्वमहिंसा क्षान्तिरार्जवम् ।
amānitvamadambhitvamahiṁsā kṣāntirārjavam
आचार्योपासनं शौचं स्थैर्यमात्मविनिग्रहः ॥ १३-७ ॥
ācāryopāsanaṁ śaucaṁ sthairyamātmavinigrahaḥ (13-7)
इन्द्रियार्थेषु वैराग्यमनहङ्कार एव च ।
indriyārtheṣu vairāgyamanahaṅkāra eva ca
जन्ममृत्युजराव्याधिदुःखदोषानुदर्शनम् ॥ १३-८ ॥
janmamṛtyujarāvyādhiduḥkhadoṣānudarśanam (13-8)
असक्तिरनभिष्वङ्गः पुत्रदारगृहादिषु ।
asaktiranabhiṣvaṅgaḥ putradāragṛhādiṣu
नित्यं च समचित्तत्वमिष्टानिष्टोपपत्तिषु ॥ १३-९ ॥
nityaṁ ca samacittatvamiṣṭāniṣṭopapattiṣu (13-9)

मयि चानन्ययोगेन भक्तिरव्यभिचारिणी ।
mayi cānanyayogena bhaktiravyabhicāriṇī
विविक्तदेशसेवित्वमरतिर्जनसंसदि ॥ १३-१० ॥
viviktadeśasevitvamaratirjanasaṁsadi (13-10)

अध्यात्मज्ञाननित्यत्वं तत्त्वज्ञानार्थदर्शनम् ।
adhyātmajñānanityatvaṁ tattvajñānārthadarśanam
एतज्ज्ञानमिति प्रोक्तमज्ञानं यदतोऽन्यथा ॥ १३-११ ॥
etajjñānamiti proktamajñānaṁ yadato'nyathā (13-11)

Humility, freedom from hypocrisy, nonviolence, forbearance, uprightness in speech and deeds, devout service to the guru, internal and external purity, steadiness, self-control, dispassion for sense objects, absence of egoism; pondering repeatedly on the pain and evil inherent in birth, death, old age and disease; non-attachment and non-identification in respect of spouse, children, home etc.; a constant equipoise of mind in both favorable and unfavorable circumstance; unwavering devotion to Me through the Yoga of non-separation; resorting to solitude; an aversion to the company of worldly beings; being ever devoted to spiritual pursuits and seeing God alone as the object of true knowledge—all this is declared to be *Jnāna* (Knowledge/Science), and that which is contrary to it is called *Ajnāna* (Nescience). (13.7-13.11)

— ॐ —

ज्ञेयं यत्तत्प्रवक्ष्यामि यज्ज्ञात्वामृतमश्नुते ।
jñeyaṁ yattatpravakṣyāmi yajjñātvāmṛtamaśnute
अनादिमत्परं ब्रह्म न सत्तन्नासदुच्यते ॥ १३-१२ ॥
anādimatparaṁ brahma na sattannāsaducyate (13-12)

Now let me tell you of The One who must be known, knowing Whom one attains to immortality. That One is the beginning-less Supreme Brahama—who is said to be neither being nor non-being. (13.12)

— ॐ —

सर्वतः पाणिपादं तत्सर्वतोऽक्षिशिरोमुखम् ।

sarvataḥ pāṇipādaṁ tatsarvato'kṣiśiromukham

सर्वतः श्रुतिमल्लोके सर्वमावृत्य तिष्ठति ॥१३-१३॥

sarvataḥ śrutimalloke sarvamāvṛtya tiṣṭhati (13-13)

With hands and feet everywhere, with eyes, heads and mouth in all directions, with ears in everyplace—It abides pervading everything in the universe. (13.13)

— ॐ —

सर्वेन्द्रियगुणाभासं सर्वेन्द्रियविवर्जितम् ।

sarvendriyaguṇābhāsaṁ sarvendriyavivarjitam

असक्तं सर्वभृच्चैव निर्गुणं गुणभोक्तृ च ॥१३-१४॥

asaktaṁ sarvabhṛccaiva nirguṇaṁ guṇabhoktṛ ca (13-14)

And though manifest in the functioning of the sense-organs, in reality It is bereft of the sense-organs; and though unattached, It is nonetheless the sustainer of all; and though void of attributes, It is the partaker of *Gunas*: the three modes of Prakriti. (13.14)

— ॐ —

बहिरन्तश्च भूतानामचरं चरमेव च ।

bahirantaśca bhūtānāmacaraṁ carameva ca

सूक्ष्मत्वात्तदविज्ञेयं दूरस्थं चान्तिके च तत् ॥१३-१५॥

sūkṣmatvāttadavijñeyaṁ dūrasthaṁ cāntike ca tat (13-15)

It exists outside and within all beings; and It is the subtle essence which stands established within all the moving and the non-moving things; and It is uncomprehensible; and It is most close and yet so far. (13.15)

— ॐ —

अविभक्तं च भूतेषु विभक्तमिव च स्थितम् ।

avibhaktaṁ ca bhūteṣu vibhaktamiva ca sthitam

भूतभर्तृ च तज्ज्ञेयं ग्रसिष्णु प्रभविष्णु च ॥१३-१६॥

bhūtabhartṛ ca tajjñeyaṁ grasiṣṇu prabhaviṣṇu ca (13-16)

It is undivided in beings and yet appears divided. That supreme Knowable who is the Sustainer of all beings, is also their Destroyer, and their Creator. (13.16)

— ॐ —

ज्योतिषामपि तज्ज्योतिस्तमसः परमुच्यते ।
jyotiṣāmapi tajjyotistamasaḥ paramucyate
ज्ञानं ज्ञेयं ज्ञानगम्यं हृदि सर्वस्य विष्ठितम् ॥ १३-१७ ॥
jñānaṁ jñeyaṁ jñānagamyaṁ hṛdi sarvasya viṣṭhitam (13-17)

That supreme Brahama is said to be the Light of lights—entirely beyond the darkness of Māyā. He is knowledge; He is the knowable; He is accessible through knowledge; He abides imbedded at the core of everything. (13.17)

— ॐ —

इति क्षेत्रं तथा ज्ञानं ज्ञेयं चोक्तं समासतः ।
iti kṣetraṁ tathā jñānaṁ jñeyaṁ coktaṁ samāsataḥ
मद्भक्त एतद्विज्ञाय मद्भावायोपपद्यते ॥ १३-१८ ॥
madbhakta etadvijñāya madbhāvāyopapadyate (13-18)

Thus has the truth of Kshetra and Knowledge and the Knowable been stated here in brief. Knowing this fully, my devotee becomes fit to attain to my Being. (13.18)

— ॐ —

प्रकृतिं पुरुषं चैव विद्ध्यनादी उभावपि ।
prakṛtiṁ puruṣaṁ caiva viddhyanādī ubhāvapi
विकारांश्च गुणांश्चैव विद्धि प्रकृतिसम्भवान् ॥ १३-१९ ॥
vikārāṁśca guṇāṁścaiva viddhi prakṛtisambhavān (13-19)

Know both *Purusha* and *Prakriti* to be beginning-less; and know the evolutes and the *Gunas* to be born of *Prakriti*. (13.19)

— ॐ —

कार्यकारणकर्तृत्वे हेतुः प्रकृतिरुच्यते ।
kāryakāraṇakartṛtve hetuḥ prakṛtirucyate
पुरुषः सुखदुःखानां भोक्तृत्वे हेतुरुच्यते ॥ १३-२० ॥
puruṣaḥ sukhaduḥkhānāṁ bhoktṛtve heturucyate (13-20)

As to the production of the effect and cause—it is the *Prakriti* which is responsible for bringing them forth; whereas the *Purusha*—as the soul—is declared to be responsible for the experiencing of the joys and sorrows. (13.20)

— ॐ —

पुरुषः प्रकृतिस्थो हि भुङ्क्ते प्रकृतिजान्गुणान् ।
puruṣaḥ prakṛtistho hi bhuṅkte prakṛtijānguṇān
कारणं गुणसङ्गोऽस्य सदसद्योनिजन्मसु ॥ १३-२१ ॥
kāraṇaṁ guṇasaṅgo'sya sadasadyonijanmasu (13-21)

The soul (*Purusha*)—which dwells in *Prakriti*—experiences the *Gunas* which are born of *Prakriti*; and it is its attachment to those *Gunas* which becomes causative for its rebirths in circumstances good and bad. (13.21)

— ॐ —

उपद्रष्टानुमन्ता च भर्ता भोक्ता महेश्वरः ।
upadraṣṭānumantā ca bhartā bhoktā maheśvaraḥ
परमात्मेति चाप्युक्तो देहेऽस्मिन्पुरुषः परः ॥ १३-२२ ॥
paramātmeti cāpyukto dehe'sminpuruṣaḥ paraḥ (13-22)

The *Purusha*—indwelling in this body—is spoken of variously as the Witness, the Guide, the Nourisher, the Protector, the Overlord, and at times the Supreme-Self as well. (13.22)

— ॐ —

य एवं वेत्ति पुरुषं प्रकृतिं च गुणैः सह ।
ya evaṁ vetti puruṣaṁ prakṛtiṁ ca guṇaiḥ saha
सर्वथा वर्तमानोऽपि न स भूयोऽभिजायते ॥ १३-२३ ॥
sarvathā vartamāno'pi na sa bhūyo'bhijāyate (13-23)

He who thus knows at its essence the nature of *Purusha* and *Prakriti*, together with the *Gunas*—such a one is not born again, whatever his mode of life. (13.23)

— ॐ —

ध्यानेनात्मनि पश्यन्ति केचिदात्मानमात्मना ।
dhyānenātmani paśyanti kecidātmānamātmanā
अन्ये साङ्ख्येन योगेन कर्मयोगेन चापरे ॥ १३-२४ ॥
anye sāṅkhyena yogena karmayogena cāpare (13-24)

Some—through meditation—see the Self, within the self, by the self; some perceive it through Knowledge; some again do so through Yoga; and some others through the path of Karma. (13.24)

— ॐ —

अन्ये त्वेवमजानन्तः श्रुत्वान्येभ्य उपासते ।
anye tvevamajānantaḥ śrutvānyebhya upāsate
तेऽपि चातितरन्त्येव मृत्युं श्रुतिपरायणाः ॥ १३-२५ ॥
te'pi cātitarantyeva mṛtyuṁ śrutiparāyaṇāḥ (13-25)

Other again—not knowing any of that—revere the Self by hearing of It from others; verily even these too—who take recourse merely to hearing etc.—are able to go beyond death. (13.25)

— ॐ —

यावत्सञ्जायते किञ्चित्सत्त्वं स्थावरजङ्गमम् ।
yāvatsañjāyate kiñcitsattvaṁ sthāvarajaṅgamam
क्षेत्रक्षेत्रज्ञसंयोगात्तद्विद्धि भरतर्षभ ॥ १३-२६ ॥
kṣetrakṣetrajñasaṁyogāttadviddhi bharatarṣabha (13-26)

Whatever being that there is—be it animate or inanimate—know that to have emerged of the union of the *Kshetra* and the *Kshetrajna* in some form or another, O Bhārata. (13.26)

— ॐ —

समं सर्वेषु भूतेषु तिष्ठन्तं परमेश्वरम् ।
samaṁ sarveṣu bhūteṣu tiṣṭhantaṁ parameśvaram
विनश्यत्स्वविनश्यन्तं यः पश्यति स पश्यति ॥ १३-२७ ॥
vinaśyatsvavinaśyantaṁ yaḥ paśyati sa paśyati (13-27)

He who perceives the supreme Lord abiding uniformly in all beings and things—who comprehends the imperishable essence concealed within the perishable—he truly sees. (13.27)

— ॐ —

समं पश्यन्हि सर्वत्र समवस्थितमीश्वरम् ।
samaṁ paśyanhi sarvatra samavasthitamīśvaram
न हिनस्त्यात्मनात्मानं ततो याति परां गतिम् ॥ १३-२८ ॥
na hinastyātmanātmānaṁ tato yāti parāṁ gatim (13-28)

By seeing the supreme Lord abiding equally everywhere, he does not injure the Self by the self—and therefore he goes on to attain the supreme abode. (13.28)

— ॐ —

प्रकृत्यैव च कर्माणि क्रियमाणानि सर्वशः ।
prakṛtyaiva ca karmāṇi kriyamāṇāni sarvaśaḥ
यः पश्यति तथात्मानमकर्तारं स पश्यति ॥ १३-२९ ॥
yaḥ paśyati tathātmānamakartāraṁ sa paśyati (13-29)

He who sees that all actions are in every way truly carried out just by the sway of *Prakriti*—and that the Self, in reality, is merely the non-doer: such a one is a true seer. (13.29)

— ॐ —

यदा भूतपृथग्भावमेकस्थमनुपश्यति ।
yadā bhūtapṛthagbhāvamekasthamanupaśyati
तत एव च विस्तारं ब्रह्म सम्पद्यते तदा ॥ १३-३० ॥
tata eva ca vistāraṁ brahma sampadyate tadā (13-30)

He who beholds all these diversified beings abiding within the One-Supreme-Soul, who sees everything sprouting forth from just that One singular source—he becomes one with that Brahama. (13.30)

— ॐ —

अनादित्वान्निर्गुणत्वात्परमात्मायमव्ययः ।
anāditvānnirguṇatvātparamātmāyamavyayaḥ
शरीरस्थोऽपि कौन्तेय न करोति न लिप्यते ॥ १३-३१ ॥
śarīrastho'pi kaunteya na karoti na lipyate (13-31)

The Supreme-Soul—which is void of attributes and without a beginning—is immutable; and although dwelling within the body, it neither acts, nor gets tainted, O Kuntī-son. (13.31)

— ॐ —

यथा सर्वगतं सौक्ष्म्यादाकाशं नोपलिप्यते ।
yathā sarvagataṁ saukṣmyādākāśaṁ nopalipyate
सर्वत्रावस्थितो देहे तथात्मा नोपलिप्यते ॥ १३-३२ ॥
sarvatrāvasthito dehe tathātmā nopalipyate (13-32)

Just as the all-pervading aether, being subtle, persists ever untouched—although permeating throughout—so too is our Self; the Self never gets affected by the attributes of body, the exterior material crust. (13.32)

— ॐ —

यथा प्रकाशयत्येकः कृत्स्नं लोकमिमं रविः ।
yathā prakāśayatyekaḥ kṛtsnaṁ lokamimaṁ raviḥ
क्षेत्रं क्षेत्री तथा कृत्स्नं प्रकाशयति भारत ॥ १३-३३ ॥
kṣetraṁ kṣetrī tathā kṛtsnaṁ prakāśayati bhārata (13-33)

Even as the one Sun illuminates the world, O Bhārata-scion, even so the One Param-Ātmā (Supreme-Soul) illumines all the bodies. (13.33)

— ॐ —

क्षेत्रक्षेत्रज्ञयोरेवमन्तरं ज्ञानचक्षुषा ।
kṣetrakṣetrajñayorevamantaraṁ jñānacakṣuṣā
भूतप्रकृतिमोक्षं च ये विदुर्यान्ति ते परम् ॥ १३-३४ ॥
bhūtaprakṛtimokṣaṁ ca ye viduryānti te param (13-34)

They who thus perceive, with the eye of wisdom, the distinction between *Kshetra* and *Kshetrajna*, as also the ways leading to freedom from *Prakriti* and *Gunas*—which's the cause of beings—they attain the supreme state." (13.34)

ॐ तत्सदिति श्रीमद्भगवद्गीतासूपनिषत्सु
om tatsaditi śrīmadbhagavadgītāsūpaniṣatsu
ब्रह्मविद्यायां योगशास्त्रे श्रीकृष्णार्जुनसंवादे
brahmavidyāyāṁ yogaśāstre śrīkṛṣṇārjunasaṁvāde
क्षेत्रक्षेत्रज्ञविभागयोगो नाम त्रयोदशोऽध्यायः ॥
kṣetrakṣetrajñavibhāgayogo nāma trayodaśo'dhyāyaḥ

In this Yogic Scripture on the Science of Brahama—the Shrimada-Bhāgvada-Gītā Upaniṣhad—hereby ends the dialogue between Shrī Krishna and Arjuna entitled:
Kshetra-Kshetrajña-Vibhāga Yoga, Canto XIII

चतुर्दशोऽध्यायः - गुणत्रयविभागयोगः

caturdaśo'dhyāyaḥ - guṇatrayavibhāgayogaḥ

:: Canto – XIV ::

- Discernment of the Three *Gunas* -

श्रीभगवानुवाच --
śrībhagavānuvāca --

परं भूयः प्रवक्ष्यामि ज्ञानानां ज्ञानमुत्तमम् ।
paraṁ bhūyaḥ pravakṣyāmi jñānānāṁ jñānamuttamam
यज्ज्ञात्वा मुनयः सर्वे परां सिद्धिमितो गताः ॥ १४-१ ॥
yajjñātvā munayaḥ sarve parāṁ siddhimito gatāḥ (14-1)

Shri Bhagwāna said: "Once more let me speak of that supreme knowledge—the greatest of all—acquiring which sages everywhere have attained to the highest perfection and felicity. (14.1)

— ॐ —

इदं ज्ञानमुपाश्रित्य मम साधर्म्यमागताः ।
idaṁ jñānamupāśritya mama sādharmyamāgatāḥ
सर्गेऽपि नोपजायन्ते प्रलये न व्यथन्ति च ॥ १४-२ ॥
sarge'pi nopajāyante pralaye na vyathanti ca (14-2)

By practicing this knowledge they, having attained to my Being, are not reborn at the time of the cosmic dawn, nor are they subjected to its sufferings at the time of cosmic dissolution. (14.2)

— ॐ —

मम योनिर्महद् ब्रह्म तस्मिन्गर्भं दधाम्यहम् ।
mama yonirmahad brahma tasmingarbhaṁ dadhāmyaham
सम्भवः सर्वभूतानां ततो भवति भारत ॥ १४-३ ॥
sambhavaḥ sarvabhūtānāṁ tato bhavati bhārata (14-3)

The great Nature is my womb. In that I place the seed of life. And from that, O Bhārata, is the origin of all beings. (14.3)

— ॐ —

सर्वयोनिषु कौन्तेय मूर्तयः सम्भवन्ति याः ।
sarvayoniṣu kaunteya mūrtayaḥ sambhavanti yāḥ
तासां ब्रह्म महद्योनिरहं बीजप्रदः पिता ॥ १४-४ ॥
tāsāṁ brahma mahadyoniraham bījapradaḥ pitā (14-4)

Whatever bods, O Kuntī-son, are born in various wombs, of them, the great Nature is the conceiving Mother, and I, the seed-giving Father. (14.4)

— ॐ —

सत्त्वं रजस्तम इति गुणाः प्रकृतिसम्भवाः ।

sattvaṁ rajastama iti guṇāḥ prakṛtisambhavāḥ

निबध्नन्ति महाबाहो देहे देहिनमव्ययम् ॥ १४-५ ॥

nibadhnanti mahābāho dehe dehinamavyayam (14-5)

Sattva, *Rājas* and *Tāmas*—these *Gunas*, which are born of Nature—bind fast the immutable, embodied soul to this body, O mighty-armed. (14.5)

— ॐ —

तत्र सत्त्वं निर्मलत्वात्प्रकाशकमनामयम् ।

tatra sattvaṁ nirmalatvātprakāśakamanāmayam

सुखसङ्गेन बध्नाति ज्ञानसङ्गेन चानघ ॥ १४-६ ॥

sukhasaṅgena badhnāti jñānasaṅgena cānagha (14-6)

Of these, *Sattva*, being immaculate, is luminous and free from evil; it binds the embodied soul through fondness for knowledge, and propensity for happiness, O sinless one. (14.6)

— ॐ —

रजो रागात्मकं विद्धि तृष्णासङ्गसमुद्भवम् ।

rajo rāgātmakaṁ viddhi tṛṣṇāsaṅgasamudbhavam

तन्निबध्नाति कौन्तेय कर्मसङ्गेन देहिनम् ॥ १४-७ ॥

tannibadhnāti kaunteya karmasaṅgena dehinam (14-7)

O Kuntī-son, know *Rājas* to be of the nature of passion—the source of all desires and attachments; it binds down the embodied soul through proclivity for actions and fruits. (14.7)

— ॐ —

तमस्त्वज्ञानजं विद्धि मोहनं सर्वदेहिनाम् ।

tamastvajñānajaṁ viddhi mohanaṁ sarvadehinām

प्रमादालस्यनिद्राभिस्तन्निबध्नाति भारत ॥ १४-८ ॥

pramādālasyanidrābhistannibadhnāti bhārata (14-8)

Know *Tāmas* to be born of Ignorance, O Bhārata; deluding all embodied beings, it binds fast the soul through error, sleep, and sloth. (14.8)

— ॐ —

सत्त्वं सुखे सञ्जयति रजः कर्मणि भारत ।
sattvaṁ sukhe sañjayati rajaḥ karmaṇi bhārata
ज्ञानमावृत्य तु तमः प्रमादे सञ्जयत्युत ॥ १४-९ ॥
jñānamāvṛtya tu tamaḥ pramāde sañjayatyuta (14-9)

Sattva binds one to joy, *Rājas* to work, and *Tāmas*—clouding wisdom—impels one to inadvertence and similar propensities, O Arjuna. (14.9)

— ॐ —

रजस्तमश्चाभिभूय सत्त्वं भवति भारत ।
rajastamaścābhibhūya sattvaṁ bhavati bhārata
रजः सत्त्वं तमश्चैव तमः सत्त्वं रजस्तथा ॥ १४-१० ॥
rajaḥ sattvaṁ tamaścaiva tamaḥ sattvaṁ rajastathā (14-10)

Overpowering *Rājas* and *Tāmas*, *Sattva* prevails; overpowering *Sattva* and *Tāmas*, *Rājas* prevails; even so, O Bhārata, overpowering *Sattva* and *Rājas*, *Tāmas* prevails. (14.10)

— ॐ —

सर्वद्वारेषु देहेऽस्मिन्प्रकाश उपजायते ।
sarvadvāreṣu dehe'sminprakāśa upajāyate
ज्ञानं यदा तदा विद्याद्विवृद्धं सत्त्वमित्युत ॥ १४-११ ॥
jñānaṁ yadā tadā vidyādvivṛddhaṁ sattvamityuta (14-11)

When the light of knowledge is found to emanate through all the sense-openings in the body—then one should know that *Sattva* predominates. (14.11)

— ॐ —

लोभः प्रवृत्तिरारम्भः कर्मणामशमः स्पृहा ।
lobhaḥ pravṛttirārambhaḥ karmaṇāmaśamaḥ spṛhā
रजस्येतानि जायन्ते विवृद्धे भरतर्षभ ॥ १४-१२ ॥
rajasyetāni jāyante vivṛddhe bharatarṣabha (14-12)

With the preponderance of *Rājas*, greed, activity, undertaking of works, restlessness and thirst for enjoyments—all these make their appearance, O best of Bhāratas. (14.12)

— ॐ —

अप्रकाशोऽप्रवृत्तिश्च प्रमादो मोह एव च ।
aprakāśo'pravṛttiśca pramādo moha eva ca
तमस्येतानि जायन्ते विवृद्धे कुरुनन्दन ॥ १४-१३ ॥
tamasyetāni jāyante vivṛddhe kurunandana (14-13)

With the outgrowth of *Tāmas*, obtuseness of the mind and senses, disinclination to perform one's obligatory duties, frivolity and stupor—all such traits become prevalent, O Kurū-scion. (14.13)

— ॐ —

यदा सत्त्वे प्रवृद्धे तु प्रलयं याति देहभृत् ।
yadā sattve pravṛddhe tu pralayaṁ yāti dehabhṛt
तदोत्तमविदां लोकानमलान्प्रतिपद्यते ॥ १४-१४ ॥
tadottamavidāṁ lokānamalānpratipadyate (14-14)

When the embodied soul leaves the body during the preponderance of *Sattva*, then he obtains those pure ethereal spheres which are designated for worshippers of the highest deities. (14.14)

— ॐ —

रजसि प्रलयं गत्वा कर्मसङ्गिषु जायते ।
rajasi pralayaṁ gatvā karmasaṅgiṣu jāyate
तथा प्रलीनस्तमसि मूढयोनिषु जायते ॥ १४-१५ ॥
tathā pralīnastamasi mūḍhayoniṣu jāyate (14-15)

Dying when *Rājas* predominates, the soul is born amongst those that are attached to action. Even so the man who meets death during preponderance of *Tāmas*, is born amongst non-cerebral species—such as insects and lowly creatures. (14.15)

— ॐ —

कर्मणः सुकृतस्याहुः सात्त्विकं निर्मलं फलम् ।
karmaṇaḥ sukṛtasyāhuḥ sāttvikaṁ nirmalaṁ phalam
रजसस्तु फलं दुःखमज्ञानं तमसः फलम् ॥ १४-१६ ॥
rajasastu phalaṁ duḥkhamajñānaṁ tamasaḥ phalam (14-16)

The result of virtuous action is said to be *Sāttvika* and pure; pain and sorrow is declared to be the fruit of *Rājasika* acts; and ignorance is the fruit of *Tāmas*. (14.16)

— ॐ —

सत्त्वात्सञ्जायते ज्ञानं रजसो लोभ एव च ।

sattvātsañjāyate jñānaṁ rajaso lobha eva ca

प्रमादमोहौ तमसो भवतोऽज्ञानमेव च ॥ १४-१७ ॥

pramādamohau tamaso bhavato'jñānameva ca (14-17)

From *Sattva* comes knowledge, from *Rājas* emanates greed, and in the wake of *Tāmas* follows only inadvertence, delusion, and ignorance. (14.17)

— ॐ —

ऊर्ध्वं गच्छन्ति सत्त्वस्था मध्ये तिष्ठन्ति राजसाः ।

ūrdhvaṁ gacchanti sattvasthā madhye tiṣṭhanti rājasāḥ

जघन्यगुणवृत्तिस्था अधो गच्छन्ति तामसाः ॥ १४-१८ ॥

jaghanyaguṇavṛttisthā adho gacchanti tāmasāḥ (14-18)

Those who abide in the quality of *Sattva*, wend their way upwards; those of *Rājasika* disposition stay in the middle; and those of a *Tāmasika* temperament—enveloped as they are in the effects of *Tamo-Guṇa*—increasingly sink downwards. (14.18)

— ॐ —

नान्यं गुणेभ्यः कर्तारं यदा द्रष्टानुपश्यति ।

nānyaṁ guṇebhyaḥ kartāraṁ yadā draṣṭānupaśyati

गुणेभ्यश्च परं वेत्ति मद्भावं सोऽधिगच्छति ॥ १४-१९ ॥

guṇebhyaśca paraṁ vetti madbhāvaṁ so'dhigacchati (14-19)

When the seer beholds no other doer other than the three *Gunas*, and when behind everything he perceives only the Supreme-Soul which is beyond the *Gunas*—then he attains to Me. (14.19)

— ॐ —

गुणानेतानतीत्य त्रीन्देही देहसमुद्भवान् ।

guṇānetānatītya trīndehī dehasamudbhavān

जन्ममृत्युजरादुःखैर्विमुक्तोऽमृतमश्नुते ॥ १४-२० ॥

janmamṛtyujarāduḥkhairvimukto'mṛtamaśnute (14-20)

Having transcended the three *Gunas*—which are the cause of this body—the embodied soul—freed from birth, decay, death, misery, sorrow—attains immortality." (14.20)

अर्जुन उवाच --
arjuna uvāca --

कैर्लिङ्गैस्त्रीन्गुणानेतानतीतो भवति प्रभो ।
kairliṅgaistrīnguṇānetānatīto bhavati prabho
किमाचारः कथं चैतांस्त्रीन्गुणानतिवर्तते ॥ १४-२१ ॥
kimācāraḥ kathaṁ caitāṁstrīnguṇānativartate (14-21)

Arjuna said: "O Lord, what are the marks of him who has risen above the three *Gunas*? What his conduct? And how does he transcend the three?" (14.21)

श्रीभगवानुवाच --
śrībhagavānuvāca --

प्रकाशं च प्रवृत्तिं च मोहमेव च पाण्डव ।
prakāśaṁ ca pravṛttiṁ ca mohameva ca pāṇḍava
न द्वेष्टि सम्प्रवृत्तानि न निवृत्तानि काङ्क्षति ॥ १४-२२ ॥
na dveṣṭi sampravṛttāni na nivṛttāni kāṅkṣati (14-22)

Shri Bhagwāna said: "O Arjuna, he who does not recoil when activity, which is born of *Rājas*, or stupor that's born of *Tāmas*, or even light which's born of *Sattva*, become prevalent, nor desires them when they have ceased; (14.22)

— ॐ —

उदासीनवदासीनो गुणैर्यो न विचाल्यते ।
udāsīnavadāsīno guṇairyo na vicālyate
गुणा वर्तन्त इत्येवं योऽवतिष्ठति नेङ्गते ॥ १४-२३ ॥
guṇā vartanta ityevaṁ yo'vatiṣṭhati neṅgate (14-23)

Who, abiding like a witness, remains unperturbed—knowing that it is the *Gunas* alone that are the actual doers—he is said to be steady and unwavering. (14.23)

— ॐ —

समदुःखसुखः स्वस्थः समलोष्टाश्मकाञ्चनः ।
samaduḥkhasukhaḥ svasthaḥ samaloṣṭāśmakāñcanaḥ
तुल्यप्रियाप्रियो धीरस्तुल्यनिन्दात्मसंस्तुतिः ॥ १४-२४ ॥
tulyapriyāpriyo dhīrastulyanindātmasaṁstutiḥ (14-24)

Who remains ever established in the Self—taking joys and sorrows alike, regarding a clod of earth, a stone and a piece of gold as of equal worth; who, possessed of wisdom, accepts agreeable and un-agreeable in the same vein, and who views bestowed praise and blame as being equal; (14.24)

— ॐ —

मानापमानयोस्तुल्यस्तुल्यो मित्रारिपक्षयोः ।
mānāpamānayostulyastulyo mitrāripakṣayoḥ
सर्वारम्भपरित्यागी गुणातीतः स उच्यते ॥ १४-२५ ॥
sarvārambhaparityāgī guṇātītaḥ sa ucyate (14-25)

who is equipoised in honor and dishonor, alike towards friend and foe, who has renounced the sense of doership in all undertakings—such a one is said to have risen above the three *Gunas*. (14.25)

— ॐ —

मां च योऽव्यभिचारेण भक्तियोगेन सेवते ।
māṁ ca yo'vyabhicāreṇa bhaktiyogena sevate
स गुणान्समतीत्यैतान्ब्रह्मभूयाय कल्पते ॥ १४-२६ ॥
sa guṇānsamatītyaitānbrahmabhūyāya kalpate (14-26)

He transcends the three Gunas and becomes fit to attain the state of Brahama who—through unswerving practice of the Yoga of Bhaktī—serves Me alone; (14.26)

— ॐ —

ब्रह्मणो हि प्रतिष्ठाहममृतस्याव्ययस्य च ।
brahmaṇo hi pratiṣṭhāhamamṛtasyāvyayasya ca
शाश्वतस्य च धर्मस्य सुखस्यैकान्तिकस्य च ॥ १४-२७ ॥
śāśvatasya ca dharmasya sukhasyaikāntikasya ca (14-27)

For, verily I am the personification of Brahama—of immutable immortality, of the eternal Dharma, and of absolute unending bliss." (14.27)

ॐ तत्सदिति श्रीमद्भगवद्गीतासूपनिषत्सु
om tatsaditi śrīmadbhagavadgītāsūpaniṣatsu
ब्रह्मविद्यायां योगशास्त्रे श्रीकृष्णार्जुनसंवादे
brahmavidyāyāṁ yogaśāstre śrīkṛṣṇārjunasaṁvāde
गुणत्रयविभागयोगो नाम चतुर्दशोऽध्यायः ॥
guṇatrayavibhāgayogo nāma caturdaśo'dhyāyaḥ .

In this Yogic Scripture on the Science of Brahama—the Shrimada-Bhāgvada-Gītā Upanishad—hereby ends the dialogue between Shrī Krishna and Arjuna entitled: Gunatraya-Vibhāga Yoga, Canto XIV

पञ्चदशोऽध्यायः - पुरुषोत्तमयोगः

pañcadaśo'dhyāyaḥ - puruṣottamayogaḥ

:: Canto – XV ::

- Path to the Supreme God-Head -

श्रीभगवानुवाच --
śrībhagavānuvāca --

ऊर्ध्वमूलमधःशाखमश्वत्थं प्राहुरव्ययम् ।
ūrdhvamūlamadhaḥśākhamaśvattham prāhuravyayam
छन्दांसि यस्य पर्णानि यस्तं वेद स वेदवित् ॥ १५-१ ॥
chandāṁsi yasya parṇāni yastaṁ veda sa vedavit (15-1)

Shri Bhagwāna said: "They speak of an immutable *Ashvattha* Tree—with its roots above, and its branches below, and which has the Vedas for its leaves—and he who knows it is the knower of the Vedas. (15.1)

— ॐ —

अधश्चोर्ध्वं प्रसृतास्तस्य शाखा गुणप्रवृद्धा विषयप्रवालाः ।
adhaścordhvaṁ prasṛtāstasya śākhā guṇapravṛddhā viṣayapravālāḥ
अधश्च मूलान्यनुसन्ततानि कर्मानुबन्धीनि मनुष्यलोके ॥ १५-२ ॥
adhaśca mūlānyanusantatāni karmānubandhīni manuṣyaloke (15-2)

Its branches, nurtured by the *Gunas*, are spread above, around, below; and its shoots are the sense-objects; and its roots hang downwards—which are the producers of actions in this world of beings. (15.2)

— ॐ —

न रूपमस्येह तथोपलभ्यते नान्तो न चादिर्न च सम्प्रतिष्ठा ।
na rūpamasyeha tathopalabhyate nānto na cādirna ca sampratiṣṭhā
अश्वत्थमेनं सुविरूढमूलं असङ्गशस्त्रेण दृढेन छित्त्वा ॥ १५-३ ॥
aśvatthamenaṁ suvirūḍhamūlaṁ asaṅgaśastreṇa dṛḍhena chittvā (15-3)

This Tree of creation—in a continuous flux and lacking constancy—has no beginning or end. One should strive to shear away this deep rooted *Ashvattha* tree with the strong axe of dispassion. (15.3)

— ॐ —

ततः पदं तत्परिमार्गितव्यं यस्मिन्गता न निवर्तन्ति भूयः ।

tataḥ padaṁ tatparimārgitavyaṁ yasmingatā na nivartanti bhūyaḥ

तमेव चाद्यं पुरुषं प्रपद्ये यतः प्रवृत्तिः प्रसृता पुराणी ॥ १५-४ ॥

tameva cādyaṁ puruṣaṁ prapadye yataḥ pravṛttiḥ prasṛtā purāṇī (15-4)

And thereafter one should diligently seek That supreme state—reaching which there is no return—by making a firm resolve: 'I take refuge in the primordial *Purusha* alone—from whom has sprung this eternal process, this great Tree of creation.' (15.4)

— ॐ —

निर्मानमोहा जितसङ्गदोषा अध्यात्मनित्या विनिवृत्तकामाः ।

nirmānamohā jitasaṅgadoṣā adhyātmanityā vinivṛttakāmāḥ

द्वन्द्वैर्विमुक्ताः सुखदुःखसंज्ञैर्गच्छन्त्यमूढाः पदमव्ययं तत् ॥ १५-५ ॥

dvandvairvimuktāḥ sukhaduḥkhasaṁjñair-
gacchantyamūḍhāḥ padamavyayaṁ tat (15-5)

Freed from pride and delusions, overcoming the evil of attachments, ever devoted to spiritual pursuits, altogether ceased of desires and rid of the throngs of dualities such as pleasures and pains—the wise will reach That Immortal State. (15.5)

— ॐ —

न तद्भासयते सूर्यो न शशाङ्को न पावकः ।

na tadbhāsayate sūryo na śaśāṅko na pāvakaḥ

यद्गत्वा न निवर्तन्ते तद्धाम परमं मम ॥ १५-६ ॥

yadgatvā na nivartante taddhāma paramaṁ mama (15-6)

The sun does not illumine That; nor the moon or fire. That supreme self-effulgent sphere—attaining Which there is no more return to the world—That is my Supreme-Abode. (15.6)

— ॐ —

ममैवांशो जीवलोके जीवभूतः सनातनः ।

mamaivāṁśo jīvaloke jīvabhūtaḥ sanātanaḥ

मनःषष्ठानीन्द्रियाणि प्रकृतिस्थानि कर्षति ॥ १५-७ ॥

manaḥṣaṣṭhānīndriyāṇi prakṛtisthāni karṣati (15-7)

Verily a fragment of my Self, having become this eternal embodied soul—the *Jīvātmā*—draws around itself the mind and the five senses which rest in Nature. (15.7)

— ॐ —

शरीरं यदवाप्नोति यच्चाप्युत्क्रामतीश्वरः ।
śarīraṁ yadavāpnoti yaccāpyutkrāmatīśvaraḥ
गृहीत्वैतानि संयाति वायुर्गन्धानिवाशयात् ॥ १५-८ ॥
gṛhītvaitāni saṁyāti vāyurgandhānivāśayāt (15-8)

Upon dropping the body behind, when the *Jīvātmā* migrates to a new body, it goes carrying away these (the mind and the senses spoken above)—just as the breeze wafts the odors away from their seats, bearing them along with it. (15.8)

— ॐ —

श्रोत्रं चक्षुः स्पर्शनं च रसनं घ्राणमेव च ।
śrotraṁ cakṣuḥ sparśanaṁ ca rasanaṁ ghrāṇameva ca
अधिष्ठाय मनश्चायं विषयानुपसेवते ॥ १५-९ ॥
adhiṣṭhāya manaścāyaṁ viṣayānupasevate (15-9)

Presiding over the sense-organs of hearing, sight, touch, taste and smell, as also the mind, it is the *Jīvātmā* who is the partaker of sense-enjoyments through the instrument of the body wherein he currently dwells. (15.9)

— ॐ —

उत्क्रामन्तं स्थितं वापि भुञ्जानं वा गुणान्वितम् ।
utkrāmantaṁ sthitaṁ vāpi bhuñjānaṁ vā guṇānvitam
विमूढा नानुपश्यन्ति पश्यन्ति ज्ञानचक्षुषः ॥ १५-१० ॥
vimūḍhā nānupaśyanti paśyanti jñānacakṣuṣaḥ (15-10)

The deluded do not know of this *Jīvātmā*—the soul—which enters and departs from the body, which is the indweller, which is the enjoyer of the sense-objects; but those endowed with the eye of wisdom, do perceive the indwelling soul alone to be the true reality in the scheme of things. (15.10)

— ॐ —

यतन्तो योगिनश्चैनं पश्यन्त्यात्मन्यवस्थितम् ।

yatanto yoginaścainaṁ paśyantyātmanyavasthitam

यतन्तोऽप्यकृतात्मानो नैनं पश्यन्त्यचेतसः ॥ १५-११ ॥

yatanto'pyakṛtātmāno nainaṁ paśyantyacetasaḥ (15-11)

Yogīs—who strive—are able to directly perceive and realize the Self that is enshrined within their body; however those who are not self-controlled—being thoughtless—will not to see It in spite of trying. (15:11)

— ॐ —

यदादित्यगतं तेजो जगद्भासयतेऽखिलम् ।

yadādityagataṁ tejo jagadbhāsayate'khilam

यच्चन्द्रमसि यच्चाग्नौ तत्तेजो विद्धि मामकम् ॥ १५-१२ ॥

yaccandramasi yaccāgnau tattejo viddhi māmakam (15-12)

The radiance in the sun which illumines the whole world, and which shines in the moon, and which gleams through the fire—know that Light to be Mine. (15.12)

— ॐ —

गामाविश्य च भूतानि धारयाम्यहमोजसा ।

gāmāviśya ca bhūtāni dhārayāmyahamojasā

पुष्णामि चौषधीः सर्वाः सोमो भूत्वा रसात्मकः ॥ १५-१३ ॥

puṣṇāmi cauṣadhīḥ sarvāḥ somo bhūtvā rasātmakaḥ (15-13)

Entering the earth with my energy, it is I who support all creation through my vitality; and becoming the sap of moon, I nourish all herbs. (15.13)

— ॐ —

अहं वैश्वानरो भूत्वा प्राणिनां देहमाश्रितः ।

ahaṁ vaiśvānaro bhūtvā prāṇināṁ dehamāśritaḥ

प्राणापानसमायुक्तः पचाम्यन्नं चतुर्विधम् ॥ १५-१४ ॥

prāṇāpānasamāyuktaḥ pacāmyannaṁ caturvidham (15-14)

Taking the form of digestive fire (*Vaishvanara*), and united with the *Prāna* and *Apāna* breaths—it is I who digests and assimilates the four kinds of foods. (15.14)

— ॐ —

सर्वस्य चाहं हृदि सन्निविष्टो मत्तः स्मृतिर्ज्ञानमपोहनञ्च ।
sarvasya cāhaṁ hṛdi sanniviṣṭo mattaḥ smṛtirjñānamapohanañca
वेदैश्च सर्वैरहमेव वेद्यो वेदान्तकृद्वेदविदेव चाहम् ॥ १५-१५ ॥
vedaiśca sarvairahameva vedyo vedāntakṛdvedavideva cāham (15-15)

It is I who remains seated in the hearts of all—as their inner controller. From Me is the knowledge and memory—or their loss. I am that ultimate import which the Vedas declare should be known in life. I am the origin of the Vedas and Vedānta; and it's I who am their Knower. (15.15)

— ॐ —

द्वाविमौ पुरुषौ लोके क्षरश्चाक्षर एव च ।
dvāvimau puruṣau loke kṣaraścākṣara eva ca
क्षरः सर्वाणि भूतानि कूटस्थोऽक्षर उच्यते ॥ १५-१६ ॥
kṣaraḥ sarvāṇi bhūtāni kūṭastho'kṣara ucyate (15-16)

Of the two in the world—the Perishable and the Imperishable—the body of beings is spoken of as the Perishable, and the indwelling *Jīvātmā* as the Imperishable. (15.16)

— ॐ —

उत्तमः पुरुषस्त्वन्यः परमात्मेत्युदाहृतः ।
uttamaḥ puruṣastvanyaḥ paramātmetyudāhṛtaḥ
यो लोकत्रयमाविश्य बिभर्त्यव्यय ईश्वरः ॥ १५-१७ ॥
yo lokatrayamāviśya bibhartyavyaya īśvaraḥ (15-17)

Apart from these there is the great Being—known as the *Param-Ātmā*, the Supreme-Soul, the immutable Lord—who, pervading the three worlds, sustains everything. (15.17)

— ॐ —

यस्मात्क्षरमतीतोऽहमक्षरादपि चोत्तमः ।
yasmātkṣaramatīto'hamakṣarādapi cottamaḥ
अतोऽस्मि लोके वेदे च प्रथितः पुरुषोत्तमः ॥ १५-१८ ॥
ato'smi loke vede ca prathitaḥ puruṣottamaḥ (15-18)

I am beyond the *Kshetra* (the perishable body), and higher even to the *Kshetrajna* (the imperishable soul); so therefore, the Vedas and the world describe Me as *Purushottama*—the Supreme Being. (15.18)

— ॐ —

यो मामेवमसम्मूढो जानाति पुरुषोत्तमम् ।
yo māmevamasammūḍho jānāti puruṣottamam
स सर्वविद्भजति मां सर्वभावेन भारत ॥ १५-१९ ॥
sa sarvavidbhajati māṁ sarvabhāvena bhārata (15-19)

Being thus undeluded, he who truly knows Me as the *Purushottama*, he truly knows it all, O Bhārata; and he naturally venerates Me in every respect. (15.19)

— ॐ —

इति गुह्यतमं शास्त्रमिदमुक्तं मयानघ ।
iti guhyatamaṁ śāstramidamuktaṁ mayānagha
एतद्बुद्ध्वा बुद्धिमान्स्यात्कृतकृत्यश्च भारत ॥ १५-२० ॥
etadbuddhvā buddhimānsyātkṛtakṛtyaśca bhārata (15-20)

Thus has this most esoteric of doctrines been expounded by me, O sinless one. Knowing this, one becomes wise; and accomplished thereby are all the duties of his life, O Bhārata." (15.20)

ॐ तत्सदिति श्रीमद्भगवद्गीतासूपनिषत्सु
oṁ tatsaditi śrīmadbhagavadgītāsūpaniṣatsu
ब्रह्मविद्यायां योगशास्त्रे श्रीकृष्णार्जुनसंवादे
brahmavidyāyāṁ yogaśāstre śrīkṛṣṇārjunasaṁvāde
पुरुषोत्तमयोगो नाम पञ्चदशोऽध्यायः ॥
puruṣottamayogo nāma pañcadaśo'dhyāyaḥ .

In this Yogic Scripture on the Science of Brahama—the Shrimada-Bhāgvada-Gītā Upanishad—hereby ends the dialogue between Shrī Krishna and Arjuna entitled: Purushottama Yoga, Canto XV

षोडशोऽध्यायः - दैवासुरसम्पद्विभागयोगः

ṣoḍaśo'dhyāyaḥ - daivāsurasampadvibhāgayogaḥ

:: Canto – XVI ::

- Divine and Demoniacal Attributes -

श्रीभगवानुवाच --

śrībhagavānuvāca --

अभयं सत्त्वसंशुद्धिर्ज्ञानयोगव्यवस्थितिः ।

abhayaṁ sattvasaṁśuddhirjñānayogavyavasthitiḥ

दानं दमश्च यज्ञश्च स्वाध्यायस्तप आर्जवम् ॥ १६-१ ॥

dānaṁ damaśca yajñaśca svādhyāyastapa ārjavam (16-1)

Shri Bhagwāna said: "Fearlessness, purity of heart, steadiness in the Yoga of Knowledge, and even so—charity, self-control, sacrifice, study of Vedas, austerity, uprightness; (16.1)

— ॐ —

अहिंसा सत्यमक्रोधस्त्यागः शान्तिरपैशुनम् ।

ahiṁsā satyamakrodhastyāgaḥ śāntirapaiśunam

दया भूतेष्वलोलुप्त्वं मार्दवं ह्रीरचापलम् ॥ १६-२ ॥

dayā bhūteṣvaloluptvaṁ mārdavaṁ hrīracāpalam (16-2)

non-injury, truthfulness, absence of anger, self-sacrifice, quietude, composure of mind, abstention from slander, compassion towards beings, non-covetousness, gentleness, modesty, refraining from frivolous pursuits; (16.2)

— ॐ —

तेजः क्षमा धृतिः शौचमद्रोहो नातिमानिता ।

tejaḥ kṣamā dhṛtiḥ śaucamadroho nātimānitā

भवन्ति सम्पदं दैवीमभिजातस्य भारत ॥ १६-३ ॥

bhavanti sampadaṁ daivīmabhijātasya bhārata (16-3)

sublimity, forgiveness, fortitude, purity, absence of hatred and conceit—these are the marks of one born of Divine endowments, O Bhārata. (16.3)

— ॐ —

दम्भो दर्पोऽभिमानश्च क्रोधः पारुष्यमेव च ।
dambho darpo'bhimānaśca krodhaḥ pāruṣyameva ca
अज्ञानं चाभिजातस्य पार्थ सम्पदमासुरीम् ॥ १६-४ ॥
ajñānaṁ cābhijātasya pārtha sampadamāsurīm (16-4)

Ostentation, arrogance, self-conceit, anger, rudeness, ignorance—these are the marks of one born with Demoniac affluence. (16.4)

— ॐ —

दैवी सम्पद्विमोक्षाय निबन्धायासुरी मता ।
daivī sampadvimokṣāya nibandhāyāsurī matā
मा शुचः सम्पदं दैवीमभिजातोऽसि पाण्डव ॥ १६-५ ॥
mā śucaḥ sampadaṁ daivīmabhijāto'si pāṇḍava (16-5)

Divine endowment has been recognized as conducive to liberation, and the demoniac as leading to bondage. Grieve not, O Pāndava, for you are born with divine propensities. (16.5)

— ॐ —

द्वौ भूतसर्गौ लोकेऽस्मिन्दैव आसुर एव च ।
dvau bhūtasargau loke'smindaiva āsura eva ca
दैवो विस्तरशः प्रोक्त आसुरं पार्थ मे श्रृणु ॥ १६-६ ॥
daivo vistaraśaḥ prokta āsuraṁ pārtha me śṛṇu (16-6)

Of beings, there are two types—the Divine and the Demoniacal. The Divine kind has been described at length; now hear from me of the Demoniacal type, O Pārtha. (16.6)

— ॐ —

प्रवृत्तिं च निवृत्तिं च जना न विदुरासुराः ।
pravṛttiṁ ca nivṛttiṁ ca janā na vidurāsurāḥ
न शौचं नापि चाचारो न सत्यं तेषु विद्यते ॥ १६-७ ॥
na śaucaṁ nāpi cācāro na satyaṁ teṣu vidyate (16-7)

Those of demoniac disposition—they are unconcerned as to what are prescribed works or prohibited acts; they have neither purity, nor proper conduct, nor truthfulness. (16.7)

— ॐ —

असत्यमप्रतिष्ठं ते जगदाहुरनीश्वरम् ।
asatyamapratiṣṭhaṁ te jagadāhuranīśvaram
अपरस्परसम्भूतं किमन्यत्कामहैतुकम् ॥ १६-८ ॥
aparasparasambhūtaṁ kimanyatkāmahaitukam (16-8)

They describe the world as without a God, without truth, without foundation, brought forth simply by the union of male and female—as nothing but originating in lust. (16.8)

— ॐ —

एतां दृष्टिमवष्टभ्य नष्टात्मानोऽल्पबुद्धयः ।
etāṁ dṛṣṭimavaṣṭabhya naṣṭātmāno'lpabuddhayaḥ
प्रभवन्त्युग्रकर्माणः क्षयाय जगतोऽहिताः ॥ १६-९ ॥
prabhavantyugrakarmāṇaḥ kṣayāya jagato'hitāḥ (16-9)

Clinging to this false view, these slow-witted men of vile disposition and terrible deeds are born only as enemies of mankind—only for the purpose of destruction of the world. (16.9)

— ॐ —

काममाश्रित्य दुष्पूरं दम्भमानमदान्विताः ।
kāmamāśritya duṣpūraṁ dambhamānamadānvitāḥ
मोहाद्गृहीत्वासद्ग्राहान्प्रवर्तन्तेऽशुचिव्रताः ॥ १६-१० ॥
mohādgṛhītvāsadgrāhānpravartante'śucivratāḥ (16-10)

Cherishing insatiable desires, embracing false doctrines, full of hypocrisy, pride and arrogance, these demoniacs of impure conduct, persist in this world holding fast to their delusional views. (16.10)

— ॐ —

चिन्तामपरिमेयां च प्रलयान्तामुपाश्रिताः ।
cintāmaparimeyāṁ ca pralayāntāmupāśritāḥ
कामोपभोगपरमा एतावदिति निश्चिताः ॥ १६-११ ॥
kāmopabhogaparamā etāvaditi niścitāḥ (16-11)

Beset with innumerable cares—which end only with their deaths—they remain devoted to the enjoyment of sensuous pleasures, convinced that this is all there is to it, firm in their belief that this is the highest limit of joy. (16.11)

— ॐ —

आशापाशशतैर्बद्धाः कामक्रोधपरायणाः ।
āśāpāśaśatairbaddhāḥ kāmakrodhaparāyaṇāḥ
ईहन्ते कामभोगार्थमन्यायेनार्थसञ्चयान् ॥ १६-१२ ॥
īhante kāmabhogārthamanyāyenārthasañcayān (16-12)

Bound by innumerable ties of expectations and given to lust and anger, they strive to amass through foul means piles of riches—only for the purpose of sense-gratifications. (16.12)

— ॐ —

इदमद्य मया लब्धमिमं प्राप्स्ये मनोरथम् ।
idamadya mayā labdhamimaṁ prāpsye manoratham
इदमस्तीदमपि मे भविष्यति पुनर्धनम् ॥ १६-१३ ॥
idamastīdamapi me bhaviṣyati punardhanam (16-13)

Full of desires they say, 'This much I have secured today, and now I shall acquire that; this much wealth is already mine, and soon that yonder too shall be mine. (16.13)

— ॐ —

असौ मया हतः शत्रुर्हनिष्ये चापरानपि ।
asau mayā hataḥ śatrurhaniṣye cāparānapi
ईश्वरोऽहमहं भोगी सिद्धोऽहं बलवान्सुखी ॥ १६-१४ ॥
īśvaro'hamahaṁ bhogī siddho'haṁ balavānsukhī (16-14)

And this opposition has been decimated by me already and those others too I shall destroy; and I am the lord; and I am full of enjoyments; and I am powerful and successful and happy; (16.14)

— ॐ —

आढ्योऽभिजनवानस्मि कोऽन्योऽस्ति सदृशो मया ।
āḍhyo'bhijanavānasmi ko'nyo'sti sadṛśo mayā
यक्ष्ये दास्यामि मोदिष्य इत्यज्ञानविमोहिताः ॥ १६-१५ ॥
yakṣye dāsyāmi modiṣya ityajñānavimohitāḥ (16-15)

अनेकचित्तविभ्रान्ता मोहजालसमावृताः ।
anekacittavibhrāntā mohajālasamāvṛtāḥ
प्रसक्ताः कामभोगेषु पतन्ति नरकेऽशुचौ ॥ १६-१६ ॥
prasaktāḥ kāmabhogeṣu patanti narake'śucau (16-16)

And I am princely, and I have big family, and who else here is equal to me? I shall make sacrifices and give endowments and I shall regale.'— Thus deluded by ignorance, ensnared in their web of delusions, addicted to the enjoyments of sensuous pleasures, with their minds bewildered by fanciful thoughts, these men of demoniacal dispositions, slide down into most foul hells. (16.15-16.16)

— ॐ —

आत्मसम्भाविताः स्तब्धा धनमानमदान्विताः ।
ātmasambhāvitāḥ stabdhā dhanamānamadānvitāḥ
यजन्ते नामयज्ञैस्ते दम्भेनाविधिपूर्वकम् ॥ १६-१७ ॥
yajante nāmayajñaiste dambhenāvidhipūrvakam (16-17)

अहङ्कारं बलं दर्पं कामं क्रोधं च संश्रिताः ।
ahaṅkāraṁ balaṁ darpaṁ kāmaṁ krodhaṁ ca saṁśritāḥ
मामात्मपरदेहेषु प्रद्विषन्तोऽभ्यसूयकाः ॥१६-१८॥
māmātmaparadeheṣu pradviṣanto'bhyasūyakāḥ (16-18)

Arrogant, vainglorious, intoxicated with wealth, haughty and ostentatious, performing sacrifices (Yajna) only in name, discarding the prescribed rites; given over to conceit, brute power, insolence, lust, anger—they perform Karmas in contempt of Me, hateful of the very soul which abides within them and others. (16.17-16.18)

— ॐ —

तानहं द्विषतः क्रूरान्संसारेषु नराधमान् ।
tānahaṁ dviṣataḥ krūrānsaṁsāreṣu narādhamān
क्षिपाम्यजस्रमशुभानासुरीष्वेव योनिषु ॥१६-१९॥
kṣipāmyajasramaśubhānāsurīṣveva yoniṣu (16-19)

Such cruel haters—these sinful and most degraded of humans—them I ever cast into the wombs of demoniacal species of the world, to revolve in an unremitting transmigratory cycle. (16.19)

— ॐ —

आसुरीं योनिमापन्ना मूढा जन्मनि जन्मनि ।
āsurīṁ yonimāpannā mūḍhā janmani janmani
मामप्राप्यैव कौन्तेय ततो यान्त्यधमां गतिम् ॥१६-२०॥
māmaprāpyaiva kaunteya tato yāntyadhamāṁ gatim (16-20)

Births after births, obtaining demoniac bodies and lives of delusional darkness, they keep sinking down into lower and still lower planes of existence—far from attaining Me. (16.20)

— ॐ —

त्रिविधं नरकस्येदं द्वारं नाशनमात्मनः ।
trividhaṁ narakasyedaṁ dvāraṁ nāśanamātmanaḥ
कामः क्रोधस्तथा लोभस्तस्मादेतत्त्रयं त्यजेत् ॥१६-२१॥
kāmaḥ krodhastathā lobhastasmādetattrayaṁ tyajet (16-21)

Lust, anger, greed—the triple gateways to hell—are destructive of the self; therefore, one should carefully shun these three. (16.21)

— ॐ —

एतैर्विमुक्तः कौन्तेय तमोद्वारैस्त्रिभिर्नरः ।

etairvimuktaḥ kaunteya tamodvāraistribhirnaraḥ

आचरत्यात्मनः श्रेयस्ततो याति परां गतिम् ॥ १६-२२ ॥

ācaratyātmanaḥ śreyastato yāti paraṁ gatim (16-22)

Whosoever manages to thwart these three gates of hell, is able to pursue what is good for the self—working for his own salvation and eventually reaching the supreme state. (16.22)

— ॐ —

यः शास्त्रविधिमुत्सृज्य वर्तते कामकारतः ।

yaḥ śāstravidhimutsṛjya vartate kāmakārataḥ

न स सिद्धिमवाप्नोति न सुखं न परां गतिम् ॥ १६-२३ ॥

na sa siddhimavāpnoti na sukhaṁ na paraṁ gatim (16-23)

But setting aside the injunctions of the scriptures, he who instead acts simply under the impulses of desires—attains neither perfection, nor happiness, nor the supreme goal. (16.23)

— ॐ —

तस्माच्छास्त्रं प्रमाणं ते कार्याकार्यव्यवस्थितौ ।

tasmācchāstraṁ pramāṇaṁ te kāryākāryavyavasthitau

ज्ञात्वा शास्त्रविधानोक्तं कर्म कर्तुमिहार्हसि ॥ १६-२४ ॥

jñātvā śāstravidhānoktaṁ karma kartumihārhasi (16-24)

So let the scriptures be your authority in ascertaining what ought to be done and what ought not to be done; and thus knowing that which is prescribed in the scriptures—act accordingly." (16.24)

ॐ तत्सदिति श्रीमद्भगवद्गीतासूपनिषत्सु

om tatsaditi śrīmadbhagavadgītāsūpaniṣatsu

ब्रह्मविद्यायां योगशास्त्रे श्रीकृष्णार्जुनसंवादे

brahmavidyāyāṁ yogaśāstre śrīkṛṣṇārjunasaṁvāde

दैवासुरसम्पद्विभागयोगो नाम षोडशोऽध्यायः ॥

daivāsurasampadvibhāgayogo nāma ṣoḍaśo'dhyāyaḥ .

In this Yogic Scripture on the Science of Brahama—the Shrimada-Bhāgvada-Gītā Upanishad—
hereby ends the dialogue between Shrī Krishna and Arjuna entitled:
Daivāsura-Sampada-Vibhāga Yoga, Canto XVI

सप्तदशोऽध्यायः - श्रद्धात्रयविभागयोगः

saptadaśo'dhyāyaḥ - śraddhātrayavibhāgayogaḥ

:: Canto – XVII ::

- Of the Three Kinds of Shraddhā -

अर्जुन उवाच --
arjuna uvāca --

ये शास्त्रविधिमुत्सृज्य यजन्ते श्रद्धयान्विताः ।
ye śāstravidhimutsṛjya yajante śraddhayānvitāḥ
तेषां निष्ठा तु का कृष्ण सत्त्वमाहो रजस्तमः ॥ १७-१ ॥
teṣāṁ niṣṭhā tu kā kṛṣṇa sattvamāho rajastamaḥ (17-1)

Arjuna said: "O Krishna, those who perform *Yajna* (sacrifice) only with *Shraddhā* (faith), setting aside the ordinance of the scriptures, where stand they: in *Sattva, Rajas* or *Tamas*?" (17.1)

श्रीभगवानुवाच --
śrībhagavānuvāca --

त्रिविधा भवति श्रद्धा देहिनां सा स्वभावजा ।
trividhā bhavati śraddhā dehināṁ sā svabhāvajā
सात्त्विकी राजसी चैव तामसी चेति तां श्रृणु ॥ १७-२ ॥
sāttvikī rājasī caiva tāmasī ceti tāṁ śṛṇu (17-2)

Shri Bhagwāna said: "The innate natural *Shraddhā* of embodied beings is of all three kinds—*Sāttvika, Rājasika* and *Tāmasika*; now hear of it from me. (17.2)

— ॐ —

सत्त्वानुरूपा सर्वस्य श्रद्धा भवति भारत ।
sattvānurūpā sarvasya śraddhā bhavati bhārata
श्रद्धामयोऽयं पुरुषो यो यच्छ्रद्धः स एव सः ॥ १७-३ ॥
śraddhāmayo'yaṁ puruṣo yo yacchraddhaḥ sa eva saḥ (17-3)

The *Shraddhā* of all is in accordance with their natural disposition. It is a person's inborn *Shraddhā* that makes him, O Bhārata; whatever the nature of his *Shraddhā*, verily one is that. (17.3)

— ॐ —

यजन्ते सात्त्विका देवान्यक्षरक्षांसि राजसाः ।
yajante sāttvikā devānyakṣarakṣāṁsi rājasāḥ
प्रेतान्भूतगणांश्चान्ये यजन्ते तामसा जनाः ॥ १७-४ ॥
pretānbhūtagaṇāṁścānye yajante tāmasā janāḥ (17-4)

The *Sāttvikas* worship gods; the *Rājasikas* worship *Yakshas* and *Rākshas*; and those of *Tāmasika* disposition, worship ghosts, spirits, goblins. (17.4)

— ॐ —

अशास्त्रविहितं घोरं तप्यन्ते ये तपो जनाः ।
aśāstravihitaṁ ghoraṁ tapyante ye tapo janāḥ
दम्भाहङ्कारसंयुक्ताः कामरागबलान्विताः ॥ १७-५ ॥
dambhāhaṅkārasaṁyuktāḥ kāmarāgabalānvitāḥ (17-5)
कर्षयन्तः शरीरस्थं भूतग्राममचेतसः ।
karṣayantaḥ śarīrasthaṁ bhūtagrāmamacetasaḥ
मां चैवान्तःशरीरस्थं तान्विद्ध्यासुरनिश्चयान् ॥ १७-६ ॥
māṁ caivāntaḥśarīrasthaṁ tānviddhyāsuraniścayān (17-6)

Given to ostentation and self-conceit, those who practice severe austerities of the arbitrary type not enjoined in the scriptures, who are possessed of desires, attachments and pride of power, who torture the elements of the body—as also Me, the spirit indwelling within—know such senseless people to be of the demoniac kind. (17.5-17.6)

— ॐ —

आहारस्त्वपि सर्वस्य त्रिविधो भवति प्रियः ।
āhārastvapi sarvasya trividho bhavati priyaḥ
यज्ञस्तपस्तथा दानं तेषां भेदमिमं शृणु ॥ १७-७ ॥
yajñastapastathā dānaṁ teṣāṁ bhedamimaṁ śṛṇu (17-7)

Agreeable to different men in accordance with their innate dispositions, the food too is of three kinds; and likewise, sacrifice, penance, and charity too are of three kinds. Hear of their respective distinction as follows. (17.7)

— ॐ —

आयुःसत्त्वबलारोग्यसुखप्रीतिविवर्धनाः ।
āyuḥsattvabalārogyasukhaprītivivardhanāḥ
रस्याः स्निग्धाः स्थिरा हृद्या आहाराः सात्त्विकप्रियाः ॥ १७-८ ॥
rasyāḥ snigdhāḥ sthirā hṛdyā āhārāḥ sāttvikapriyāḥ (17-8)

Foods that augment life, intelligence, vigor, health, happiness, joy; which are savory, succulent, nourishing and naturally agreeable—they are liked by those of *Sāttvika* nature. (17.8)

— ॐ —

कट्वम्ललवणात्युष्णतीक्ष्णरूक्षविदाहिनः ।
kaṭvamlalavaṇātyuṣṇatīkṣṇarūkṣavidāhinaḥ
आहारा राजसस्येष्टा दुःखशोकामयप्रदाः ॥ १७-९ ॥
āhārā rājasasyeṣṭā duḥkhaśokāmayapradāḥ (17-9)

Foods that are very bitter, sour, saltish, over-hot, pungent, dry and burning—they are very dear to the *Rājasikas* and are productive of pain, grief and disease. (17.9)

— ॐ —

यातयामं गतरसं पूति पर्युषितं च यत् ।
yātayāmaṁ gatarasaṁ pūti paryuṣitaṁ ca yat
उच्छिष्टमपि चामेध्यं भोजनं तामसप्रियम् ॥ १७-१० ॥
ucchiṣṭamapi cāmedhyaṁ bhojanaṁ tāmasapriyam (17-10)

Food that is ill-cooked, unripe, insipid, putrid, stale, partly eaten and impure too—that comes to be relished by men of *Tāmasika* dispositions. (17.10)

— ॐ —

अफलाकाङ्क्षिभिर्यज्ञो विधिदृष्टो य इज्यते ।
aphalākāṅkṣibhiryajño vidhidṛṣṭo ya ijyate
यष्टव्यमेवेति मनः समाधाय स सात्त्विकः ॥ १७-११ ॥
yaṣṭavyameveti manaḥ samādhāya sa sāttvikaḥ (17-11)

A *Yajna* (sacrifice) undertaken for its own sake desiring no fruits thereof, which is performed in ways prescribed by scriptural injunctions and with an intent mind—that *Yajna* is termed *Sāttvika*. (17.11)

— ॐ —

अभिसन्धाय तु फलं दम्भार्थमपि चैव यत् ।

abhisandhāya tu phalaṁ dambhārthamapi caiva yat

इज्यते भरतश्रेष्ठ तं यज्ञं विद्धि राजसम् ॥ १७-१२ ॥

ijyate bharataśreṣṭha taṁ yajñaṁ viddhi rājasam (17-12)

A sacrifice which is offered with an objective to gain fruits or merely for ostentation—know that to be *Rājasika*, O Bhārata. (17.12)

— ॐ —

विधिहीनमसृष्टान्नं मन्त्रहीनमदक्षिणम् ।

vidhihīnamasṛṣṭānnaṁ mantrahīnamadakṣiṇam

श्रद्धाविरहितं यज्ञं तामसं परिचक्षते ॥ १७-१३ ॥

śraddhāvirahitaṁ yajñaṁ tāmasaṁ paricakṣate (17-13)

A sacrifice which is contrary to scriptural injunctions, in which no food is distributed, which is devoid of faith or Mantras or gifts to the priests—that is said to be *Tāmasika*. (17.13)

— ॐ —

देवद्विजगुरुप्राज्ञपूजनं शौचमार्जवम् ।

devadvijaguruprājñapūjanaṁ śaucamārjavam

ब्रह्मचर्यमहिंसा च शारीरं तप उच्यते ॥ १७-१४ ॥

brahmacaryamahiṁsā ca śārīraṁ tapa ucyate (17-14)

Worship of the gods, the twice-born, the gurus, and the wise; purity, straightforwardness, continence and non-injury—these are said to be austerities of the body. (17.14)

— ॐ —

अनुद्वेगकरं वाक्यं सत्यं प्रियहितं च यत् ।

anudvegakaraṁ vākyaṁ satyaṁ priyahitaṁ ca yat

स्वाध्यायाभ्यसनं चैव वाङ्मयं तप उच्यते ॥ १७-१५ ॥

svādhyāyābhyasanaṁ caiva vāṅmayaṁ tapa ucyate (17-15)

Speech that is agreeable and beneficial and truthful too, which causes no aggravation; and the study of the Vedas and the holy-scriptures and the chanting of divine name—these are known as the austerities of speech. (17.15)

— ॐ —

मनः प्रसादः सौम्यत्वं मौनमात्मविनिग्रहः ।
manaḥ prasādaḥ saumyatvaṁ maunamātmavinigrahaḥ
भावसंशुद्धिरित्येतत्तपो मानसमुच्यते ॥ १७-१६ ॥
bhāvasaṁśuddhirityetattapo mānasamucyate (17-16)

Likewise, serenity of mind, kindliness, quietude, self-control, and purity of heart—these are said to be mortifications of the mental kind. (17.16)

— ॐ —

श्रद्धया परया तप्तं तपस्तत्त्रिविधं नरैः ।
śraddhayā parayā taptaṁ tapastattrividhaṁ naraiḥ
अफलाकाङ्क्षिभिर्युक्तैः सात्त्विकं परिचक्षते ॥ १७-१७ ॥
aphalākāṅkṣibhiryuktaiḥ sāttvikaṁ paricakṣate (17-17)

This threefold austerity practiced with great faith by Yogīs who are steadfast, with no expectations in return, is called the *Sāttvika Tapam*. (17.17)

— ॐ —

सत्कारमानपूजार्थं तपो दम्भेन चैव यत् ।
satkāramānapūjārthaṁ tapo dambhena caiva yat
क्रियते तदिह प्रोक्तं राजसं चलमध्रुवम् ॥ १७-१८ ॥
kriyate tadiha proktaṁ rājasaṁ calamadhruvam (17-18)

That austerity which is performed with a view to gain renown, honor, adoration, or for similar selfish gains, or made by way of display, and which is uncertain and transitory in its yield—that has been termed as *Rājasika*. (17.18)

— ॐ —

मूढग्राहेणात्मनो यत्पीडया क्रियते तपः ।
mūḍhagrāheṇātmano yatpīḍayā kriyate tapaḥ
परस्योत्सादनार्थं वा तत्तामसमुदाहृतम् ॥ १७-१९ ॥
parasyotsādanārthaṁ vā tattāmasamudāhṛtam (17-19)

Mortification that is resorted to out of foolish obstinacy, accompanied with self-torture, or done with the purpose of ruining others—that is declared to be *Tāmasika*. (17.19)

— ॐ —

दातव्यमिति यद्दानं दीयतेऽनुपकारिणे ।

dātavyamiti yaddānaṁ dīyate'nupakāriṇe

देशे काले च पात्रे च तद्दानं सात्त्विकं स्मृतम् ॥ १७-२० ॥

deśe kāle ca pātre ca taddānaṁ sāttvikaṁ smṛtam (17-20)

'To give is a duty'—a gift *(Dāna)* which is made with that sense of duty; which is bestowed upon someone from whom no return is expected; which is given at a proper place and time and unto a fit recipient—such a gift has been declared to be *Sāttvika*. (17.20)

— ॐ —

यत्तु प्रत्युपकारार्थं फलमुद्दिश्य वा पुनः ।

yattu pratyupakārārthaṁ phalamuddiśya vā punaḥ

दीयते च परिक्लिष्टं तद्दानं राजसं स्मृतम् ॥ १७-२१ ॥

dīyate ca parikliṣṭaṁ taddānaṁ rājasaṁ smṛtam (17-21)

A gift that is given in a grudging manner, or in the hope of obtaining reward, or for getting some service in return—that is called *Rājasika*. (17.21)

— ॐ —

अदेशकाले यद्दानमपात्रेभ्यश्च दीयते ।

adeśakāle yaddānamapātrebhyaśca dīyate

असत्कृतमवज्ञातं तत्तामसमुदाहृतम् ॥ १७-२२ ॥

asatkṛtamavajñātaṁ tattāmasamudāhṛtam (17-22)

A gift that is made disdainfully and without regard, given at the wrong place and time, bestowed upon a person who is unworthy—that is said to be *Tāmasika*. (17.22)

— ॐ —

ॐतत्सदिति निर्देशो ब्रह्मणस्त्रिविधः स्मृतः ।

omtatsaditi nirdeśo brahmaṇastrividhaḥ smṛtaḥ

ब्राह्मणास्तेन वेदाश्च यज्ञाश्च विहिताः पुरा ॥ १७-२३ ॥

brāhmaṇāstena vedāśca yajñāśca vihitāḥ purā (17-23)

'*Om-Tat-Sata*': this has been declared to be the three-fold representations of Brahama—who is Existence-Consciousness-Bliss. From That egressed—at the time of cosmic dawn—the Brahmins, the Vedas, and the *Yajna*. (17.23)

— ॐ —

तस्मादोमित्युदाहृत्य यज्ञदानतपःक्रियाः ।
tasmādomityudāhṛtya yajñadānatapaḥkriyāḥ
प्रवर्तन्ते विधानोक्ताः सततं ब्रह्मवादिनाम् ॥ १७-२४ ॥
pravartante vidhānoktāḥ satataṁ brahmavādinām (17-24)

Therefore acts of sacrifice, charity and austerity are begun well by invoking the divine word '*Om*', in accordance with the prescriptions of Vedic injunctions. (17.24)

— ॐ —

तदित्यनभिसन्धाय फलं यज्ञतपःक्रियाः ।
tadityanabhisandhāya phalaṁ yajñatapaḥkriyāḥ
दानक्रियाश्च विविधाः क्रियन्ते मोक्षकाङ्क्षिभिः ॥ १७-२५ ॥
dānakriyāśca vividhāḥ kriyante mokṣakāṅkṣibhiḥ (17-25)

Those who seek just liberation and want no material returns therefrom—they utter the word '*Tat*' when performing the various Vedic acts of sacrifice, austerity, charity. (17.25)

— ॐ —

सद्भावे साधुभावे च सदित्येतत्प्रयुज्यते ।
sadbhāve sādhubhāve ca sadityetatprayujyate
प्रशस्ते कर्मणि तथा सच्छब्दः पार्थ युज्यते ॥ १७-२६ ॥
praśaste karmaṇi tathā sacchabdaḥ pārtha yujyate (17-26)

The sound '*Sata*' is used to denote existence, reality, goodness, and also it is used in the sense of worthy, auspicious activities, O Pārtha. (17.26)

— ॐ —

यज्ञे तपसि दाने च स्थितिः सदिति चोच्यते ।
yajñe tapasi dāne ca sthitiḥ saditi cocyate
कर्म चैव तदर्थीयं सदित्येवाभिधीयते ॥ १७-२७ ॥
karma caiva tadarthīyaṁ sadityevābhidhīyate (17-27)

Steadfastness in sacrifice, austerity and gift is also spoken of as '*Sata*'; and all work done—even indirectly—for the sake of the Lord-God, is called '*Sata*' as well. (17.27)

— ॐ —

अश्रद्धया हुतं दत्तं तपस्तप्तं कृतं च यत् ।
aśraddhayā hutaṁ dattaṁ tapastaptaṁ kṛtaṁ ca yat
असदित्युच्यते पार्थ न च तत्प्रेत्य नो इह ॥ १७-२८॥
asadityucyate pārtha na ca tatpretya no iha (17-28)

By contrast, an oblation offered, a gift given, an austerity practiced, a good deed performed, or anything else which is void of *Shraddhā* (faith)—that is termed as *'A-sata'*: non-existent, void, insubstantial; and therefore it is of no avail here or hereafter." (17.28)

ॐ तत्सदिति श्रीमद्भगवद्गीतासूपनिषत्सु
om tatsaditi śrīmadbhagavadgītāsūpaniṣatsu
ब्रह्मविद्यायां योगशास्त्रे श्रीकृष्णार्जुनसंवादे
brahmavidyāyāṁ yogaśāstre śrīkṛṣṇārjunasaṁvāde
श्रद्धात्रयविभागयोगो नाम सप्तदशोऽध्यायः ॥
śraddhātrayavibhāgayogo nāma saptadaśo'dhyāyaḥ .

In this Yogic Scripture on the Science of Brahama—the Shrimada-Bhāgvada-Gītā Upanishad—hereby ends the dialogue between Shrī Krishna and Arjuna entitled: Śraddhātraya-Vibhāga Yoga, Canto XVII

अष्टादशोऽध्यायः - मोक्षसंन्यासयोगः

aṣṭādaśo'dhyāyaḥ - mokṣasaṁnyāsayogaḥ

:: Canto – XVIII ::

- The Path of Renunciation -

अर्जुन उवाच --
arjuna uvāca --

संन्यासस्य महाबाहो तत्त्वमिच्छामि वेदितुम् ।
saṁnyāsasya mahābāho tattvamicchāmi veditum
त्यागस्य च हृषीकेश पृथक्केशिनिषूदन ॥ १८-१ ॥
tyāgasya ca hṛṣīkeśa pṛthakkeśiniṣūdana (18-1)

Arjuna said: "I wish to know distinctly the true nature of *Sanyāsa* (renunciation), as also *Tyāga* (relinquishment), O mighty-armed, O inner controller of all, O Slayer of Keshi." (18.1)

श्रीभगवानुवाच --
śrībhagavānuvāca --

काम्यानां कर्मणां न्यासं संन्यासं कवयो विदुः ।
kāmyānāṁ karmaṇāṁ nyāsaṁ saṁnyāsaṁ kavayo viduḥ
सर्वकर्मफलत्यागं प्राहुस्त्यागं विचक्षणाः ॥ १८-२ ॥
sarvakarmaphalatyāgaṁ prāhustyāgaṁ vicakṣaṇāḥ (18-2)

Shri Bhagwāna said: "Sages understand *Sanyāsa* to be the giving up of such actions that fulfill desires, and the learned declare that relinquishing the fruits of all actions comprises *Tyāga*. (18.2)

— ॐ —

त्याज्यं दोषवदित्येके कर्म प्राहुर्मनीषिणः ।
tyājyaṁ doṣavadityeke karma prāhurmanīṣiṇaḥ
यज्ञदानतपःकर्म न त्याज्यमिति चापरे ॥ १८-३ ॥
yajñadānatapaḥkarma na tyājyamiti cāpare (18-3)

Some philosophers judiciously declare that all actions should be relinquished—contain as they do some measure of evil; while some aver that acts which are performed towards *Yajna*, charity and austerities should not to be given up. (18.3)

— ॐ —

निश्चयं शृणु मे तत्र त्यागे भरतसत्तम ।
niścayaṁ śṛṇu me tatra tyāge bharatasattama
त्यागो हि पुरुषव्याघ्र त्रिविधः सम्प्रकीर्तितः ॥ १८-४ ॥
tyāgo hi puruṣavyāghra trividhaḥ samprakīrtitaḥ (18-4)

Hear now my final conclusion on this subject, O Bhārata, for *Tyāga* is truly declared to be of three kinds: *Sāttvika*, *Rājasika* and *Tāmasika*. (18.4)

— ॐ —

यज्ञदानतपःकर्म न त्याज्यं कार्यमेव तत् ।
yajñadānatapaḥkarma na tyājyaṁ kāryameva tat
यज्ञो दानं तपश्चैव पावनानि मनीषिणाम् ॥ १८-५ ॥
yajño dānaṁ tapaścaiva pāvanāni manīṣiṇām (18-5)

Acts of sacrifice, charity and penance should not be relinquished, rather they must be diligently performed indeed. Verily sacrifice-charity-penance—all these Karmas are sanctifying unto the wise. (18.5)

— ॐ —

एतान्यपि तु कर्माणि सङ्गं त्यक्त्वा फलानि च ।
etānyapi tu karmāṇi saṅgaṁ tyaktvā phalāni ca
कर्तव्यानीति मे पार्थ निश्चितं मतमुत्तमम् ॥ १८-६ ॥
kartavyānīti me pārtha niścitaṁ matamuttamam (18-6)

But even these acts of obligatory duties must be performed without attachments and with no expectations of reward—that is my decided and final conclusion, O Arjuna. (18.6)

— ॐ —

नियतस्य तु संन्यासः कर्मणो नोपपद्यते ।
niyatasya tu saṁnyāsaḥ karmaṇo nopapadyate
मोहात्तस्य परित्यागस्तामसः परिकीर्तितः ॥ १८-७ ॥
mohāttasya parityāgastāmasaḥ parikīrtitaḥ (18-7)

The relinquishment of incumbent duty is deemed highly inappropriate; and this abandonment—which arises out of delusion—has been declared to be *Tāmasika Tyāga*. (18.7)

— ॐ —

दुःखमित्येव यत्कर्म कायक्लेशभयात्त्यजेत् ।

duḥkhamityeva yatkarma kāyakleśabhayāttyajet

स कृत्वा राजसं त्यागं नैव त्यागफलं लभेत् ॥ १८-८ ॥

sa kṛtvā rājasaṁ tyāgaṁ naiva tyāgaphalaṁ labhet (18-8)

He who gives up his duties out of fear of physical strain or thinking them to be irksome—thereby practices what is termed as *Rājasika Tyāga*; and he does not gain the result which ensue from true renunciation. (18.8)

— ॐ —

कार्यमित्येव यत्कर्म नियतं क्रियतेऽर्जुन ।

kāryamityeva yatkarma niyataṁ kriyate'rjuna

सङ्गं त्यक्त्वा फलं चैव स त्यागः सात्त्विको मतः ॥ १८-९ ॥

saṅgaṁ tyaktvā phalaṁ caiva sa tyāgaḥ sāttviko mataḥ (18-9)

An obligatory duty that is performed simply because it ought to be performed—while simultaneously relinquishing the fruits and attachments inherent in that Karma—that alone has been recognized to be true renunciation: the *Sāttvika* Tyāga. (18.9)

— ॐ —

न द्वेष्ट्यकुशलं कर्म कुशले नानुषज्जते ।

na dveṣṭyakuśalaṁ karma kuśale nānuṣajjate

त्यागी सत्त्वसमाविष्टो मेधावी छिन्नसंशयः ॥ १८-१० ॥

tyāgī sattvasamāviṣṭo medhāvī chinnasaṁśayaḥ (18-10)

Imbued with the quality of goodness, and of an unwavering understanding, and with all his doubts resolved—a man of true renunciation neither shuns disagreeable work, nor hankers after the agreeable. (18.10)

— ॐ —

न हि देहभृता शक्यं त्यक्तुं कर्माण्यशेषतः ।

na hi dehabhṛtā śakyaṁ tyaktuṁ karmāṇyaśeṣataḥ

यस्तु कर्मफलत्यागी स त्यागीत्यभिधीयते ॥ १८-११ ॥

yastu karmaphalatyāgī sa tyāgītyabhidhīyate (18-11)

Actions cannot really be given up in their entirety—by souls having taken up this human body; so therefore he alone is a true *Tyāgī* (renunciant), who relinquishes the fruit which is inherent in Karma. (18.11)

— ॐ —

अनिष्टमिष्टं मिश्रं च त्रिविधं कर्मणः फलम् ।

aniṣṭamiṣṭaṁ miśraṁ ca trividhaṁ karmaṇaḥ phalam

भवत्यत्यागिनां प्रेत्य न तु संन्यासिनां क्वचित् ॥ १८-१२ ॥

bhavatyatyāgināṁ pretya na tu saṁnyāsināṁ kvacit (18-12)

From Karmas performed during life—agreeable, disagreeable and mixed—threefold indeed is the fruit that accrues upon death unto the [non-relinquisher] doer; but no Karma accrues whatsoever to those who have renounced the fruits already—even while performing the act. (18.12)

— ॐ —

पञ्चैतानि महाबाहो कारणानि निबोध मे ।

pañcaitāni mahābāho kāraṇāni nibodha me

साङ्ख्ये कृतान्ते प्रोक्तानि सिद्धये सर्वकर्मणाम् ॥ १८-१३ ॥

sāṅkhye kṛtānte proktāni siddhaye sarvakarmaṇām (18-13)

In *Sānkhya*—which prescribes the means for neutralizing of actions—five factors have been mentioned in the process of performing all Karmas, O mighty armed; now hear of them from me. (18.13)

— ॐ —

अधिष्ठानं तथा कर्ता करणं च पृथग्विधम् ।

adhiṣṭhānaṁ tathā kartā karaṇaṁ ca pṛthagvidham

विविधाश्च पृथक्चेष्टा दैवं चैवात्र पञ्चमम् ॥ १८-१४ ॥

vividhāśca pṛthakceṣṭā daivaṁ caivātra pañcamam (18-14)

These are: the seat of action and likewise the agent, the various senses, and the different manifold efforts—with *Daiva* (providence, or latencies of past lives) being the fifth. (18.14)

— ॐ —

शरीरवाङ्मनोभिर्यत्कर्म प्रारभते नरः ।

śarīravāṅmanobhiryatkarma prārabhate naraḥ

न्याय्यं वा विपरीतं वा पञ्चैते तस्य हेतवः ॥ १८-१५ ॥

nyāyyaṁ vā viparītaṁ vā pañcaite tasya hetavaḥ (18-15)

These five are the contributing causes of all Karmas—proper or improper—that one performs with body, speech, mind. (18.15)

— ॐ —

तत्रैवं सति कर्तारमात्मानं केवलं तु यः ।
tatraivaṁ sati kartāramātmānaṁ kevalaṁ tu yaḥ
पश्यत्यकृतबुद्धित्वान्न स पश्यति दुर्मतिः ॥ १८-१६ ॥
paśyatyakṛtabuddhitvānna sa paśyati durmatiḥ (18-16)

Such being the case, he who—owing to his perverse unrefined understanding—regards the absolute, taintless Self to be the agent here, does not view aright. (18.16)

— ॐ —

यस्य नाहङ्कृतो भावो बुद्धिर्यस्य न लिप्यते ।
yasya nāhaṅkṛto bhāvo buddhiryasya na lipyate
हत्वाऽपि स इमाँल्लोकान्न हन्ति न निबध्यते ॥ १८-१७ ॥
hatvā'pi sa imāṁllokānna hanti na nibadhyate (18-17)

He whose mind is free from the sense of doership, whose reason is not obstructed by the sway of worldly things, he—though having killed these beings—does not really kill; nor does he become bound to the sins accrued thereof. (18.17)

— ॐ —

ज्ञानं ज्ञेयं परिज्ञाता त्रिविधा कर्मचोदना ।
jñānaṁ jñeyaṁ parijñātā trividhā karmacodanā
करणं कर्म कर्तेति त्रिविधः कर्मसङ्ग्रहः ॥ १८-१८ ॥
karaṇaṁ karma karteti trividhaḥ karmasaṅgrahaḥ (18-18)

The knower, the object, and its knowledge—this is the threefold impulse to action; the agent (doer), the instrument (sense-organs), and the resultant activity (objective)—this is the threefold basis of action. (18.18)

— ॐ —

ज्ञानं कर्म च कर्ता च त्रिधैव गुणभेदतः ।
jñānaṁ karma ca kartā ca tridhaiva guṇabhedataḥ
प्रोच्यते गुणसङ्ख्याने यथावच्छृणु तान्यपि ॥ १८-१९ ॥
procyate guṇasaṅkhyāne yathāvacchṛṇu tānyapi (18-19)

Knowledge, action and the agent, these too—in the branch of science which deals with the *Gunas*—have been declared to be of three kinds in accordance with the nature predominant in each. Hear of them from me now. (18.19)

— ॐ —

सर्वभूतेषु येनैकं भावमव्ययमीक्षते ।

sarvabhūteṣu yenaikaṁ bhāvamavyayamīkṣate

अविभक्तं विभक्तेषु तज्ज्ञानं विद्धि सात्त्विकम् ॥ १८-२० ॥

avibhaktaṁ vibhakteṣu tajjñānaṁ viddhi sāttvikam (18-20)

That knowledge by which man perceives One imperishable divine existence—undivided and equally present in all diverse beings—know that knowledge to be of the *Sāttvika* kind. (18.20)

— ॐ —

पृथक्त्वेन तु यज्ज्ञानं नानाभावान्पृथग्विधान् ।

pṛthaktvena tu yajjñānaṁ nānābhāvānpṛthagvidhān

वेत्ति सर्वेषु भूतेषु तज्ज्ञानं विद्धि राजसम् ॥ १८-२१ ॥

vetti sarveṣu bhūteṣu tajjñānaṁ viddhi rājasam (18-21)

The knowledge by which one cognizes within creation, the many existences of various kinds—all apart and distinct and bereft of any oneness—know that knowledge to be *Rājasika*. (18.21)

— ॐ —

यत्तु कृत्स्नवदेकस्मिन्कार्ये सक्तमहैतुकम् ।

yattu kṛtsnavadekasminkārye saktamahaitukam

अतत्त्वार्थवदल्पं च तत्तामसमुदाहृतम् ॥ १८-२२ ॥

atattvārthavadalpaṁ ca tattāmasamudāhṛtam (18-22)

The knowledge which is irrational and trivial, which has no real grasp of truth, which clings to a single part as if it were the whole—that has been declared to be *Tāmasika*. (18.22)

— ॐ —

नियतं सङ्गरहितमरागद्वेषतः कृतम् ।

niyataṁ saṅgarahitamarāgadveṣataḥ kṛtam

अफलप्रेप्सुना कर्म यत्तत्सात्त्विकमुच्यते ॥ १८-२३ ॥

aphalaprepsunā karma yattatsāttvikamucyate (18-23)

Actions prescribed by scriptures, performed bereft of sense of doership, free of attraction or repulsion, and without coveting anything in return—such are called *Sattvika* Karmas. (18.23)

— ॐ —

यत्तु कामेप्सुना कर्म साहङ्कारेण वा पुनः ।

yattu kāmepsunā karma sāhaṅkāreṇa vā punaḥ

क्रियते बहुलायासं तद्राजसमुदाहृतम् ॥ १८-२४ ॥

kriyate bahulāyāsaṁ tadrājasamudāhṛtam (18-24)

Actions that are performed possessed of conceit and with a view to appease desires, and which involve too much trouble—such have been spoken of as *Rājasika*. (18.24)

— ॐ —

अनुबन्धं क्षयं हिंसामनपेक्ष्य च पौरुषम् ।

anubandhaṁ kṣayaṁ hiṁsāmanapekṣya ca pauruṣam

मोहादारभ्यते कर्म यत्तत्तामसमुच्यते ॥ १८-२५ ॥

mohādārabhyate karma yattattāmasamucyate (18-25)

Work performed through sheer delusion—without regard to capacity, consequence, hurtfulness and loss to oneself or others—such is declared to be *Tāmasika*. (18.25)

— ॐ —

मुक्तसङ्गोऽनहंवादी धृत्युत्साहसमन्वितः ।

muktasaṅgo'nahaṁvādī dhṛtyutsāhasamanvitaḥ

सिद्ध्यसिद्ध्योर्निर्विकारः कर्ता सात्त्विक उच्यते ॥ १८-२६ ॥

siddhyasiddhyornirvikāraḥ kartā sāttvika ucyate (18-26)

Free from attachments, non-egoistic, endowed with zeal and fortitude, unaffected by success or failure—such a doer of work is said to be *Sāttvika*. (18.26)

— ॐ —

रागी कर्मफलप्रेप्सुर्लुब्धो हिंसात्मकोऽशुचिः ।

rāgī karmaphalaprepsurlubdho hiṁsātmako'śuciḥ

हर्षशोकान्वितः कर्ता राजसः परिकीर्तितः ॥ १८-२७ ॥

harṣaśokānvitaḥ kartā rājasaḥ parikīrtitaḥ (18-27)

The doer who is full of attachments and desirous of fruits of work, who is greedy, malefic, impure, and subject to sways of elation and dejection—he is declared to be *Rājasika*. (18.27)

— ॐ —

अयुक्तः प्राकृतः स्तब्धः शठो नैष्कृतिकोऽलसः ।
ayuktaḥ prākṛtaḥ stabdhaḥ śaṭho naiṣkṛtiko'lasaḥ
विषादी दीर्घसूत्री च कर्ता तामस उच्यते ॥१८-२८॥
viṣādī dīrghasūtrī ca kartā tāmasa ucyate (18-28)

Lacking piety and self-control, uncultured, arrogant, deceitful, overbearing, indolent, despondent and procrastinating—such a doer of Karmas is called *Tāmasika*. (18.28)

— ॐ —

बुद्धेर्भेदं धृतेश्चैव गुणतस्त्रिविधं शृणु ।
buddherbhedaṁ dhṛteścaiva guṇatastrividhaṁ śṛṇu
प्रोच्यमानमशेषेण पृथक्त्वेन धनञ्जय ॥१८-२९॥
procyamānamaśeṣeṇa pṛthaktvena dhanañjaya (18-29)

Now let me exposit exhaustively and respectively, O Dhananjaya, on the threefold divisions of *Buddhī* (understanding) and *Dhritī* (tenacity), in accordance with the predominant *Gunas* prevalent in each. (18.29)

— ॐ —

प्रवृत्तिं च निवृत्तिं च कार्याकार्ये भयाभये ।
pravṛttiṁ ca nivṛttiṁ ca kāryākārye bhayābhaye
बन्धं मोक्षं च या वेत्ति बुद्धिः सा पार्थ सात्त्विकी ॥१८-३०॥
bandhaṁ mokṣaṁ ca yā vetti buddhiḥ sā pārtha sāttvikī (18-30)

The understanding which distinguishes inclination and abstention, which correctly discerns what ought to be done and what ought not to be done, which knows fear and absence of fear, and bondage and liberation—that understanding is said to be *Sāttvika*. (18.30)

— ॐ —

यया धर्ममधर्मं च कार्यं चाकार्यमेव च ।
yayā dharmamadharmaṁ ca kāryaṁ cākāryameva ca
अयथावत्प्रजानाति बुद्धिः सा पार्थ राजसी ॥१८-३१॥
ayathāvatprajānāti buddhiḥ sā pārtha rājasī (18-31)

The understanding by which one knows—albeit confusedly—of what is Dharma and what Adharma, and what ought to be done and what ought not be—that understanding is *Rājasika*. (18.31)

— ॐ —

अधर्मं धर्ममिति या मन्यते तमसावृता ।
adharmaṁ dharmamiti yā manyate tamasāvṛtā
सर्वार्थान्विपरीतांश्च बुद्धिः सा पार्थ तामसी ॥ १८-३२ ॥
sarvārthānviparītāṁśca buddhiḥ sā pārtha tāmasī (18-32)

Completely false comprehension which is wrapped in ignorance, which imagines Adharma to be Dharma and perceives things in an inverted way—the very obverse of what things are—that understanding is deemed *Tāmasika*, O Pārtha. (18.32)

— ॐ —

धृत्या यया धारयते मनःप्राणेन्द्रियक्रियाः ।
dhṛtyā yayā dhārayate manaḥprāṇendriyakriyāḥ
योगेनाव्यभिचारिण्या धृतिः सा पार्थ सात्त्विकी ॥ १८-३३ ॥
yogenāvyabhicāriṇyā dhṛtiḥ sā pārtha sāttvikī (18-33)

Perseverance and tenacity by which one controls the functions of the mind, the vital airs, and the sense-organs through an unswerving practice of Yoga—that resolve is held to be *Sāttvika Dhritī,* O Pārtha. (18.33)

— ॐ —

यया तु धर्मकामार्थान्धृत्या धारयतेऽर्जुन ।
yayā tu dharmakāmārthāndhṛtyā dhārayate'rjuna
प्रसङ्गेन फलाकाङ्क्षी धृतिः सा पार्थ राजसी ॥ १८-३४ ॥
prasaṅgena phalākāṅkṣī dhṛtiḥ sā pārtha rājasī (18-34)

Tenacity by which one holds fast to work, pleasures, and wealth, desiring their fruits because of attachments—that is said to be *Rājasika,* O Pārtha. (18.34)

— ॐ —

यया स्वप्नं भयं शोकं विषादं मदमेव च ।
yayā svapnaṁ bhayaṁ śokaṁ viṣādaṁ madameva ca
न विमुञ्चति दुर्मेधा धृतिः सा पार्थ तामसी ॥ १८-३५ ॥
na vimuñcati durmedhā dhṛtiḥ sā pārtha tāmasī (18-35)

Tenacity of the anserine—which makes them to hold tenaciously to sleep, fear, anxiety, grief, depression, and vanity—that tenacity is *Tāmasika.* (18.35)

— ॐ —

सुखं त्विदानीं त्रिविधं श्रृणु मे भरतर्षभ ।

sukhaṁ tvidānīṁ trividhaṁ śṛṇu me bharatarṣabha

अभ्यासाद्रमते यत्र दुःखान्तं च निगच्छति ॥ १८-३६ ॥

abhyāsādramate yatra duḥkhāntaṁ ca nigacchati (18-36)

यत्तदग्रे विषमिव परिणामेऽमृतोपमम् ।

yattadagre viṣamiva pariṇāme'mṛtopamam

तत्सुखं सात्त्विकं प्रोक्तमात्मबुद्धिप्रसादजम् ॥ १८-३७ ॥

tatsukhaṁ sāttvikaṁ proktamātmabuddhiprasādajam (18-37)

Now hear from me of the threefold felicity as well, O prince amongst Bhāratas. Happiness which one reaches through practice; in which one comes to the end of all pain; which, though appearing as poison in the beginning, tastes like ambrosia in the end—that has been declared to be *Sāttvika*: born of the serenity of understanding emanating just from the Self. (18.36-18.37)

— ॐ —

विषयेन्द्रियसंयोगाद्यत्तदग्रेऽमृतोपमम् ।

viṣayendriyasaṁyogādyattadagre'mṛtopamam

परिणामे विषमिव तत्सुखं राजसं स्मृतम् ॥ १८-३८ ॥

pariṇāme viṣamiva tatsukhaṁ rājasaṁ smṛtam (18-38)

Pleasure which arises from contact between the sense-organs and sense-objects, which though appearing nectar-like at first, is discovered to be like poison in the end—it is said to be *Rājasika*. (18.38)

— ॐ —

यदग्रे चानुबन्धे च सुखं मोहनमात्मनः ।

yadagre cānubandhe ca sukhaṁ mohanamātmanaḥ

निद्रालस्यप्रमादोत्थं तत्तामसमुदाहृतम् ॥ १८-३९ ॥

nidrālasyapramādotthaṁ tattāmasamudāhṛtam (18-39)

Enchantment that is delusional , which stupefies the self during its partaking as also in its end, which arises through sleep, lassitude, and inadvertence—that is termed to be *Tāmasika*. (18.39)

— ॐ —

न तदस्ति पृथिव्यां वा दिवि देवेषु वा पुनः ।

na tadasti pṛthivyāṁ vā divi deveṣu vā punaḥ

सत्त्वं प्रकृतिजैर्मुक्तं यदेभिः स्यात्त्रिभिर्गुणैः ॥ १८-४० ॥

sattvaṁ prakṛtijairmuktaṁ yadebhiḥ syāttribhirguṇaiḥ (18-40)

There is no being—on earth, or heaven, or anywhere else, even amongst gods—who is free from these three *Gunas* born of Nature. (18.40)

— ॐ —

ब्राह्मणक्षत्रियविशां शूद्राणां च परन्तप ।

brāhmaṇakṣatriyaviśāṁ śūdrāṇāṁ ca parantapa

कर्माणि प्रविभक्तानि स्वभावप्रभवैर्गुणैः ॥ १८-४१ ॥

karmāṇi pravibhaktāni svabhāvaprabhavairguṇaiḥ (18-41)

The duties of the *Brahmins*, *Kshatriyas*, *Vaishyas* and *Shūdras*: have all been assigned in accordance with the disposition born of their innate respective natures, O Arjuna. (18.41)

— ॐ —

शमो दमस्तपः शौचं क्षान्तिरार्जवमेव च ।

śamo damastapaḥ śaucaṁ kṣāntirārjavameva ca

ज्ञानं विज्ञानमास्तिक्यं ब्रह्मकर्म स्वभावजम् ॥ १८-४२ ॥

jñānaṁ vijñānamāstikyaṁ brahmakarma svabhāvajam (18-42)

Calmness, self-control, austerity, purity, forbearance, and also uprightness, learning, knowledge, realization and faith—these constitute the natural duties of a *Brahmin*. (18.42)

— ॐ —

शौर्यं तेजो धृतिर्दाक्ष्यं युद्धे चाप्यपलायनम् ।

śauryaṁ tejo dhṛtirdākṣyaṁ yuddhe cāpyapalāyanam

दानमीश्वरभावश्च क्षात्रं कर्म स्वभावजम् ॥ १८-४३ ॥

dānamīśvarabhāvaśca kṣātraṁ karma svabhāvajam (18-43)

Heroism, daring, firmness, diligence, audacity in battle, generosity, majesty, lordliness—these are the duties of a *Kshatriya* born of his inner nature. (18.43)

— ॐ —

कृषिगौरक्ष्यवाणिज्यं वैश्यकर्म स्वभावजम् ।
kṛṣigaurakṣyavāṇijyaṁ vaiśyakarma svabhāvajam
परिचर्यात्मकं कर्म शूद्रस्यापि स्वभावजम् ॥ १८-४४ ॥
paricaryātmakaṁ karma śūdrasyāpi svabhāvajam (18-44)

Agriculture, cattle-rearing, and trade—these constitute the natural duties of a *Vaishya*; and work of the nature of service—that is the duty of a *Shūdra* in line with his nature. (18.44)

— ॐ —

स्वे स्वे कर्मण्यभिरतः संसिद्धिं लभते नरः ।
sve sve karmaṇyabhirataḥ saṁsiddhiṁ labhate naraḥ
स्वकर्मनिरतः सिद्धिं यथा विन्दति तच्छृणु ॥ १८-४५ ॥
svakarmanirataḥ siddhiṁ yathā vindati tacchṛṇu (18-45)

Know that devoted to one's innate duty, man attains perfection. Hear now how, through remaining engaged in one's natural duties, one reaches that paragon. (18.45)

— ॐ —

यतः प्रवृत्तिर्भूतानां येन सर्वमिदं ततम् ।
yataḥ pravṛttirbhūtānāṁ yena sarvamidaṁ tatam
स्वकर्मणा तमभ्यर्च्य सिद्धिं विन्दति मानवः ॥ १८-४६ ॥
svakarmaṇā tamabhyarcya siddhiṁ vindati mānavaḥ (18-46)

From whom all beings come into being, and by whom the whole universe stands pervaded—worshipping Him through the performance of his duties, man reaches perfection. (18.46)

— ॐ —

श्रेयान्स्वधर्मो विगुणः परधर्मात्स्वनुष्ठितात् ।
śreyānsvadharmo viguṇaḥ paradharmātsvanuṣṭhitāt
स्वभावनियतं कर्म कुर्वन्नाप्नोति किल्बिषम् ॥ १८-४७ ॥
svabhāvaniyataṁ karma kurvannāpnoti kilbiṣam (18-47)

Better is one's own well-performed duty—even though perceived to be defective—than the duty of another one. Performing the duty ordained by his inborn nature, one incurs no sin. (18.47)

— ॐ —

सहजं कर्म कौन्तेय सदोषमपि न त्यजेत् ।
sahajaṁ karma kaunteya sadoṣamapi na tyajet
सर्वारम्भा हि दोषेण धूमेनाग्निरिवावृताः ॥ १८-४८ ॥
sarvārambhā hi doṣeṇa dhūmenāgnirivāvṛtāḥ (18-48)

One should not, O Kuntī-son, relinquish the duty to which one is born—even though it may be attended with a measure of fault—because all undertakings are covered with some blemish or another, just as fire is shrouded in smoke. (18.48)

— ॐ —

असक्तबुद्धिः सर्वत्र जितात्मा विगतस्पृहः ।
asaktabuddhiḥ sarvatra jitātmā vigataspṛhaḥ
नैष्कर्म्यसिद्धिं परमां संन्यासेनाधिगच्छति ॥ १८-४९ ॥
naiṣkarmyasiddhiṁ paramāṁ saṁnyāsenādhigacchati (18-49)

Whose undertakings remain free of attachments in every respect, whose mind stands conquered, whose hunger for desires has completely abated, he attains thereby, through such mental renunciation, the supreme state of freedom from action. (18.49)

— ॐ —

सिद्धिं प्राप्तो यथा ब्रह्म तथाप्नोति निबोध मे ।
siddhiṁ prāpto yathā brahma tathāpnoti nibodha me
समासेनैव कौन्तेय निष्ठा ज्ञानस्य या परा ॥ १८-५० ॥
samāsenaiva kaunteya niṣṭhā jñānasya yā parā (18-50)

Learn from me in brief how reaching that perfection, O Kuntī-son, such a one attains to the state of Brahama—the supreme consummation, the culmination of knowledge. (18.50)

— ॐ —

बुद्ध्या विशुद्धया युक्तो धृत्यात्मानं नियम्य च ।
buddhyā viśuddhayā yukto dhṛtyātmānaṁ niyamya ca
शब्दादीन्विषयांस्त्यक्त्वा रागद्वेषौ व्युदस्य च ॥ १८-५१ ॥
śabdādīnviṣayāṁstyaktvā rāgadveṣau vyudasya ca (18-51)
विविक्तसेवी लघ्वाशी यतवाक्कायमानसः ।
viviktasevī laghvāśī yatavākkāyamānasaḥ
ध्यानयोगपरो नित्यं वैराग्यं समुपाश्रितः ॥ १८-५२ ॥
dhyānayogaparo nityaṁ vairāgyaṁ samupāśritaḥ (18-52)

अहङ्कारं बलं दर्पं कामं क्रोधं परिग्रहम् ।
ahaṅkāraṁ balaṁ darpaṁ kāmaṁ krodhaṁ parigraham
विमुच्य निर्ममः शान्तो ब्रह्मभूयाय कल्पते ॥ १८-५३ ॥
vimucya nirmamaḥ śānto brahmabhūyāya kalpate (18-53)

Endowed with pure understanding; controlling the mind with tenacity; relinquishing sense-objects such as sound, touch etc.; setting aside likes and dislikes; seeking solitude; of a pure diet and eating little; restrained in speech, body, mind; remaining ever devoted to the Yoga of contemplation; cultivating dispassion; abandoning egotism, power, arrogance, lust, anger and superfluous things; tranquil in heart; and free from the notion of 'me & mine'—who has perfected that, that one is fit for oneness in Brahama: the ocean of Existence, Consciousness, Bliss. (18.51-18.53)

— ॐ —

ब्रह्मभूतः प्रसन्नात्मा न शोचति न काङ्क्षति ।
brahmabhūtaḥ prasannātmā na śocati na kāṅkṣati
समः सर्वेषु भूतेषु मद्भक्तिं लभते पराम् ॥ १८-५४ ॥
samaḥ sarveṣu bhūteṣu madbhaktiṁ labhate parām (18-54)

Established in identity with Brahama, that tranquil-minded being neither craves nor grieves; alike to all beings, he achieves supreme devotion towards Me. (18.54)

— ॐ —

भक्त्या मामभिजानाति यावान्यश्चास्मि तत्त्वतः ।
bhaktyā māmabhijānāti yāvānyaścāsmi tattvataḥ
ततो मां तत्त्वतो ज्ञात्वा विशते तदनन्तरम् ॥ १८-५५ ॥
tato māṁ tattvato jñātvā viśate tadanantaram (18-55)

Through devotion he comes to know Me for what I am—at the very essence; and once having known Me truly, he forthwith enters My Being. (18.55)

— ॐ —

सर्वकर्माण्यपि सदा कुर्वाणो मद्व्यपाश्रयः ।
sarvakarmāṇyapi sadā kurvāṇo madvyapāśrayaḥ
मत्प्रसादादवाप्नोति शाश्वतं पदमव्ययम् ॥ १८-५६ ॥
matprasādādavāpnoti śāśvataṁ padamavyayam (18-56)

And even though outwardly performing all the works all the while, he attains the immutable, eternal, highest state, through My grace—having taken refuge in Me. (18.56)

— ॐ —

चेतसा सर्वकर्माणि मयि संन्यस्य मत्परः ।
cetasā sarvakarmāṇi mayi saṁnyasya matparaḥ
बुद्धियोगमुपाश्रित्य मच्चित्तः सततं भव ॥ १८-५७ ॥
buddhiyogamupāśritya maccittaḥ satataṁ bhava (18-57)

Mentally resigning all Karmas unto Me; regarding Me as the highest goal; taking to the Yoga of equanimity through the intellect—ever dwell with your mind fixed upon Me. (18.57)

— ॐ —

मच्चित्तः सर्वदुर्गाणि मत्प्रसादात्तरिष्यसि ।
maccittaḥ sarvadurgāṇi matprasādāttariṣyasi
अथ चेत्त्वमहङ्कारान्न श्रोष्यसि विनङ्क्ष्यसि ॥ १८-५८ ॥
atha cettvamahaṅkārānna śroṣyasi vinaṅkṣyasi (18-58)

In this way, with your mind devoted to Me, you shall overcome every difficulty through my grace; but burdened with self-conceit, if you do not listen and pay heed—you shall end up ruined. (18.58)

— ॐ —

यदहङ्कारमाश्रित्य न योत्स्य इति मन्यसे ।
yadahaṅkāramāśritya na yotsya iti manyase
मिथ्यैष व्यवसायस्ते प्रकृतिस्त्वां नियोक्ष्यति ॥ १८-५९ ॥
mithyaiṣa vyavasāyaste prakṛtistvāṁ niyokṣyati (18-59)

If indulging in self-conceit you decide: 'I shall not fight'—vain is this resolve of yours; because your very nature will compel and force you towards that. (18.59)

— ॐ —

स्वभावजेन कौन्तेय निबद्धः स्वेन कर्मणा ।
svabhāvajena kaunteya nibaddhaḥ svena karmaṇā
कर्तुं नेच्छसि यन्मोहात्करिष्यस्यवशोऽपि तत् ॥ १८-६० ॥
kartuṁ necchasi yanmohātkariṣyasyavaśo'pi tat (18-60)

That very action, O Kuntī-son, which through ignorance you are unwilling to undertake, you will perform in spite of yourself: impelled by the dictates born of your innate nature. (18.60)

— ॐ —

ईश्वरः सर्वभूतानां हृद्देशेऽर्जुन तिष्ठति ।

īśvaraḥ sarvabhūtānāṁ hṛddeśe'rjuna tiṣṭhati

भ्रामयन्सर्वभूतानि यन्त्रारूढानि मायया ॥ १८-६१ ॥

bhrāmayansarvabhūtāni yantrārūḍhāni māyayā (18-61)

In the hearts of all beings, O Arjuna, abides the Lord who, through his Māyā, causes everyone to whirl and move about—as if mounted on an automaton. (18.61)

— ॐ —

तमेव शरणं गच्छ सर्वभावेन भारत ।

tameva śaraṇaṁ gaccha sarvabhāvena bhārata

तत्प्रसादात्परां शान्तिं स्थानं प्राप्स्यसि शाश्वतम् ॥ १८-६२ ॥

tatprasādātparāṁ śāntiṁ sthānaṁ prāpsyasi śāśvatam (18-62)

So take refuge in Him alone with all your heart, O Bhārata, for only through His grace you shall attain supreme peace and the eternal abode of His. (18.62)

— ॐ —

इति ते ज्ञानमाख्यातं गुह्याद्गुह्यतरं मया ।

iti te jñānamākhyātaṁ guhyādguhyataraṁ mayā

विमृश्यैतदशेषेण यथेच्छसि तथा कुरु ॥ १८-६३ ॥

vimṛśyaitadaśeṣeṇa yathecchasi tathā kuru (18-63)

Thus has this sacred wisdom—the most profound of all secrets—been declared unto you; reflect upon it deeply and then act as you deem fit. (18.63)

— ॐ —

सर्वगुह्यतमं भूयः शृणु मे परमं वचः ।

sarvaguhyatamaṁ bhūyaḥ śṛṇu me paramaṁ vacaḥ

इष्टोऽसि मे दृढमिति ततो वक्ष्यामि ते हितम् ॥ १८-६४ ॥

iṣṭo'si me dṛḍhamiti tato vakṣyāmi te hitam (18-64)

Hear again the essence of this profound teaching of mine—the most esoteric of truths—because you are a dearly beloved of mine and I speak only that which is good for you: (18.64)

— ॐ —

मन्मना भव मद्भक्तो मद्याजी मां नमस्कुरु ।
manmanā bhava madbhakto madyājī māṁ namaskuru
मामेवैष्यसि सत्यं ते प्रतिजाने प्रियोऽसि मे ॥ १८-६५ ॥
māmevaiṣyasi satyaṁ te pratijāne priyo'si me (18-65)

Fix your mind upon Me, be devoted to Me, offer venerations, and surrender yourself unto Me—and you shall come to Me; I truly promise you that—for you are very dear to Me. (18.65)

— ॐ —

सर्वधर्मान्परित्यज्य मामेकं शरणं व्रज ।
sarvadharmānparityajya māmekaṁ śaraṇaṁ vraja
अहं त्वा सर्वपापेभ्यो मोक्षयिष्यामि मा शुचः ॥ १८-६६ ॥
ahaṁ tvā sarvapāpebhyo mokṣayiṣyāmi mā śucaḥ (18-66)

Resigning all your duties, just take refuge in Me alone; I shall liberate you from all sins, do not grieve. (18.66)

— ॐ —

इदं ते नातपस्काय नाभक्ताय कदाचन ।
idaṁ te nātapaskāya nābhaktāya kadācana
न चाशुश्रूषवे वाच्यं न च मां योऽभ्यसूयति ॥ १८-६७ ॥
na cāśuśrūṣave vācyaṁ na ca māṁ yo'bhyasūyati (18-67)

Never by you should this secret gospel be divulged to one who lacks in austerity or is wanting in faith, or to a quibbler or to one unwilling to listen. (18.67)

— ॐ —

य इदं परमं गुह्यं मद्भक्तेष्वभिधास्यति ।
ya idaṁ paramaṁ guhyaṁ madbhakteṣvabhidhāsyati
भक्तिं मयि परां कृत्वा मामेवैष्यत्यसंशयः ॥ १८-६८ ॥
bhaktiṁ mayi parāṁ kṛtvā māmevaiṣyatyasaṁśayaḥ (18-68)

One who imparts this most profound wisdom to My devotees, manifests thereby the highest devotion towards Me; freed of doubts, such a one shall undoubtedly reach Me. (18.68)

— ॐ —

न च तस्मान्मनुष्येषु कश्चिन्मे प्रियकृत्तमः ।

na ca tasmānmanuṣyeṣu kaścinme priyakṛttamaḥ

भविता न च मे तस्मादन्यः प्रियतरो भुवि ॥ १८-६९ ॥

bhavitā na ca me tasmādanyaḥ priyataro bhuvi (18-69)

There is none amongst humans—now, or in future—who thereby carries out a more devout act of service than that; and none whom I hold more dear. (18.69)

— ॐ —

अध्येष्यते च य इमं धर्म्यं संवादमावयोः ।

adhyeṣyate ca ya imaṁ dharmyaṁ saṁvādamāvayoḥ

ज्ञानयज्ञेन तेनाहमिष्टः स्यामिति मे मतिः ॥ १८-७० ॥

jñānayajñena tenāhamiṣṭaḥ syāmiti me matiḥ (18-70)

Whosoever studies this sacred dialogue of ours: by them too shall I stand worshipped by the Yajna of Knowledge—this I declare. (18.70)

— ॐ —

श्रद्धावाननसूयश्च श्रृणुयादपि यो नरः ।

śraddhāvānanasūyaśca śṛṇuyādapi yo naraḥ

सोऽपि मुक्तः शुभाँल्लोकान्प्राप्नुयात्पुण्यकर्मणाम् ॥ १८-७१ ॥

so'pi muktaḥ śubhām̐llokānprāpnuyātpuṇyakarmaṇām (18-71)

Even he who merely listens to this dialogue with reverence and without caviling, shall stand freed and will reach those very exalted realms which are designated for people of most righteous deeds. (18.71)

— ॐ —

कच्चिदेतच्छ्रुतं पार्थ त्वयैकाग्रेण चेतसा ।

kaccidetacchrutaṁ pārtha tvayaikāgreṇa cetasā

कच्चिदज्ञानसम्मोहः प्रनष्टस्ते धनञ्जय ॥ १८-७२ ॥

kaccidajñānasammohaḥ pranaṣṭaste dhanañjaya (18-72)

O Pārtha, did you listen to this gospel with an attentive mind? Has your delusion, born of ignorance, been decimated, O Dhananjaya?" (18.72)

अर्जुन उवाच --
arjuna uvāca --

नष्टो मोहः स्मृतिर्लब्धा त्वत्प्रसादान्मयाच्युत ।
naṣṭo mohaḥ smṛtirlabdhā tvatprasādānmayācyuta
स्थितोऽस्मि गतसन्देहः करिष्ये वचनं तव ॥ १८-७३ ॥
sthito'smi gatasandehaḥ kariṣye vacanaṁ tava (18-73)

Arjuna said: "Destroyed is my ignorance and delusion! By your grace, I have gained retentivity. I stand freed of doubts. I will now carry out your behest, O Achyuta." (18.73)

सञ्जय उवाच --
sañjaya uvāca --

इत्यहं वासुदेवस्य पार्थस्य च महात्मनः ।
ityahaṁ vāsudevasya pārthasya ca mahātmanaḥ
संवादमिममश्रौषमद्भुतं रोमहर्षणम् ॥ १८-७४ ॥
saṁvādamimamaśrauṣamadbhutaṁ romaharṣaṇam (18-74)

Sanjay said: Thus I have heard this most wonderful dialogue between Vāsudeva and the high-souled Pārtha—which causes my hair to stand on end. (18.74)

— ॐ —

व्यासप्रसादाच्छ्रुतवानेतद्गुह्यमहं परम् ।
vyāsaprasādācchrutavānetadguhyamahaṁ param
योगं योगेश्वरात्कृष्णात्साक्षात्कथयतः स्वयम् ॥ १८-७५ ॥
yogaṁ yogeśvarātkṛṣṇātsākṣātkathayataḥ svayam (18-75)

Having acquired a divine vision through the grace of Shri Vyāsa, I directly heard this supremely secret gospel of Shri Krishna, the Lord of Yoga, when He himself declared it unto Arjuna. (18.75)

— ॐ —

राजन्संस्मृत्य संस्मृत्य संवादमिममद्भुतम् ।
rājansaṁsmṛtya saṁsmṛtya saṁvādamimamadbhutam
केशवार्जुनयोः पुण्यं हृष्यामि च मुहुर्मुहुः ॥ १८-७६ ॥
keśavārjunayoḥ puṇyaṁ hṛṣyāmi ca muhurmuhuḥ (18-76)

Recollecting over and over this most wonderful and sacred dialogue between Keshava and Arjuna, I rejoice with deep exhilaration again and again! (18.76)

— ॐ —

तच्च संस्मृत्य संस्मृत्य रूपमत्यद्भुतं हरेः ।
tacca saṁsmṛtya saṁsmṛtya rūpamatyadbhutaṁ hareḥ
विस्मयो मे महान् राजन्हृष्यामि च पुनः पुनः ॥ १८-७७ ॥
vismayo me mahān rājanhṛṣyāmi ca punaḥ punaḥ (18-77)

And repeatedly recalling that most wonderful form of Shri Hari, such great is my wonderment, O king! And I thrill over again and again! (18.77)

— ॐ —

यत्र योगेश्वरः कृष्णो यत्र पार्थो धनुर्धरः ।
yatra yogeśvaraḥ kṛṣṇo yatra pārtho dhanurdharaḥ
तत्र श्रीर्विजयो भूतिर्ध्रुवा नीतिर्मतिर्मम ॥ १८-७८ ॥
tatra śrīrvijayo bhūtirdhruvā nītirmatirmama (18-78)

Verily wherever there is Bhagwāna Krishna—the Lord of Yoga—and wherever there is Arjuna—the wielder of the bow—there shall prevail every goodness, every prosperity, victory, glory and unfailing righteousness. That is my conviction." (18.78)

ॐ तत्सदिति श्रीमद्भगवद्गीतासूपनिषत्सु
om tatsaditi śrīmadbhagavadgītāsūpaniṣatsu
ब्रह्मविद्यायां योगशास्त्रे श्रीकृष्णार्जुनसंवादे
brahmavidyāyāṁ yogaśāstre śrīkṛṣṇārjunasaṁvāde
मोक्षसंन्यासयोगो नाम अष्टादशोऽध्यायः ॥
mokṣasaṁnyāsayogo nāma aṣṭādaśo'dhyāyaḥ .

In this Yogic Scripture on the Science of Brahama—the Shrimada-Bhāgvada-Gītā Upanishad—hereby ends the dialogue between Shrī Krishna and Arjuna entitled:
Moksha-Sanyāsa Yoga, Canto XVIII

ॐ ॐ ॐ ॐ ॐ ॐ ॐ ॐ ॐ ॐ ॐ ॐ ॐ ॐ ॐ ॐ

ॐ शान्तिः शान्तिः शान्तिः — ॐ शान्तिः शान्तिः शान्तिः — ॐ शान्तिः शान्तिः शान्तिः
om śantiḥ śantiḥ śantiḥ — om śantiḥ śantiḥ śantiḥ — om śantiḥ śantiḥ śantiḥ

ॐ ॐ ॐ ॐ ॐ ॐ ॐ ॐ ॐ ॐ ॐ ॐ ॐ ॐ ॐ ॐ

ॐ

श्रीरामचरणार्पणमस्तु

śrī rāma caraṇāarpaṇamastu

Hereby dedicated to the Lotus Feet of
Lord-God Shrī Rāma.

कायेन वाचा मनसेंद्रियैर्वा । बुद्ध्यात्मना वा प्रकृतिस्वभावात् ।

kāyena vācā manasemdriyairvā ,
buddhyātmanā vā prakṛtisvabhāvāt ,

करोमि यद्यत् सकलं परस्मै । नारायणायेति समर्पयामि ॥

karomi yadyat sakalaṁ parasmai ,
nārāyaṇāyeti samarpayāmi .

Whatever it is I do—through body, mind, speech, or sense-organs, or with my intellect and soul, or with my innate natural tendencies—whatever it be—I offer it all unto Narayana.

गीतामाहात्म्यम्

gītāmāhātmyam

[Verses on the glory and import of the Bhagavad-Gītā]

गीताशास्त्रमिदं पुण्यं यः पठेत्प्रयतः पुमान् ।

gītāśāstramidaṁ puṇyaṁ yaḥ paṭhetprayataḥ pumān ,

विष्णोः पदमवाप्नोति भयशोकादिवर्जितः ॥

viṣṇoḥ padamavāpnoti bhayaśokādivarjitaḥ .

One who diligently studies this Bhagavad-Gītā—the bestower of all virtues—with firm devotion and a regulated mind—verily attains Vaikuntha—the holy abode of Māhā-Vishnu—and he stands freed of all the fears and sorrows of this mundane world. (1)

गीताध्ययनशीलस्य प्राणायामपरस्य च ।

gītādhyayanaśīlasya prāṇāyāmaparasya ca ,

नैव सन्ति हि पापानि पूर्वजन्मकृतानि च ॥

naiva santi hi pāpāni pūrvajanmakṛtāni ca .

One who performs Prāṇāyāms and studies the Bhagavad-Gītā regularly and sincerely—all his sins melt away, even those from all prior lives. (2)

— ॐ —

मलनिर्मोचनं पुंसां जलस्नानं दिने दिने ।

malanirmocanaṁ puṁsāṁ jalasnānaṁ dine dine ,

सकृद्गीताम्भसि स्नानं संसारमलनाशनम् ॥

sakṛdgītāmbhasi snānaṁ saṁsāramalanāśanam .

A daily bath removes external bodily taints, but a single bath in the sacred waters of Bhagavad-Gītā is enough to remove all the taints of this Saṁsāra—this polluting worldly existence of joys, sorrows, births, and deaths. (3)

— ॐ —

गीता सुगीता कर्तव्या किमन्यैः शास्त्रविस्तरैः ।

gītā sugītā kartavyā kimanyaiḥ śāstravistaraiḥ ,

या स्वयं पद्मनाभस्य मुखपद्माद्विनिःसृता ॥

yā svayaṁ padmanābhasya mukhapadmādviniḥsṛtā .

Why go in for other elaborate scriptures, when you can chant the Gītā—the essence of all Vedic scriptures—which issued forth from the lotus mouth of Māhā-Vishnu Himself—on whose navel is the lotus of Creation. (4)

— ॐ —

भारतामृतसर्वस्वं विष्णोर्वक्त्राद्विनिःसृतम् ।

bhāratāmṛtasarvasvaṁ viṣṇorvaktrādviniḥsṛtam ,

गीतागङ्गोदकं पीत्वा पुनर्जन्म न विद्यते ॥

gītāgaṅgodakaṁ pītvā punarjanma na vidyate .

There is no more rebirth for one who partakes of the sacred waters of the Gītā-Gangā—the holy stream which flowed out from the lotus lips of Shri Māhā-Vishnu—the nectar which is the quintessence of Māhā-Bhārata. (5)

— ॐ —

एकं शास्त्रं देवकीपुत्रगीतमेको देवो देवकीपुत्र एव ।

ekaṁ śāstraṁ devakīputragītameko devo devakīputra eva ,

एको मन्त्रस्तस्य नामानि यानि कर्माप्येकं तस्य देवस्य सेवा ॥

eko mantrastasya nāmāni yāni karmāpyekaṁ tasya devasya sevā .

The holy Gītā of Krishna—son of Devakī—is the One Scripture; Krishna—son of Devakī—is the One God; the name Krishna—son of Devakī—is the One Mantra; service to Him—son of Devakī—is the One and only Duty. (6)

— ॐ — ॐ — ॐ — ॐ — ॐ — ॐ

—— Some other books you may like ——

Below is reproduced from **Tulsi Ramayana, Sanatana Dharma Holy Book, by Baldev Prasad Saxena & Vidya Wati** ISBNs: **978-1-945739-60-6** (Paperback) / **978-1-945739-61-3** (Hardback)

———————————————————————————

(Excerpts shown below are in reduced font-size)

[Below are the beginning verses of Tulsi Rāmāyana]

श्लोक-*śloka:*

वर्णानामर्थसंघानां रसानां छन्दसामपि ।
varṇānāmarthasaṁghānāṁ rasānāṁ chandasāmapi,
मङ्गलानां च कर्त्तारौ वन्दे वाणीविनायकौ ॥ १ ॥
maṅgalānāṁ ca karttārau vande vāṇīvināyakau. 1.

Trans:

I venerate Vānī and Vināyak, the originators of the alphabet and of the multitudinous expressions of those letters; the creators of the poetic styles, of cadence, of metre; and the begetters of all blessings.

भवानीशङ्करौ वन्दे श्रद्धाविश्वासरूपिणौ ।
bhavānīśaṅkarau vande śraddhāviśvāsarūpiṇau,
याभ्यां विना न पश्यन्ति सिद्धाःस्वान्तःस्थमीश्वरम् ॥ २ ॥
yābhyāṁ vinā na paśyanti siddhāḥsvāntaḥsthamīśvaram. 2.

Trans:

I reverence Bhawānī and Shankar, the embodiments of reverence and faith, without whom, not even the adept may see the Great Spirit which is enshrined in their very own hearts.

वन्दे बोधमयं नित्यं गुरुं शङ्कररूपिणम् ।
vande bodhamayaṁ nityaṁ guruṁ śaṅkararūpiṇam,
यमाश्रितो हि वक्रोऽपि चन्द्रः सर्वत्र वन्द्यते ॥ ३ ॥
yamāśrito hi vakro'pi candraḥ sarvatra vandyate. 3.

Trans:

I make obeisance to the eternal preceptor in the form of Shankar, who is all wisdom, and resting on whose crest the crescent moon, though crooked in shape, is everywhere honored.

सीतारामगुणग्रामपुण्यारण्यविहारिणौ ।
sītārāmaguṇagrāmapuṇyāraṇyavihāriṇau,
वन्दे विशुद्धविज्ञानौ कवीश्वरकपीश्वरौ ॥ ४ ॥
vande viśuddhavijñānau kavīśvarakapīśvarau. 4.

Trans:

I reverence the king of bards (Vālmikī) and the king of monkeys (Hanumān), of pure intelligence, who ever linger with delight in the holy woods in the shape of glories of Sītā-Rāma.

उद्भवस्थितिसंहारकारिणीं क्लेशहारिणीम् ।
udbhavasthitisaṁhārakāriṇīṁ kleśahāriṇīm,
सर्वश्रेयस्करीं सीतां नतोऽहं रामवल्लभाम् ॥ ५ ॥
sarvaśreyaskarīṁ sītāṁ nato'haṁ rāmavallabhām. 5.

Trans:

I bow to Sītā—the beloved consort of Rāma—She who's the responsible cause of creation, sustenance and dissolution of the universe—She who removes all afflictions and begets every blessing.

यन्मायावशवर्त्ति विश्वमखिलं ब्रह्मादिदेवासुरा
yanmāyāvaśavartti viśvamakhilaṁ brahmādidevāsurā
यत्सत्त्वादमृषैव भाति सकलं रज्जौ यथाहेर्भ्रमः ।
yatsattvādamṛṣaiva bhāti sakalaṁ rajjau yathāherbhramaḥ,
यत्पादप्लवमेकमेव हि भवाम्भोधेस्तितीर्षावतां
yatpādaplavamekameva hi bhavāmbhodhestitīrṣāvatāṁ
वन्देऽहं तमशेषकारणपरं रामाख्यमीशं हरिम् ॥ ६ ॥
vande'haṁ tamaśeṣakāraṇaparaṁ rāmākhyamīśaṁ harim. 6.

Trans:

I reverence Lord Harī, known by the name of Shrī Rāma—the Supreme causative Cause—whose Māyā holds sway over the entire universe, upon every being and supernatural beings from Brahmmā downwards—whose presence lends positive reality to the world of appearances: just as the false notion of serpent is imagined in a rope—and whose feet are the only bark for those eager to cross this worldly ocean of existence.

नानापुराणनिगमागमसम्मतं यद् रामायणे निगदितं क्वचिदन्यतोऽपि ।
nānāpurāṇanigamāgamasammataṁ yad
rāmāyaṇe nigaditaṁ kvacidanyato'pi,
स्वान्तःसुखाय तुलसी रघुनाथगाथाभाषानिबन्धमतिमञ्जुलमातनोति ॥ ७ ॥
svāntaḥsukhāya tulasī raghunāthagāthā-
bhāṣānibandhamatimañjulamātanoti. 7.

Trans:

In accord with the various Purānas, Vedas, Agamas (Tantras), and with what has been recorded in the Rāmāyana and elsewhere, I, Tulsīdās, for the delight of my own heart, have composed these verses of the exquisite saga of Raghunāth in the common parlance.

सोरठा-*soratha:*

जो सुमिरत सिधि होइ गन नायक करिबर बदन ।
jo sumirata sidhi hoi gana nāyaka karibara badana,
करउ अनुग्रह सोइ बुद्धि रासि सुभ गुन सदन ॥ १ ॥
karau anugraha soi buddhi rāsi subha guna sadana. 1.

Trans:

The mention of whose very name ensures success, who carries on his shoulders the head of beautiful elephant, who is a repository of wisdom and an abode of blessed qualities, may Ganesh, the leader of Shiva's retinue, shower his grace.

मूक होइ बाचाल पंगु चढइ गिरिबर गहन ।
mūka hoi bācāla paṁgu caḍhai giribara gahana,
जासु कृपाँ सो दयाल द्रवउ सकल कलि मल दहन ॥ २ ॥
jāsu kṛpām̐ so dayāla dravau sakala kali mala dahana. 2.

Trans:

By whose favor the dumb become eloquent and the cripple ascend formidable mountains; He, who burns all the impurities of the Kali-Yug—may that merciful Harī, be moved to pity.

नील सरोरुह स्याम तरुन अरुन बारिज नयन ।
nīla saroruha syāma taruna aruna bārija nayana,
करउ सो मम उर धाम सदा छीरसागर सयन ॥ ३ ॥
karau so mama ura dhāma sadā chīrasāgara sayana. 3.

Trans:

O Harī, thou who ever slumbers on the milky ocean, thou whose body is dark as a blue lotus, thou with eyes lustrous as freshly bloomed red water-lilies—do take up thy abode in my heart as well.

कुंद इंदु सम देह उमा रमन करुना अयन ।
kuṁda iṁdu sama deha umā ramana karunā ayana,
जाहि दीन पर नेह करउ कृपा मर्दन मयन ॥ ४ ॥
jāhi dīna para neha karau kṛpā mardana mayana. 4.

Trans:

O Hara, Destroyer-of-Kāmdev, whose form resembles in color the jasmine flower and the moon, who is an abode of compassion, who is the refuge of the afflicted, O spouse of Umā, be thou gracious to me.

बंदउँ गुरु पद कंज कृपा सिंधु नररूप हरि ।
baṁdaum̐ guru pada kaṁja kṛpā siṁdhu nararūpa hari,
महामोह तम पुंज जासु बचन रबि कर निकर ॥ ५ ॥
mahāmoha tama puṁja jāsu bacana rabi kara nikara. 5.

Trans:

I bow to the lotus feet of my Gurū, who is an ocean of mercy and is none other than Harī in human form, and whose words are a deluge of sunshine upon the darkness of Ignorance and Infatuation.

[Below are the ending verses of Tulsi Rāmāyana]

दोहा-dohā:

मो सम दीन न दीन हित तुम्ह समान रघुबीर ।
mo sama dīna na dīna hita tumha samāna raghubīra,
अस बिचारि रघुबंस मनि हरहु बिषम भव भीर ॥१३०क॥
asa bicāri raghubaṁsa mani harahu biṣama bhava bhīra. 130(ka).
कामिहि नारि पिआरि जिमि लोभिहि प्रिय जिमि दाम ।
kāmihi nāri piāri jimi lobhihi priya jimi dāma,
तिमि रघुनाथ निरंतर प्रिय लागहु मोहि राम ॥१३०ख॥
timi raghunātha niraṁtara priya lāgahu mohi rāma. 130(kha).

Trans:

There is no one as pathetic as I am and no one as gracious to the piteous as you, O Raghubīr: remember this, O glory of the race of Raghu, and rid me of the grievous burden of existence. As an amorous person is infatuated over their lover, and just as a greedy miser hankers after money, so for ever and ever, may you be always dear to me, O Rāma.

श्लोक-śloka:

यत्पूर्वं प्रभुणा कृतं सुकविना श्रीशम्भुना दुर्गमं
yatpūrvaṁ prabhuṇā kṛtaṁ sukavinā śrīśambhunā durgamaṁ
श्रीमद्रामपदाब्जभक्तिमनिशं प्राप्त्यै तु रामायणम् ।
śrīmadrāmapadābjabhaktimaniśaṁ prāptyai tu rāmāyaṇam,
मत्वा तद्रघुनाथमनिरतं स्वान्तस्तमःशान्तये
matvā tadraghunāthamaniratam svāntastamaḥśāntaye
भाषाबद्धमिदं चकार तुलसीदासस्तथा मानसम् ॥१॥
bhāṣābaddhamidaṁ cakāra tulasīdāsastathā mānasam. 1.

Trans:

The same esoteric Mānas-Rāmāyana, the Holy Lake of enactments of Shrī Rāma, that was brought to fore, in days of yore, by the blessed Shambhu, the foremost amongst poets—with the object of developing unceasing devotion to the beautiful lotus-feet of our beloved Lord: the all-merciful Rāma—has been likewise rendered into the common lingo by Tulsīdās for dispersing the gloom of his own soul, which it does—rife as it is with the name Rāma that alone gives this work a substance.

पुण्यं पापहरं सदा शिवकरं विज्ञानभक्तिप्रदं
puṇyaṁ pāpaharaṁ sadā śivakaraṁ vijñānabhaktipradaṁ
मायामोहमलापहं सुविमलं प्रेमाम्बुपूरं शुभम् ।
māyāmohamalāpahaṁ suvimalaṁ premāmbupūraṁ śubham,
श्रीमद्रामचरित्रमानसमिदं भक्त्यावगाहन्ति ये
śrīmadrāmacaritramānasamidaṁ bhaktyāvagāhanti ye
ते संसारपतङ्गघोरकिरणैर्दह्यन्ति नो मानवाः ॥२॥
te saṁsārapataṅgaghorakiraṇairdahyanti no mānavāḥ. 2.

Trans:

This glorious, purifying, blessed most limpid holy Mānas Lake of Shrī Rāma's enactments ever begets happiness. Verily, it bestows both Wisdom and Devotion; and it washes away delusion, infatuation and impurity; and brimful with a stream of love it inundates one with bliss supreme. Never scorched by the burning rays of the sun of worldly illusions are those who take a plunge in this most Holy-Lake of the Glories of Shrī Rāma.

सीताराम सीताराम सीताराम सीताराम सीताराम सीताराम सीताराम सीताराम सीताराम सीताराम सीताराम सीताराम सीताराम सीताराम सीताराम सीताराम सीताराम सीताराम सीताराम सीताराम
सीताराम सीताराम सीताराम सीताराम सीताराम सीताराम सीताराम सीताराम सीताराम सीताराम सीताराम सीताराम सीताराम सीताराम सीताराम सीताराम सीताराम सीताराम सीताराम सीताराम

Below is reproduced from **Sundarakanda: The Fifth-Ascent of Tulsi Ramayana, by Subhash Chandra.**

ISBNs: 978-1-945739-05-7 / 978-1-945739-15-6 / 978-1-945739-90-3 / 978-1-945739-91-0

(Excerpts shown below are in reduced font-size)

श्लोक-śloka:

शान्तं शाश्वतमप्रमेयमनघं निर्वाणशान्तिप्रदं
śāntaṁ śāśvatamaprameyamanaghaṁ nirvāṇaśāntipradaṁ
ब्रह्माशम्भुफणीन्द्रसेव्यमनिशं वेदान्तवेद्यं विभुम् ।
brahmāśambhuphaṇīndrasevyamaniśaṁ vedāntavedyaṁ vibhum,
रामाख्यं जगदीश्वरं सुरगुरुं मायामनुष्यं हरिं
rāmākhyaṁ jagadīśvaraṁ suraguruṁ māyāmanuṣyaṁ hariṁ
वन्देऽहं करुणाकरं रघुवरं भूपालचूडामणिम् ॥१॥
vande'haṁ karuṇākaraṁ raghuvaraṁ bhūpālacūrāmaṇim. 1.

Trans:

I adore the Lord of the universe—immeasurable, all pervading and eternal, the very theme of Vedanta, beyond ordinary means of cognition, the all-merciful God of gods constantly worshipped by Brahmmā, Shambhu and Shesha; the dispeller of all sins, bestower of the supreme beatitude of emancipation, a veritable mine of compassion, the Lord God Hari appearing through his Māyā in the form of man, the King of kings, the chief of Raghus—Shrī Rāma.

नान्या स्पृहा रघुपते हृदयेऽस्मदीये
nānyā spṛhā raghupate hṛdaye'smadīye
सत्यं वदामि च भवानखिलान्तरात्मा ।
satyaṁ vadāmi ca bhavānakhilāntarātmā,
भक्तिं प्रयच्छ रघुपुङ्गव निर्भरां मे
bhaktiṁ prayaccha raghupuṅgava nirbharāṁ me
कामादिदोषरहितं कुरु मानसं च ॥२॥
kāmādidoṣarahitaṁ kuru mānasaṁ ca. 2.

Trans:

There is no other craving in my heart, O Lord, and I speak the truth and you know my inmost thoughts—for you are the indwelling Spirit in the hearts of all—do please grant me, O crest-jewel of Raghus, the intense-most devotion to Thy Holy Feet; and make my heart clean of lust and every other sin.

अतुलितबलधामं हेमशैलाभदेहं
atulitabaladhāmaṁ hemaśailābhadehaṁ
दनुजवनकृशानुं ज्ञानिनामग्रगण्यम् ।
danujavanakṛśānuṁ jñānināmagragaṇyam,
सकलगुणनिधानं वानराणामधीशं
sakalaguṇanidhānaṁ vānarāṇāmadhīśaṁ
रघुपतिप्रियभक्तं वातजातं नमामि ॥३॥
raghupatipriyabhaktaṁ vātajātaṁ namāmi. 3.

Trans:

Repeatedly I bow to the son-of-wind-god: repository of immeasurable might, with his body shining like a mountain of gold, the very blazing fire that devours the forest in the shape of demons; the abode of virtues, the noblest messenger of Raghupati, foremost amongst the wise, the chief of the monkeys: Shrī Hanumān, the most beloved devotee of Shrī Rāma.

चौपाई-caupāī:

जामवंत के बचन सुहाए । सुनि हनुमंत हृदय अति भाए ॥
jāmavaṁta ke bacana suhāe, suni hanumaṁta hṛdaya ati bhāe.
तब लगि मोहि परिखेहु तुम्ह भाई । सहि दुख कंद मूल फल खाई ॥
taba lagi mohi parikhehu tumha bhāī, sahi dukha kaṁda mūla phala khāī.
जब लगि आवौं सीतहि देखी । होइहि काजु मोहि हरष बिसेषी ॥
jaba lagi āvauṁ sītahi dekhī, hoihi kāju mohi haraṣa biseṣī.
यह कहि नाइ सबन्हि कहुँ माथा । चलेउ हरषि हियँ धरि रघुनाथा ॥
yaha kahi nāi sabanhi kahuṁ māthā, caleu haraṣi hiyaṁ dhari raghunāthā.
सिंधु तीर एक भूधर सुंदर । कौतुक कूदि चढ़ेउ ता ऊपर ॥
siṁdhu tīra eka bhūdhara suṁdara, kautuka kūdi caṛheu tā ūpara.
बार बार रघुबीर सँभारी । तरकेउ पवनतनय बल भारी ॥
bāra bāra raghubīra saṁbhārī, tarakeu pavanatanaya bala bhārī.
जेहिं गिरि चरन देइ हनुमंता । चलेउ सो गा पाताल तुरंता ॥
jehiṁ giri carana dei hanumaṁtā, caleu so gā pātāla turaṁtā.
जिमि अमोघ रघुपति कर बाना । एही भाँति चलेउ हनुमाना ॥
jimi amogha raghupati kara bānā, ehī bhāṁti caleu hanumānā.
जलनिधि रघुपति दूत बिचारी । तैं मैनाक होहि श्रमहारी ॥
jalanidhi raghupati dūta bicārī, taiṁ maināka hohi śramahārī.

Trans:

Hearing the heartening speech of Jāmavaṁt, Hanumān greatly rejoiced in his heart and said, "Endure these hardships my brothers, and with roots, herbs, fruits as your food, await here my return—till I am back with the news of Mā Sītā. My objective will surely be accomplished—I experience this great exhilaration in my heart." Saying so he bowed his head to them all; and then, with the image of Shrī Rāma enshrined in his heart, and full of exuberance, Hanumān sallied forth. There was a majestic rock by the seashore and Hanumān sprang upon its top in mere sport. Then again and again invoking the name of Raghubīr, the son-of-wind leaped with all his might. And the hill upon which he had planted his foot instantly sank—recoiling into the nethermost world. And just like an exceeding unerring arrow fired by Raghupati, Hanumān sped away. On the way—and knowing Hanumān to be the emissary of Shrī Rāma—the deity presiding over the Ocean told Mainăk, "Relieve him of his fatigue."

दोहा-dohā:

हनूमान तेहि परसा कर पुनि कीन्ह प्रनाम ।
hanūmāna tehi parasā kara puni kīnha pranāma,
राम काजु कीन्हें बिनु मोहि कहाँ बिश्राम ॥१॥
rāma kāju kīnheṁ binu mohi kahāṁ biśrāma. 1.

Trans:

[Mount Mainăk raised himself up from the sea and stood before, in welcome,] but Hanumān merely touched it with his hand, and saluting to it said, "There can be no rest for me until I have accomplished the work of Shri Rāma."

Below is reproduced from **Ashtavakra Gita, A Fiery Octave in Ascension, by Vidya Wati.**

ISBNs: **978-1-945739-42-2** (Journal format) / **978-1-945739-46-0** (Paperback) / **978-1-945739-48-4** (Pocket-sized) / **978-1-945739-47-7** (Hardback)

(Excerpts shown below are in reduced font-size)

अहं कर्तेत्यहंमानमहाकृष्णाहिदंशितः ।
ahaṁ kartetyahaṁmānamahākṛṣṇāhidaṁśitaḥ ,
नाहं कर्तेति विश्वासामृतं पीत्वा सुखी भव ॥१-८॥
nāhaṁ karteti viśvāsāmṛtaṁ pītvā sukhī bhava (1-8)

May thou
—who have been bitten by the deadly serpent of egoism,
who persist delirious in its venom,
hallucinating, "I am the Doer"—
drink of the antidote of faith
—partake of the curative reality—
which avers: "I am not the Doer";
and replete with that nectar,
may thou abide ever glad.

एको विशुद्धबोधोऽहमिति निश्चयवह्निना ।
eko viśuddhabodho'hamiti niścayavahninā ,
प्रज्वाल्याज्ञानगहनं वीतशोकः सुखी भव ॥१-९॥
prajvālyājñānagahanaṁ vītaśokaḥ sukhī bhava (1-9)

Burn down this wilderness of Ignorance in the
Fiery Knowledge-of-the-Self,
the essence of which Truth is the firm conviction that proclaims,
"I am the One Reality,
the all-pervading pristine Consciousness";
and thus freed of pain grief sorrows,
may thou abide in supreme happiness.

कूटस्थं बोधमद्वैतमात्मानं परिभावय ।
kūṭasthaṁ bodhamadvaitamātmānaṁ paribhāvaya ,
आभासोऽहं भ्रमं मुक्त्वा भावं बाह्यमथान्तरम् ॥१-१३॥
ābhāso'haṁ bhramaṁ muktvā bhāvaṁ bāhyamathāntaram (1-13)

Giving up the mistaken identification with the body,
the external crust;
and rid also of identifying yourself
as being the ego and mind
—the superimposed delusions which are but
reflections of the Ātmā—
meditate on yourself as being none of these but purely the Ātmā:
Immutable Consciousness,
the One without a second.

यथा न तोयतो भिन्नास्तरङ्गाः फेनबुद्बुदाः ।
yathā na toyato bhinnāstaraṅgāḥ phenabudbudāḥ ,
आत्मनो न तथा भिन्नं विश्वमात्मविनिर्गतम् ॥२-४॥
ātmano na tathā bhinnaṁ viśvamātmavinirgatam (2-4)

Just as
the waves foam and bubbles
are identical to the water of which they are made,
even so this seemingly real universe
has emanated from the Param-Ātmā,
and is none other than the Ātmā
—my Self.

प्रकाशो मे निजं रूपं नातिरिक्तोऽस्म्यहं ततः ।
prakāśo me nijaṁ rūpaṁ nātirikto'smyahaṁ tataḥ ,
यदा प्रकाशते विश्वं तदाहं भास एव हि ॥२-८॥
yadā prakāśate viśvaṁ tadāhaṁ bhāsa eva hi (2-8)

My innate essence is a Fiery Light—
and other than the effulgence of Consciousness
I am nothing else.
When the universe shines forth,
it does so borrowing the glow of my brilliance.
Through and through everything which is manifest anywhere,
there is nothing except for the Fiery Ātmā
shining all splendorous.

मत्तो विनिर्गतं विश्वं मय्येव लयमेष्यति ।
matto vinirgataṁ viśvaṁ mayyeva layameṣyati ,
मृदि कुम्भो जले वीचिः कनके कटकं यथा ॥२-१०॥
mṛdi kumbho jale vīciḥ kanake kaṭakaṁ yathā (2-10)

All this here, emerges out of me;
it exists in me;
and within me again it becomes dissolved
—like an earthen jar returning to its
component clay,
...or a wave
blending back into the water again,
...or a gold bracelet
melting into the pureness of its element
—having become bereft of form
bereft of name.

द्वैतमूलमहो दुःखं नान्यत्तस्याऽस्ति भेषजम् ।
dvaitamūlamaho duḥkhaṁ nānyattasyā'sti bheṣajam ,
दृश्यमेतन् मृषा सर्वमेकोऽहं चिद्रसोमलः ॥२-१६॥
dṛśyametan mṛṣā sarvameko'haṁ cidrasomalaḥ (2-16)

The notion of duality
is at the root of all grief and misery.
There is no other cure for sorrow
except the realization of the Truth, that
"There are no two here—it is all just One."

All this perceived multifariousness
is just an apparition,
and behind it all is just the One pristine Reality void of defilements,
comprised in bliss and consciousness.

नाहं देहो न मे देहो जीवो नाहमहं हि चित् ।
nāhaṁ deho na me deho jīvo nāhamahaṁ hi cit ,
अयमेव हि मे बन्ध आसीद्या जीविते स्पृहा ॥२-२२॥
ayameva hi me bandha āsīdyā jīvite spṛhā (2-22)

I am not this body
—and nor had I ever a body—
I am not the Jīva,
I am nothing but a Pure Consciousness.
This indeed was my bondage:
that I once had this 'me' and 'mine';
and that I thirsted for life
in greed, desires, covetousness;
and that I fancied little bites of joys
—while in fact
the entire ocean of bliss was just I myself.

यत् पदं प्रेप्सवो दीनाः शक्राद्याः सर्वदेवताः ।
yat padaṁ prepsavo dīnāḥ śakrādyāḥ sarvadevatāḥ ,
अहो तत्र स्थितो योगी न हर्षमुपगच्छति ॥४-२॥
aho tatra sthito yogī na harṣamupagacchati (4-2)

Even suffering the state of mirthful revelries
—those ravishing spheres of pleasures which even gods like Indra yearn for disconsolately—
the yogi finds no excitement existing in them
—being that he always abides
in That-Ocean-of-Bliss
where such morsels of delights
are but tiny fleeting waves
...flapping away

न ते सङ्गोऽस्ति केनापि किं शुद्धस्त्यक्तुमिच्छसि ।
na te saṅgo'sti kenāpi kiṁ śuddhastyaktumicchasi ,
सङ्घातविलयं कुर्वन्नेवमेव लयं व्रज ॥५-१॥
saṅghātavilayaṁ kurvannevameva layaṁ vraja (5-1)

There is nothing at all here attached to which you lie bound in fetters.
Pure and taintless you already are—
so what is that you must needs give up?

Renounce simply the idea of a body—
set aside this composite organism to rest.
Give up identifying yourself with this assemblage of skin, bone, organs.
Abide Dissolved,
knowing that you are not anything material
but the Ātmā pure.

यस्य बोधोदये तावत्स्वप्नवद् भवति भ्रमः ।
yasya bodhodaye tāvatsvapnavad bhavati bhramaḥ ,
तस्मै सुखैकरूपाय नमः शान्ताय तेजसे ॥१८-१॥
tasmai sukhaikarūpāya namaḥ śāntāya tejase (18-1)

Salutation to that Fiery Light—
self-effulgent, self-existent, independent,
which is pristine consciousness
which is tranquility,
which is bliss,
which is abiding existence—
in whose dawn,
this dark delusive universe
—which has you enslaved—

vanishes away
like the dream of a dark night.

व्यामोहमात्रविरतौ स्वरूपादानमात्रतः ।
vyāmohamātraviratau svarūpādānamātrataḥ ,
वीतशोका विराजन्ते निरावरणदृष्टयः ॥१८-६॥
vītaśokā virājante nirāvaraṇadṛṣṭayaḥ (18-6)

With their delusions dispelled,
those who abide cognized of the Self
—the fiery glow of pure consciousness shining within—
their distress is now at end;
and they live free of sorrows
—in a completeness of Bliss.

क्व विक्षेपः क्व चैकाग्र्यं क्व निर्बोधः क्व मूढता ।
kva vikṣepaḥ kva caikāgryaṁ kva nirbodhaḥ kva mūḍhatā ,
क्व हर्षः क्व विषादो वा सर्वदा निष्क्रियस्य मे ॥२०-९॥
kva harṣaḥ kva viṣādo vā sarvadā niṣkriyasya me (20-9)

Whither went concentration?
...and what happened to all those distractions?
...whither the deluded soul?
...and whither the burdensome bag of delusions?
...where went charms and delights of the world?
...and where went sorrows?
For me, it has all coalesced into a oneness.
Bereft of any karmas,
I am just the Ātmā now.

सीताराम सीताराम सीताराम सीताराम सीताराम सीताराम सीताराम सीताराम सीताराम सीताराम सीताराम सीताराम सीताराम सीताराम सीताराम सीताराम सीताराम सीताराम सीताराम सीताराम
सीताराम सीताराम सीताराम सीताराम सीताराम सीताराम सीताराम सीताराम सीताराम सीताराम सीताराम सीताराम सीताराम सीताराम सीताराम सीताराम सीताराम सीताराम सीताराम सीताराम

Below is reproduced from **Vivekachūḍāmani of Shankaracharya, the Fiery Crest-Jewel of Wisdom, by Vidya Wati.** ISBNs: **978-1-945739-41-5** (Journal format) / **978-1-945739-44-6**(Paperback) / **978-1-945739-79-8**(Pocket-sized) / **978-1-945739-45-3**(Hardback)

(Excerpts shown below are in reduced font-size)

लब्ध्वा कथञ्चिन्नरजन्म दुर्लभं तत्रापि पुंस्त्वं श्रुतिपारदर्शनम् ।
labdhvā kathañcinnarajanma durlabhaṁ tatrāpi puṁstvaṁ śrutipāradarśanam ,
यस्त्वात्ममुक्तौ न यतेत मूढधीः स ह्यात्महा स्वं विनिहन्त्यसद्ग्रहात् ॥४॥
yastvātmamuktau na yateta mūḍhadhīḥ sa hyātmahā svaṁ vinihantyasadgrahāt (4)

He who, having by some means obtained this privileged human birth born a man—and furthermore having knowledge and learning and grasp of the sacred scriptures—does not exert himself for self-liberation, that fool is certainly committing suicide thereby—for he imperils himself by holding as life-support those very things which themselves are tenuous and unreal.

ब्रह्म सत्यं जगन्मिथ्येत्येवंरूपो विनिश्चयः ।
brahma satyaṁ jaganmithyetyevaṁrūpo viniścayaḥ ,
सोऽयं नित्यानित्यवस्तुविवेकः समुदाहृतः ॥२०॥
so'yaṁ nityānityavastuvivekaḥ samudāhṛtaḥ (20)

"*Brahama* alone is Real (self-existent), and the universe non-Real (not self-existent)"—the insight, discernment, and firm conviction by which one comprehends this Vedic dictum: that is designated to be *Viveka* (or Discrimination between the Real and the non-Real).

अहङ्कारादिदेहान्तान् बन्धानज्ञानकल्पितान् ।
ahaṅkārādidehāntān bandhānajñānakalpitān ,
स्वस्वरूपावबोधेन मोक्तुमिच्छा मुमुक्षुता ॥२७॥
svasvarūpāvabodhena moktumicchā mumukṣutā (27)

An intense yearning for Freedom—to be released of all bondages, from that of egoism to that of body, to be relieved of all thralldoms superimposed by dint of Ignorance—by realizing one's Real Nature: that is designated to be *Mumukshutā* (or Longing for Liberation).

मोक्षकारणसामग्र्यां भक्तिरेव गरीयसी ।
mokṣakāraṇasāmagryāṁ bhaktireva garīyasī ,
स्वस्वरूपानुसन्धानं भक्तिरित्यभिधीयते ॥३१॥
svasvarūpānusandhānaṁ bhaktirityabhidhīyate (31)

Among the means most conducive to Liberation, *Bhaktī* holds a supreme spot. A constant contemplation and seeking of one's true Self, one's Real Nature—that is designated to be *Bhaktī* (Devotion).

ऋणमोचनकर्तारः पितुः सन्ति सुतादयः ।
ṛṇamocanakartāraḥ pituḥ santi sutādayaḥ ,
बन्धमोचनकर्ता तु स्वस्मादन्यो न कश्चन ॥५१॥
bandhamocanakartā tu svasmādanyo na kaścana (51)

A father may have his sons and others to redeem him from his financial debts, but there is no one other than one's own Self to deliver one from the within bondages that are upon the Self (and which are self-imposed).

तस्मात्सर्वप्रयत्नेन भवबन्धविमुक्तये ।
tasmātsarvaprayatnena bhavabandhavimuktaye ,
स्वैरेव यत्नः कर्तव्यो रोगादाविव पण्डितैः ॥६६॥
svaireva yatnaḥ kartavyo rogādāviva paṇḍitaiḥ (66)

Therefore—just as in the case of bodily diseases and internal maladies—the wise should strive personally and with every means in his power, to free himself from the bondages of this dreadful transmigratory disease of repeated births and deaths.

मा भैष्ट विद्वंस्तव नास्त्यपायः संसारसिन्धोस्तरणेऽस्त्युपायः ।
mā bhaiṣṭa vidvaṁstava nāstyapāyaḥ saṁsārasindhostaraṇe'styupāyaḥ ,
येनैव याता यतयोऽस्य पारं तमेव मार्गं तव निर्दिशामि ॥४३॥
yenaiva yātā yatayo'sya pāraṁ tameva mārgaṁ tava nirdiśāmi (43)

Fear not, O learned one, there is no death for thee; verily there is a sovereign means of crossing this sea of relative existence. That very supreme path, treading which our ancient sages of yore have managed to go beyond—that very way I shall now inculcate to thee.

www.ingramcontent.com/pod-product-compliance
Lightning Source LLC
Chambersburg PA
CBHW051803100526
44592CB00016B/2544
* 9 7 8 1 9 4 5 7 3 9 5 5 2 *